GETTING
THINGS
DONE

GETTING THINGS DONE

Concepts and Skills for Leaders

Lyle E. Schaller

ILLUSTRATED BY
EDWARD LEE TUCKER

ABINGDON PRESS NASHVILLE

GETTING THINGS DONE
Concepts and Skills for Leaders

Copyright © 1986 by Abingdon Press

Second Printing 1986

This book is printed on acid-free paper.

Library of Congress Cataloging in Publication Data

SCHALLER, LYLE E.
  Getting things done.
  Bibliography: p.
  1. Christian leadership.   I. Title.

BV652.1.S34   1986   253'.2   85-23020

ISBN 0-687-14141-9
(pbk.: alk. paper)

MANUFACTURED BY THE PARTHENON PRESS AT
NASHVILLE, TENNESSEE, UNITED STATES OF AMERICA

To
Uncle Murray
and six of his boys:
Bob, Jim, Tom, Doug, Alan, and Earl

C O N T E N T S

PREFACE..9

CHAPTER 1
Prologue..12

CHAPTER 2
Tribes, Movements, and Organizations...................27
    What Is a Tribe?...28
    Why Bother?...32
    What Is a Social Movement?...........................34
    What Are You Seeking to Change?..................37
    The Other End of the Spectrum.....................39
    Four Basic Differences...................................43
    Questions for Self-Evaluation.........................46

CHAPTER 3
Leaders Know How to Organize.............................48
    The New Mission Becomes a Congregation.....50
    When Women Organize Around Missions.......50
    Where Are Today's Women?...........................52
    An Ancient Organizing Principle....................53
    Rewards and Punishments...............................54
    Organizing Principles for Large Groups..........54
    Three Questions...58
    The Redevelopment of the Anglo Urban Church.....59
    The Sunday Morning Fellowship Period............68
    The Fifth-Grade Sunday School Class.............70

CHAPTER 4
Leaders Do Lead!...75
    Do Leaders Manipulate?.................................77

Six Central Characteristics...78
Leaders, Cultures, and Values..80

CHAPTER 5
Type, Role, and Style..86
    Who Wants to Be Called an Authoritarian Leader?..87
    How Do You Define Democratic?...90
    Administrative Manager or Initiating Leader?..95
    Alternative Categories...100
    What Is the Context?..102
    What Is Your Leadership Style?..106

CHAPTER 6
The Future of a New Idea..110
    Twenty-Seven Thousand Cookies..112

CHAPTER 7
Allies, Coalitions, and Meetings...116
    Supporters or Allies?..118
    The Value of Coalitions...119
    Disagreement or Apathy?...122
    Dual Leadership..122
    Committees and Meetings..123
        How Large?..124
        Who Is in Charge?...125
        What Is the Purpose?...125
        Dual Leadership..126
        The Setting...126
        Refreshments...126
        Overcoming Negativism..127
        Is Anyone Listening?..128
        Pace and Style..128
        Time for Second Thoughts...129
        The Value of Shared Experiences..129
        Do We Trust Subcommittees?...129

CHAPTER 8
What Do We Seek in Our Next Minister?...131
    Job Descriptions, Tests, or Competencies?..133
    The Question of Structure..136
    Who Will Be the Leaders in 2015?..138

NOTES..140

W hy are certain individuals exceptionally effective leaders, sometimes apparently without any great effort, while others fail as leaders? Why do some organizations succeed in attaining their goals, and others, that appear to be equally worthy, fail?

Those two questions are being asked all across our society today. Sometimes the focus of the discussion is national political leadership; in other groups the concern is with the future of American business, and frequently the subject is the success or failure of a political party or a college or a service club or a city government or a denomination or a congregation or an association of churches.

When the large corporation contemplates creating a new regional office, nearly everyone agrees it is essential that the right person be found to head up that new branch. When the university decides to launch a new program, the president or dean looks for the right individual to organize and supervise the new center or department. When a political party loses the contest for the presidency, the talk immediately turns to a discussion of who might be a winning candidate four years hence. When an inner-city elementary or high school that has been on the decline for years turns the corner, the credit for that transformation usually is accorded to the new principal. When the discussion turns to organizing a new congregation, nearly everyone agrees the key is finding the right minister to serve as the founding pastor or mission developer.

Everywhere the cry is for more competent and attractive leaders. Nearly everyone appears to be searching for more and better leaders.

One facet of the current debate is whether leadership is a gift, with which one is born, or whether it is a skill that can be taught and learned. Increasingly the answer today echoes the sentiment of Dwight D. Eisenhower when he declared, "It would be unwise to assume that the qualities of leadership cannot be improved by teaching." At least a score of colleges and universities are now offering programs in leadership development.

This list includes Dartmouth, Columbia, Harvard, Princeton, Northwestern, Wisconsin, Minnesota, and the University of Texas. Most of the leadership development programs today, however, are offered, not by the traditional academic institutions, but rather by profit-making corporations, professional associations, retreat centers, the military services, the YMCA, governmental organizations, centers for adult education, and other organizations not seen as a part of academia. Perhaps three out of every four dollars spent in leadership development programs go into training events offered by agencies that are not a part of the traditional academic community. Today, for example, most of the larger and better known theological seminaries tend to model themselves after the university graduate school that emphasizes scholarship, rather than on the model of an institution concerned with producing leaders for the churches.

All these leadership development programs have been organized on the assumption that leadership skills can be identified, transmitted, and learned. Most of them also operate on the assumption that it is impossible to teach an adult anything that person does not want to learn and therefore that the participants in a leadership development program should (a) already be on the job and (b) enroll on their own initiative as part of a voluntary continuing education plan, rather than as a prerequisite for being employed in the first place or continued employment.

In other words, the critical debate is not on whether leadership skills can be taught, that is now widely accepted, but rather on when is the best time to teach those skills. The predominant opinion appears to be on post-entry experiences rather than on pre-entry preparation into a specific vocation, profession, or occupation.

This discussion introduces three of the basic assumptions on which this book is based. First, it is assumed that leadership can be taught and learned. The first chapter is a composite account that illustrates a number of lessons in leadership.

Second, and perhaps the most widely ignored of any of these assumptions, it is assumed that it is difficult to teach anyone anything that person does not want to learn. This book has been written for inquisitive people who want to learn more than the absolute essentials. This book is intended for the intellectually curious who are as much concerned with the "Why?" as with the "How?" That is why the second chapter is devoted to tribes and movements.

Third, it is assumed that an analysis of leadership and a discussion of basic organizing principles are but two sides of the same coin. That is the theme of the third chapter. Effective leaders are both willing to lead and also know how to organize for action. Useful basic organizing principles can be identified, conceptualized, taught, and adapted to a particular situation by any creative leader.

The fourth, and the clearest assumption on which this book is based, is that by definition leaders are individuals who accept the responsibility of leading. That means a proactive or initiating stance in contrast with the reactive posture of many managers. That is the focus of the fourth chapter, and it raises fundamental questions on terminology, values, and goals.

The fifth, and perhaps the most controversial assumption, is that using terms such as *authoritarian* or *laissez faire* or *democratic* to categorize basic types of leadership is at best obsolete and at worst counterproductive. The fifth chapter discusses the origin of these terms, which are still widely used in ecclesiastical circles, and suggests that a better conceptual framework includes differentiating between role and style.

A sixth assumption is that occasionally leaders must take the initiative, usually with relatively few supporters, in instituting changes. A good manager may be all the organization needs until the day arrives when the status quo no longer is acceptable. That is also the day when the effective leader needs the skills of an agent of intentional change, and that is the focus of the sixth chapter.

A seventh assumption on which this book is based is that effective leaders recognize and affirm the value of coalitions, know how to enlist allies, and also are willing and able to function comfortably and creatively with committees. That is the subject of the seventh chapter.

An impressive amount of research has been conducted during the past half century, and especially during the past quarter century, on the qualities of good leaders and on how to identify potential leaders. Therefore the eighth assumption on which this book rests is that it would be foolish to ignore that research. A brief introduction to that subject constitutes the eighth chapter.

Once upon a time many people believed that leaders created the epoch which provided the context for their work. Today the overwhelming weight of opinion is that leaders are greatly influenced, and often energized, by the era in which they function. In simple terms the question is did Julius Caesar create the Roman Empire, or were the conditions such that called forth a leader with Caesar's gifts? Was Abraham Lincoln a great natural leader, or did the outbreak of the Civil War make Lincoln a notable president? Did Hitler create Nazi Germany, or did postwar conditions in Germany create the conditions calling for a strong leader? The ninth assumption on which this and all of this author's previous books are based is that the size and type of the church, the congregational culture, and the role and style of the most influential recent predecessor are exceptionally influential factors that affect the leadership roles of both the laity and the clergy. This assumption is part of the foundation of every chapter.

A tenth assumption is that no two people are exactly alike, but that effective leaders do have much in common. That is both the reason for writing a book on leadership that is directed to a general audience and also for the admonition that every leader should identify his or her gifts, skills, talents, and experiences and build on these strengths in shaping a role and in developing a distinctive leadership style. Thus the perceptive reader will be able to shrug off some of the suggestions and advice offered here with a comment, "That doesn't fit me," and go on, without any feelings of guilt, to the next section. Discard what does not fit.

The eleventh of these twelve assumptions is that it is never too late to learn! Therefore the contents of the entire book are set in the context of the life of the worshiping congregation. No one is expected to learn everything while in school. There is life after graduation, and for many that is the best time to learn new concepts and to master new skills in leadership.

Finally, the last of these twelve assumptions, and far and away the most important one, is that God is still at work in the world He created. Unlike those who are convinced that God is off in some faraway corner of the universe alternately laughing and crying as He watches what these sinful human beings are doing to His creation, this writer is convinced that God still is interacting with what He created. That may mean that the most significant act of any leader is to keep the door open to the Holy Spirit!

The story of a composite character named Jerry Buchanan, who agrees with all these assumptions, provides an introduction to the operational expression of what is contained in subsequent chapters. By accepting the role of an initiating leader, Jerry illustrates many of the essential concepts of leadership and of the use of central organizing principles. Jerry's first year as the pastor at Trinity Church also illustrates the point that no one leader is always able to make everyone happy. Remember that!

PROLOGUE

"I realize it's too far away for you or anyone else to come see me, but I've decided I'm no longer able to live here by myself. The time has come for me to go to a nursing home, and I've been accepted by the Hillcrest Home," explained the eighty-three-year-old Mrs. Albert Porter to her pastor at Trinity Church.

"I know it's almost two hundred miles from here," continued Mrs. Porter, "but it's less than a mile from what everyone agrees is the best hospital anywhere around. Nelda Brice, who has been a lifelong friend, has been living there for nearly two years, and she writes me once a week. In every letter she tells me what a wonderful place it is and has begged me to consider coming to share a room with her. It's also almost exactly halfway between where my daughter and her husband live and where my son and his family now live. He used to live over here in Reedtown, but when he got this new job, they had to move, and they now live nearly three hundred fifty miles from here."

"But you'll be leaving your sister, Rose, behind as well as all your old friends here at Trinity and in this community," protested the minister. "Are you sure you want to move that far away? There are a lot of good nursing homes within twenty-five miles of right here."

"Yes, Rose is absolutely against my doing this," replied Mrs. Porter, "but she's been trying to run my life for more than eighty years now, so I'm used to that. She opposed my going off to school sixty-five years ago, and she was against my marrying Albert. When he died nineteen years ago, she wanted me to move in with her so she could boss me around, and I'm sure glad I didn't do that. Think what it would have been like living with her for the past nineteen years! About half of my old friends already have died, and several more already are failing. I know that if I move, I'll have to make some new friends, but I would have to do that if I went into a home here. Now don't worry about me, Reverend, I'll be all right. I know what I'm doing. I realize it's too far away to expect you to come see me, so if you want to see me one more time, drop by next Friday. My son is coming over Friday evening, and Saturday morning we're leaving."

The following Friday the minister stopped in to say good-bye to a remarkably cheerful Mrs. Porter. As he drove away in his car, he promised himself that one of these days he would surprise her by dropping in to see her when he was over in that part of the state. Two years later, however, when he left Trinity to begin serving another church, the opportunity to drop in on Mrs. Porter had not yet arrived.

* * * *

One of the first assignments the Reverend Jerry Buchanan gave himself when he arrived as the new pastor at Trinity Church was to gather three highly knowledgeable longtime members together one evening. He already had listed the names of the 243 resident and nonresident members in a six-by-nine inch looseleaf notebook. That evening he asked for identifying comments about each member. He was especially interested in learning who were identified as being relatively inactive. He was a little surprised at how many people were identified as active but also rarely attended worship and the even larger number who attended no more than once a month. Jerry had been told before coming that worship attendance had been dropping gradually for the past several years. One explanation was that many of the younger members had moved away to find jobs. Another was "church attendance is down all over." A third explanation was that the congregation was composed largely of older members, many of whom found it increasingly difficult to get out to church. It appeared to Jerry, however, that perhaps the biggest factor was that a substantial number of members, many of whom once were regular attenders, now were coming to church only occasionally.

On a bright June day a month later the new minister said to his wife, "Next Tuesday is my day off as well as yours. Let's take a trip if the weather looks promising." The following Tuesday morning Jerry, his thirty-eight-year-old wife, Mildred, and their two children, ages nine and seven, were on the highway by eight o'clock. Two hundred miles later they were enjoying a picnic lunch in a beautiful city park. A little after one o'clock Jerry said to his wife, "If you'll look after the kids for an hour, I need to make a pastoral visit."

Fifteen minutes later Jerry was introducing himself to a very surprised Mrs. Albert Porter. "So you're the new minister!" she exclaimed. "How did you ever find me way out here?"

"No one at Trinity has forgotten you. Ever since we arrived, people have been telling about what a wonderful person you are and how much they miss you. So I had to come see for myself," explained Jerry.

"Well, I'm delighted to see you, but you shouldn't have done it. Coming way over here this far to see me and driving back will take up a whole day. You can't spend a whole day simply visiting one old woman in a nursing home. When you come this far to see me, that means you're neglecting everyone else. There are members at Trinity who'll think you don't know how to make good use of your time if they learn you wasted a whole day coming way over here just to see me. Somebody's bound to figure out how much it's costing for you to make this one call," protested Mrs. Porter. "You should be back there calling on the active members."

"You're wrong," replied Jerry. "No one can object to this call. This is my day off. How I spend my day off is my business."

"You came all this way on your day off to see someone you've never met before!" exclaimed an amazed, flattered, and pleased Mrs. Porter.

Forty-five minutes later Jerry left and drove by the park to pick up Mildred and their boys. On the way home they took a slightly longer route that allowed them to spend three hours climbing the hills of a lovely state park. From the top of one of the hills they gained a breathtaking view of a beautiful lake and beach. After a brief swim in the lake, they resumed their journey and at ten o'clock that evening were back home. The next morning Jerry resumed the task of getting acquainted with his new parish while Mrs. Buchanan went back to her new job at the local municipal hospital where she worked a nine-hour day as a laboratory technician Wednesday through Saturday.

Within a week, nine different households at Trinity Church had received joy-filled letters from Mrs. Albert Porter bragging about what a wonderful pastor Jerry is and explaining how he had taken his day off to come see her. Two months later Jerry wrote Mrs. Porter a condolence note mailed to arrive on the twentieth anniversary of Albert's death. A couple of months later he mailed her birthday greetings on her eighty-fourth birthday; in December he sent her a congratulatory note following the arrival of her first great-grandchild, and the following May he mailed her a photograph of Rose's granddaughter's wedding. Although she lived two hundred miles away, Mrs. Porter was one of the most ardent supporters of the new minister at Trinity, and rarely did anyone back at Trinity receive a letter from Mrs. Porter that did not include a word of praise for the new minister.

"I simply cannot tell you how much your visits mean to me," declared Ethel Powell, a fifty-three-year-old member of Trinity who was dying of cancer, as Jerry Buchanan came to see her again that Tuesday in late August. "I'll have to tell the truth. I broke down and cried last spring when I heard our pastor was moving. I prayed I would die before he left. I didn't want to be buried by a stranger. I knew I didn't have much time left, and I was afraid I would be gone before I had a chance to get acquainted with a new minister. My husband brought me back to the hospital the day you moved here. While he can't bring himself to talk about it, he knows and I know that I'll never go home again. Two days later you came in to see me, and you've been the only one who has been willing to talk to me about death. Even the doctors and the nurses here won't talk to me about death. They keep telling me to cheer up, that God works miracles and that one of these days I'll be walking out of here and going home to my family. I know better and they know better. I've desperately needed someone that I could talk to about what it's really like to know you're dying. You've been the only one, Reverend Buchanan, and before I go, I want you to know how much you've meant to me. Your prayers, your willingness to listen to me ramble, your ministry to my husband and to our children all have meant so much to me. Before it's too late, I want you to know that I cannot imagine how anyone could have been a better pastor."

Ten days later the Reverend Jerry Buchanan conducted the funeral service for Ethel Powell. As they walked across the churchyard after the service, Betty Wagner said to Martha Hayes, "Ethel and I grew up together. We went to school together for twelve years. I was the maid of honor when she was married, and she stood up with us when Harold and I were married. We were the closest of friends, but I believe Reverend Buchanan was closer to Ethel at the end than even her husband or I. When he spoke about his conversations with Ethel as she lay there knowing she was dying, I cried. One of the reasons I cried was because I couldn't talk to Ethel about death."

"Well, that's what a minister is supposed to be able to do," commented Martha. "A minister is trained to comfort the dying and to console the bereaved."

"That may be true," replied Betty, "but I don't think I've ever met a minister before who was so sensitive to both the feelings of the person who was dying and to the survivors. I think Reverend Buchanan did an absolutely wonderful job with what had to be a very difficult responsibility today. He recaptured the spirit of Ethel in a way I'll never forget. I don't suppose he will be, but I sure hope he's still around here when the time comes for me to go."

Three years earlier Mrs. Elmer Wood, the choir director and organist at Trinity for the past seventeen years, had asked that the chancel be enlarged so she could see the choir more easily while she played the organ. Her request had been rejected, and four reasons could be identified behind that decision. Several people strongly believed that while Mrs. Wood was a superb organist, she left much to be desired as a choir director. This faction wanted her job to be divided with someone else recruited to direct the choir. The second reason for the rejection of the idea was that Phil Stephenson and Eddie Heath, the two most influential leaders at Trinity Church, did not like Elmer Wood, and both disliked Elmer's wife even more intensely. The third reason was that the proposed remodeling would cost at least $3,800 and perhaps as much as $6,000, depending on the extent of the work. Finally, the family that had given nearly half the cost of that new organ nine years earlier was afraid the console would be damaged if it were moved. So nothing was done. Mrs. Wood was still unhappy, but no one, including most of the fourteen regulars in the choir, was ready to go into battle again.

Within three months following his arrival Jerry Buchanan heard nine different versions of that story. He agreed the chancel was too small, that it looked shabby, and was poorly lighted. He also agreed it was an awkward arrangement for Mrs. Wood to both play the organ and direct the choir. He disagreed, however, with her critics. In neither of the two previous churches he had served was the choir director either as competent or as cooperative as Mrs. Wood.

Shortly after his arrival Jerry had begun to discuss with both the worship committee (which had not met for nearly three years) and with the Christian education committee the merits of planning two services for Christmas Eve. That was a new idea at Trinity. The 7:30 P.M. Christmas Eve service was a tradition of at least forty years' standing in this ninety-four-year-old congregation. Jerry explained, however, that for many young parents who had dropped out of church when they were teenagers, Christmas Eve was the number one reentry point back into the church. When he pointed out that the nave could seat only 185, and the congregation reported 243 resident confirmed members, one response was that many members were away on Christmas. Another response was that people enjoyed the feeling of a packed house for such a festive occasion.

Eventually, however, Jerry gained tentative approval of a plan for a 7:00 P.M. service on Christmas Eve that would be planned with a major emphasis on children and an 11:00 P.M. communion service planned primarily for adults with the chancel choir providing the special music. Laura Miller, Eddie Heath's twenty-three-year-old granddaughter, who taught music in the public schools but was married to a man who rarely came to church, was enlisted to organize and direct a children's choir for that early service. Her two most valuble assistants were the twin daughters of Phil Stephenson. The first practices were scheduled for early October.

The last Sunday in October Phil Stephenson and Eddie Heath cornered Jerry Buchanan between Sunday school and worship. "Reverend, we have to talk to you about building a platform out in front of the chancel for Christmas Eve. Laura says she has more kids lined up for the Christmas Eve program than she can get in the chancel. Could you meet us over here about two o'clock this afternoon so we can talk about it?"

That afternoon Phil, Eddie, Laura, and the minister met and discussed the alternative possibilities. When they adjourned, it was agreed that Phil Stephenson would get an estimate for the cost of a temporary platform that would require removal of the three front pews. Nine days later, at the monthly Board meeting, Phil came in with two detailed plans. A temporary expansion of the chancel platform would cost $900 including labor. The contractor had suggested that for $3,700 he could provide a much more attractive permanent enlargement of the chancel complete with a new railing and better lighting.

As she examined the sketches, Laura Miller pointed out, "I like the permanent arrangement much better, but it won't work for what we have in mind unless we move the organ console over to this side."

One of the choir members, who was a close friend of the choir director and also a member of the Board, commented that on the basis of the estimates they had received three years earlier, it probably would cost another $600 to $800 to move the organ console to where Laura wanted it—which also was where the choir director wanted it to be placed.

By the second Saturday in December (a) a special committee had been approved, appointed, and had been working, (b) the permanent enlargement of the chancel had been completed, (c) a total of $5,300 had been received in designated second-mile giving toward the actual cost of $4,489, (d) it had been agreed that the beautiful new chancel and the improved lighting made the robes worn by the adult choir look rather shabby so the money left over from the remodeling would go toward the purchase of twenty new choir robes, (e) Mrs. Elmer Wood, the choir director, who had been kept informed by the minister of what was going on, was surprised, delighted, and grateful, and (f) on the following Sunday morning those in attendance were impressed and pleased with the attractive new chancel.

The previous year the attendance on Christmas Eve had been 227 including the choir, people seated in chairs in the aisles and behind the back pews, and nearly a dozen who had to stand. This year, thanks to the removal of those three pews as a part of the expansion of the chancel, the crowd appeared to be equally large although the ushers reported only 199 at the 7:00 P.M. service. The 11:00 P.M. service drew 188, including nearly three dozen who also had attended the earlier service.

While many of the people, and especially the choir director, saw that remodeled chancel as the number one accomplishment of the year, a larger number were even more impressed with the fact that "We filled this church twice on Christmas Eve. That certainly reflects a new spirit here since our new minister came."

Jerry Buchanan, however, was not satisfied. Dozens of members had explained to him that he should not be discouraged with the fact that during his first summer, worship attendance had fluctuated between 110 and 120, with the exception of 171 on his first Sunday. "Our attendance always slacks off during the summer." "At our peak about twelve years ago, when Reverend Harrison was here, we only averaged 165, and you did better than that on your first Sunday here."

At the July meeting with the Christian education committee Jerry had suggested the second Sunday in September be designated as Rally Day and that an intensive effort be made to start off the fall with a big attendance in Sunday school. This received a positive response since the previous minister had not displayed much interest in the Sunday school. Jerry also offered to help organize and teach a new adult class beginning in September if a place could be found for a new class to meet. Willard Jones, who lived next door to the church, offered his living room for that purpose.

The previous spring the Sunday school attendance had averaged 113. That fall the attendance fluctuated between 140 and 150, including fifteen in the new class taught by the new minister. One fringe benefit was that in the fall, worship attendance climbed to an average of 165, a significant increase from the average of 130 for the previous calendar year.

While making his get-acquainted pastoral calls that summer and fall, Jerry had met three couples all in their early forties. All three of the husbands were Vietnam veterans. The three couples socialized together, but rarely attended church. Two of the three husbands were third-generation members of Trinity Church, and the third had married a girl whose parents and grandparents were pillars at Trinity. None of the six had been to church since Jerry's arrival, and Jerry soon discovered that they rarely attended during his predecessor's seven-year pastorate.

When one of the men discovered that Jerry had started theological seminary in the late 1960s, he asked him point-blank, "Did you go to seminary to dodge the draft?" Jerry explained that he had felt a call to the ministry while in high school and had never given a thought to any other vocation. He stated that while in seminary he knew several students who were quite open about the fact that they saw the seminary as a means of avoiding the draft, but he did not consider himself to be in that category.

One Sunday afternoon in October Jerry dropped in unannounced on the couple with whom he had become fairly well acquainted after three previous visits. They were sitting out in the backyard talking with the other two couples. When Jerry attempted to excuse himself after a few minutes, they all insisted he stay. Two hours later, following a question from Jerry, all three men not only had agreed they would be present, but they also would do their best to encourage several other veterans to attend as Jerry described his plans for a special service on the second Sunday in November at which the special contributions of veterans would be recognized.

To his surprise all three couples were in church the Sunday following his unannounced visit—they also were at worship on nearly every Sunday for the rest of Jerry's pastorate at Trinity. Several years later, when Jerry and his wife were entertaining these three couples at the parsonage, one of the men said, "Jerry, I've been wanting to tell you this for a long time, but I never was quite sure how to say it. You're the only minister I've ever met who has not made me feel guilty about being in Vietnam. You're not only a great pastor, you're a great man. I want you to know I appreciate you."

"That goes for all of us," added one of the other men, who quickly changed the subject to ask Jerry what kind of mileage he was getting on his new car.

At the January Board meeting, which began with a brief review of the success of the new Christmas Eve schedule and was followed by a report from the treasurer in which he happily pointed out that all bills had been paid in full including the denominational obligations, and they were beginning the new year with an unprecedented surplus of $3,831, the Reverend Jerry Buchanan introduced what he feared would be seen by some as a radical idea.

"It seems to me the time has come to consider two services on Sunday morning. The experts tell us that when your average attendance on Sunday morning is more than 80 percent of the capacity of the sanctuary, you have four choices. One is to build. A second is to go to two services. A third is to expect people to begin to attend less frequently. A fourth is to stop expecting first-time visitors to return. We can seat 185 in the nave plus 16 in the choir. Eighty percent of that is 160. For the past several weeks we've been running between 160 and 180 including the choir. I've been thinking the best time to begin two services would be the first Sunday in Lent. Laura Miller tells me that her new youth choir will be ready by then. They could sing at the first service, and the adult could sing at the second service."

"Well, we have to do something," declared one of the ushers. "We've had to bring chairs in on three of the last seven Sundays."

"If you were more careful in filling up every pew, you wouldn't have to bring in more chairs," retorted a Board member who obviously was opposed to Jerry's idea.

"We can't split up families," explained the usher. "If four people in one family come together, you can't put one here, two over there, and one up front."

"I like the feeling of a full house, Reverend," commented someone else. "If we go to two services, we'll divide the congregation. We'll have eighty at the first service, and they'll feel like the church is half empty because it will be half empty."

"Going to two services will undercut the congregational singing," complained someone else. "Why can't we have the youth choir sing at eleven o'clock on odd-numbered Sundays and let the adult choir sing on even-numbered Sundays?"

"All that would do would be to encourage people to attend every other Sunday," argued someone else. "Why don't we give a two-service schedule a try?"

"I think we ought to wait awhile and see if this increase in attendance is just a passing phenomenon before we make any big changes," suggested a longtime member.

"I believe we ought to encourage the youth, and this is one way to do it," declared Eddie Heath. "I move we change the schedule to two services on Sunday morning beginning with the first Sunday in Lent and give the minister the authority to determine the exact time."

"I second that motion," announced Phil Stephenson in a categorical tone of voice. The motion carried with one negative vote. It appeared that four members of the Board abstained, but no one commented on that.

"I move we evaluate the success of this idea at our May meeting and decide at that meeting whether or not we want to continue it," moved the one person who had voiced the only negative vote a minute earlier.

"That's a good idea," urged Jerry. "That will allow us enough time to see how people respond to two services. By May we should be able to tell." Without further discussion that motion was seconded and approved.

By the third Sunday in Lent the attendance at the first service was running close to 100, and for the period ending with the last Sunday in April the first service averaged 108 (including 160 on Easter) while the second service averaged 137 (including 187 on Easter). These figures included an average of nearly 40 children who were not yet of confirmation age, 9 constituents and 11 visitors. When these figures were reported at the May meeting of the Board, no one questioned the need to continue the new schedule.

One reason for the sharp increase in the average attendance was the change to two services. Experience suggests that if five congregations change from one worship experience on Sunday morning to two, four of them will experience an increase that will average about 15 percent while one out of five will experience no increase or may even drop a little.

A second, and more influential reason for the sharp increase in Sunday morning worship attendance at Trinity Church was the new minister's long-term strategy to expand the number of special Sundays. In addition to Palm Sunday, Easter, and Mother's Day, during his first eighteen months at Trinity Church Jerry Buchanan planned special services for Rally Day, World Communion Sunday, Reformation Sunday, Laity Sunday, World Peace Sunday, Veterans' Sunday, Thanksgiving Sunday, every Sunday in Advent, the birthday of Martin Luther King, Jr., every Sunday in Lent, One Great Hour of Sharing, Pentecost, the ninety-fifth anniversary of the founding of Trinity Church on the last Sunday in April, Missionary Sunday, Independence Sunday, World Hunger Sunday, and that second Sunday in February when all couples married for twenty-five years or more who chose to do so came forward to renew their marriage vows.

For each of these special Sundays Jerry organized a committee of three to ten persons who helped plan the day and also worked at publicizing in advance the special significance of that special occasion.

The third factor in that increase in worship attendance, and it could be argued this was the most influential factor, was that the Reverend Jerry Buchanan strongly believed it is good for Christians to come together to praise God and to worship Him. This was clearly a central theme in Jerry's ministry. He worked hard to increase attendance.

Another example of Jerry's determination to increase the worship attendance was his response the next summer to the traditional summer slump. During his first summer at Trinity Jerry had been advised that Trinity always cut back during the summer. Many members were on vacation, and an increasing number spent their weekends at their cottages on one of the lakes fifty miles to the north. The choir was on vacation for July and August, and the Sunday school closed down during August.

At the April meeting of the Board Jerry raised this issue. The first response came from the head usher who declared, "Sometimes we even have a hard time finding three people to take up the offering in August."

Undeterred, Jerry suggested, "I would like to try an experiment. Let's not schedule the summer slump this year. We've arranged our family's vacation so I'll be gone only one Sunday during July and August. Let's see if we can maintain the momentum we've built up during the spring by maintaining a full program for the summer."

The Sunday school superintendent replied, "The only way I can get teachers is by promising them they won't have to teach in August." The only tenor in the choir said, "I'll be gone all of August, and I know Mrs. Wood plans to be gone in July, so I don't see how we can have a choir."

After nearly two hours' discussion, it was decided to (a) continue the worship schedule for the entire summer, (b) plan intergenerational classes for the Sunday school during August, (c) arrange for special music, including two Sundays with a men's and boys' chorus and one Sunday with a women's chorus, so the choir could continue the custom of not being expected to sing during July and August, and (d) designate six of those nine Sundays as special days.

For those nine Sundays, worship attendance averaged 191 including what everyone saw as a surprisingly large number of visitors.

Finally, many of the members at Trinity attributed the increased attendance to Jerry's calling. Exclusive of trips to the hospitals and nursing homes, Jerry set for himself a goal of 500 calls a year with one-third of these on prospective new members and constituents. That not only enabled him to enlist people for all the short-term committees he created, it also was a powerful counterforce to the natural tendency of many members to drift into a less active role. Jerry was firmly convinced that involved members are more likely to be in church on Sunday than those who are not actively involved in some specific facet of the life and ministry of that congregation.

While much was accomplished during Jerry Buchanan's first year at Trinity Church, the road was not completely smooth. One major disturbance and several minor ones upset several members. The first came in early August when Marilyn Cahoon, the mother of a sixteen-year-old son and a fourteen-year-old daughter asked Jerry, "What are you intending to do about a youth group? We haven't had a decent youth program here for several years and some of us parents have been hoping you'll make organizing and leading a youth group a top priority. We were hoping that by now you would have announced something that would bring the kids together soon after school starts this fall."

"You're not the first one to raise this, Marilyn," replied Jerry. "I agree on the need, but so far we've not found any volunteers who will lead it. This came up at last month's meeting of the Christian education committee, but the only members anyone could identify as possible counselors were Jack and Loretta Russell, and they're moving away at the end of this month."

"Well, I was hoping you would take it on yourself," urged Mrs. Cahoon. "Or maybe you or your wife could do it together. We really do need to get something started soon, or the kids will get so involved in school activities that they won't have time for it."

"Sorry, but there are two things I don't do," declared Jerry. "One is I do not volunteer my wife for anything. The second is I don't do youth ministries. That's not my gift. I'll be glad to help organize it and to work with the counselors if we can find three or four volunteers who will carry the basic responsibility, but I will not take the lead."

In February Mickey Brown stopped by the office one Tuesday morning and said, "Jerry, our last minister always appreciated it when I acted as his eyes and ears for him, and I thought maybe I could help you get off to a smooth start here. Please do not misunderstand me; this is not criticism. It's simply I've been hearing some things that I thought you might not know, but you should know. There are at least four couples here who are beginning to complain that you haven't stopped by to see them since you made that first round of visits last summer."

"Are they shut-ins?" asked Jerry.

"No, all four are in good health and able to get out. In fact, three of them are in church nearly every Sunday," replied Mickey Brown.

"Are they complaining that they've asked me to call, but I haven't done so?" was Jerry's next question.

"No, I don't think so," came the reply. "They just think it would be nice if you would drop in on them three or four times a year like your predecessor did. They're a little lonely, and they simply would like a little more attention."

"I really do appreciate your stopping by and telling me," explained Jerry, recognizing this was an excellent opportunity to plug into one of the largest intake valves in the local grapevine. "Let me take a minute of your time and explain how I try to schedule my week. As you probably remember, shortly after I came, I explained that I planned to call in every home before Easter. I'm about 95 percent of the way toward accomplishing that goal. It seems as if a few of our members are never home when I'm free. I visit all three of the hospitals our people go to whenever I know someone is in the hospital. I've also tried to make it clear that I'll respond whenever anyone asks me to stop by. One thing I can't do, however, if I'm going to be able to do all the other things I have to do here, is a lot of dropping in on people without any particular point to that visit."

"Well, I know you're real busy, what with having two services now, but here are the names of those four couples in case you do find yourself with a little extra time," responded Mickey, placing a piece of paper on Jerry's desk and walking out without another word.

A few weeks after the new Sunday morning schedule had been inaugurated, another member said to Jerry, "I've got an idea for increasing the attendance at this first service. Why don't you take a few minutes every morning, ask the little kids to come up and tell them a story. I think a children's sermon would add a lot to that first service."

"That's a good idea," acknowledged Jerry, "but I'm not the one to do it. I've never felt comfortable talking to three- and four- and five-year-olds. I do a lot better with adults. Maybe I can find someone, however, who can do it." A month later Jerry had persuaded Mrs. Arthur Zimmerman, a sixty-three-year-old grandmother of seven to try it. She agreed, on the condition that Jerry would bring her some books with sermons for little children. Beginning with the Sunday after Easter, the children's message became a regular part of the early service at Trinity. During the following twelve months Mrs. Zimmerman fulfilled that role on forty Sundays, her substitute did it ten times, and twice Jerry delivered the children's sermon. Each time he tried it he knew he had made a wise decision in asking Mrs. Zimmerman to do it. Jerry's wife and two sons agreed with him on both occasions.

The least significant of these points of dissension came up about four months after Jerry's arrival. The chairperson of the finance committee remained after worship one Sunday to talk to Jerry alone. "I need a minute of your time, Reverend, before our meeting Tuesday night. As you know, every fall we recruit a group of callers who go out and visit all the members and ask them for their pledge for the coming year. What you may not know is that for a dozen years or more, the custom here has been for the minister to call on five of our biggest contributors. We've found they're a little more generous in their response when it's the minister who asks them for their pledge. The minister who started this approached a couple of them on the golf course, and I know he took one other couple out to dinner to sort of warm them up for the occasion. We don't care how you do it, but I thought I had better tell you about that custom before it comes up at our Tuesday night meeting."

"This is all news to me, and I certainly do appreciate your telling me about it before we get to the finance committee meeting," replied Jerry with genuine gratitude in his voice, "but I don't ask people for money. I know that a great many ministers do, and some of them do it very effectively. Long ago, however, I decided that while I'll be glad to preach on stewardship and to work with the finance committee, I won't do the calling that's involved in asking people for pledges. I do not want to do anything that might cause people to think when they see me coming to their front door, that I'll be asking them for money."

"That's fair enough," replied this sixty-six-year-old lifetime member of Trinity, who was also the father of one of the three Vietnam veterans Jerry had been visiting. "If you do the pastoral work, I guess our committee can take care of the finances." The subject of Jerry's calling on potential big contributors did not come up at the Tuesday evening meeting, and afterward some of the members wondered to themselves why it had not been discussed, but they did not pursue it.

At the April meeting of the Board someone inquired, "I just heard the other day that we're going to run our own vacation Bible school this summer. How come? We've always done that cooperatively with our three neighboring churches for as long as I can remember. Who made the decision that we should go it alone this year?"

"That was decided at our meeting last week," explained the person who had chaired the Christian education committee for the past seven years. "We discussed in great detail the question of whether we should run our own or run it as a joint project of the four churches. One of the facts that came up was that nearly one-third of our own children do not participate in those years when it is scheduled to be held in one of the other three churches. We get our best participation from our own families every fourth year, when it is held here at Trinity. A second fact was that last year was the fourth year in a row that our total enrollment had dropped."

"Is this a final decision?" interrupted the man who had raised the issue. "If it is, I'm sorry to hear it. I believe very strongly in interchurch cooperation, and I wish Trinity would do more, rather than cut back on cooperating with other churches. I was disappointed that we would have our own Thanksgiving service here, rather than cooperate in the union service on Thursday morning as we used to do."

"That was one of the factors that made our committee think seriously about going it alone this summer," continued the chairperson who had been interrupted. "When Jerry pointed out that our special Thanksgiving service here on Wednesday evening drew nearly two hundred, and we had never had any more than that when the four churches had a union service on Thursday morning, we concluded that we probably could reach more people by having our own vacation Bible school."

"I have friends in each of those other three congregations," observed another member of the Board, "and already I've been hearing questions about why Trinity no longer wants to cooperate with anyone else."

At this point Jerry took the floor and asked, "Let me take a few minutes to tell you a little about who I am. When I was seven years old, an uncle came by one summer day with his two sons to take my ten-year-old brother and me for an all-day picnic in a state park. That afternoon we went down to the beach, and my uncle, his two boys, and my older brother went in swimming while I played in the sand on the beach. They kept asking me to join them, but I refused since I didn't know how to swim. Finally my uncle came over, picked me up, carried me out to where the water must have been five- or six-feet deep and said, 'The way you learn to swim is by swimming,' and dropped me in. I didn't know anything about swimming, and I almost drowned. I was absolutely terrified. I can still remember how scared I was that I was going to drown. He finally fished me out and took me back to the beach where someone helped him pump the water out of me that I had swallowed. He told me he guessed I needed a few lessons.

"Several years later I tried to swim, but I simply couldn't keep my head under water. When I got to college, I was told I couldn't graduate until I learned to swim, so I enrolled for swimming lessons. After almost drowning a couple of times, I got a waiver from a doctor at the infirmary so I could graduate. My wife, Mildred, is an excellent swimmer and both of our boys are good swimmers, and I'm glad they are. A long time ago Mildred gave up on nagging me to learn to swim, but the boys still insist I should learn. I explain that what I do best is stay away from large bodies of deep water.

"Now the point of that story is not to explain why I don't swim," continued Jerry to an intently listening Board. "The point of that story is there are a number of things I don't do. I believe I've been in the pastorate long enough to be able to recognize most of my strengths as well as my weaknesses. One of things I don't do is swim. Another is I don't feel comfortable asking members for money or pledges. A third is I never have been comfortable with teenagers, so that explains why we're still looking for volunteers to serve as counselors for a high school youth group. I never have felt comfortable about my ability to communicate with young children so that's why I've asked Lillian Zimmerman to do the children's sermon. I don't believe I can afford the time to do a lot of social calling on folks who would enjoy having the preacher drop in on them every few weeks. As you all know, I do a fair amount of calling, but I believe every call must have a purpose.

"One more thing I no longer do is to encourage intercongregational cooperation in program and ministry. While I was in seminary, I was taught that it was good to cooperate with other churches, and we did a lot of that in my first pastorate. About halfway through my second pastorate, however, I discovered that intercongregational cooperation in program and ministry is not compatible with numerical growth in a church. I didn't want to believe that, and I still wish it weren't true, but all the evidence I've seen points in that direction. That's why I suggested we have our own Thanksgiving service last fall and why I urged the Christian education committee last week that we plan to have our own vacation Bible school. One of the things I don't do anymore is to promote intercongregational cooperation in programming."

After a long pause the chairperson of the Board said, "That was an interesting statement, Jerry, and we appreciate your candor. I guess we're not used to a minister's laying everything on the line so clearly. I do want you to know that if you come up to our cabin on the lake this summer, I'll be glad to pitch horseshoes with you while the others go swimming. I don't swim either."

"Thanks for the invitation," replied Jerry, "but you also should know that I never learned to pitch horseshoes. In fact, there's a whole long list of other things I don't do. I don't expect to take my turn in the crib room, I can't sing well enough to be in the choir as one of my predecessors did, I don't play golf, and I can't play the piano or guitar."

As they drove home together, Larry Ward said to his neighbor, "You know, Lynn, I was a litle surprised to hear Jerry be so categorical about what he won't do. I know there're a lot of parents who were hoping when he came that he and his wife would take the lead in building a strong youth program. I don't think I've ever heard a minister be so blunt about what he wouldn't do. The ministers I've known over the years tend to feel they have to be able to do everything and are always talking about all the different things they do. I suspect a few of

"Some just arrive on time while others charge in with a plan in mind!"

— FRIAR TUCK

the Board members were a little upset with that speech of Jerry's tonight. Some of us believe that one way we grow is by accepting challenges to learn to do things we've never done before."

"I was a little surprised, too," agreed Lynn Howell, "and perhaps most of all by the tone of his voice, but I'm glad he said what he did. I admire people who know what they don't do, and you have to admit Jerry is a real leader!"

Although this story is a composite, drawn from three different ministers' experiences in that honeymoon first year of a new pastorate, it does illustrate several issues for those concerned with ministerial leadership roles and styles.

First, and perhaps most obvious, is that Jerry Buchanan represents a proactive leadership stance. Instead of waiting and responding to others, he was willing to take the initiative. A limited historical foundation does exist for the conventional wisdom that suggests a newly arrived minister should not rock the boat during that first year. In perhaps three-quarters of all situations, however, that is bad advice for the newly arrived pastor. Frequently the new minister encounters a sea of passivity. Rather than attempt to out-passive the passive, the new minister would be well advised to accept the role of an initiating leader. Jerry is an example of a pastor who could be assertive without being aggressive and who could persuade people to follow his leadership. Obviously it is a style that not every minister will find to be comfortable.

Too many ministers come out of seminary with a laissez-faire version of the enabler concept and adopt a noninterference or reactive approach to leadership. The overwhelming majority of congregations today want a minister who is willing and able to function as an initiating leader. Jerry Buchanan accepted that role.

A second clue to Jerry's leadership approach was illustrated by the need to enlarge the chancel. Rather than reactivate the old alliances that had come to a stalemate on that issue three years earlier, Jerry built new alliances. He made sure that key leaders from the old opposition were now involved in pushing for that overdue remodeling. Jerry also recognized that "something for the children" would have broader appeal than would a remodeling program perceived largely in response to the need of "making our choir director happy." Jerry redefined the issue and built new alliances around that new definition of the issue.

Third, Jerry was and is a self-confident individual. He has confidence in himself, in the gift God has given him, in his competence as a pastor, in his ideas, and in his intuition. The leader who exudes self-confidence finds it compratively easy to enlist allies and supporters. Winston Churchill and Franklin D. Roosevelt stand out as among the best known self-confident leaders of this century. Like them, Jerry has a strong ego.

This strong ego enabled Jerry to be open with people about what he does not do. He acted from strength, not from weakness. Instead of apologizing for not organizing and leading a new youth group or for not doing the children's sermon or for not following the tradition of a predecessor in making a lot of "drop in" pastoral visits, Jerry knew what he believed he was called to be and to do. Knowing what one does not do often clarifies that. His forthright statements on what he does not do illustrated three important characteristics of an effective leader. He was able to identify and share with people what he does not feel his strengths to be. He was able to do this without apology. Most significant of all, he was able to allocate large amounts of time to those responsibilities that would have significant long-term implications for that congregation while he neglected those tasks that either someone else could do or were not of long-term significance for that congregation. That is one mark of a leader with a healthy ego.

Fourth, and perhaps most significant, the new minister recognized that in the typical small or middle-sized congregation, the most highly prized competence in a minister is the ability to accept the role as the local expert in the Christian view of death. This is especially true in smaller communities. Jerry's ministry with the terminally ill Ethel Powell and her funeral service demonstrated that the new minister was willing to accept that role.

Fifth, in most congregations, and in nearly all small towns, the local grapevine is the most widely used channel of communication for disseminating reactions to the new minister. Jerry understood that and was willing to invest a day off in a combination family outing and feeding the grapevine some good news about the new minister.

Sixth, unlike many people of his generation, Jerry was able to separate his own personal feelings about the war in Vietnam from his attitudes toward those who had participated in that conflict. His persistent and nonjudgmental pastoral approach brought three alienated veterans and their families back into the church.

His relationships with these three couples, with the choir director, his long trip to visit Mrs. Albert Porter, and his ministry with the dying Ethel Powell also illustrate what many of the parishioners at Trinity lifted up when asked about Jerry's number one gift. "He likes people" was the response most often given to that question. The leader who loves people has a tremendous advantage over the leader who does not like or is uncomfortable with people. Although it is listed here as seventh, many of the parishioners at Trinity placed it at the top of their list of reasons why Jerry is an effective pastor.

Eighth, this was Jerry's third pastorate, not his first. He had had a chance to reflect on his experiences and to learn from those experiences. That is a mark of a mature leader. Leaders grow with the passing of time.

A ninth point about leadership that is illustrated by this account is the value of a long-term central goal. A long-term central objective or goal is essential for anyone who seeks to be an intentional leader, who is planning an internally consistent and coherent approach to program development, and who is discontented with the status quo. Jerry's goal was to increase the proportion of the members who gathered every Sunday to worship God. He did not believe that all the members had to meet together and discuss it in order to gain a sense of "ownership" of that goal. Jerry was convinced that the centrality of Word and Sacrament was a given and undebateable aspect of being a part of Christ's church.

Jerry recognized that only when a widely perceived crisis exists is there much chance of changing the status quo by majority vote. Most of the time the majority will favor a continuation of the present conditions over change. Jerry was able to deal effectively with this predictable tendency because he understood the biblical narrative to be the story of God's repeated intervention into the world to change the status quo. The Bible is not a brief for maintaining the status quo. Moses (Exod. 3:16) and Paul (Acts 15) were two of Jerry's models of leadership, and neither of them waited for the majority to tell them what to do. Jerry acted on the conviction that leaders have the responsibility to initiate rather than to wait and respond to someone else's initiative.

One day a fellow minister questioned him about what this friend perceived as a unilateral streak in Jerry's approach to leadership.

"Let me use an analogy," explained Jerry. "When Mildred and I were over to visit you and your wife a month ago, we played that new table game you had just purchased. Remember when we had a dispute over how you counted up the points? To settle the dispute you read the rules very carefully, and we all accepted what that person had written in the rules. I pointed out to you that what we were doing was accepting, without question, the statement of someone none of us had ever met, who might even be dead by now, and who had never consulted any of us before writing that set of rules. You replied that when we agreed to play that game, that also implied we were going to follow the rules that went with the game. That's how I see it. When anyone unites with the congregation where I am the pastor, they play by the rules that go with that game. One of the rules is to be in church to worship God every Sunday morning. I don't think it's any more necessary to bring everyone together to discuss that and adopt it than it was for us to meet with the person who wrote the rules for that table game. When we agreed to play the game, we accepted the rules."

This distinction between being involved in the creation of a new idea or a goal and accepting a goal created by someone else is a central component of Jerry's approach to leadership. He followed it in unilaterally deciding to designate nearly a score of Sundays as special days. From the Board he sought only the withholding of a veto as he suggested additional special Sundays. The acceptance came when various members agreed to serve on specific ad hoc committees to plan and publicize those special Sundays. Likewise Jerry unilaterally invented the proposal for two services on Christmas Eve. Acceptance came with the creation of that new children's choir and by the unprecedented attendance. Jerry also unilaterally announced his intention to organize and teach a new adult class if a space could be found for that class to meet. Acceptance came from (a) the Christian education committee and (b) the fifteen people who joined that class.

Another value of a central long-term goal is that after that goal has been formulated, it becomes possible to develop a variety of mutually compatible programs that reinforce that central goal.

At Trinity Church the expansion of the Sunday church school, the revival of Rally Day, the creation of several special Sundays, the remodeling of the chancel, the decision not to schedule the traditional summer slump, and the pastoral calling all reinforced that central goal. Jerry's ego was sufficiently strong that he could affirm the fact that when the pastor is willing to organize and teach a proposed new adult class, that greatly enhances the possibility that class will still be in existence a year later. The scheduling of two worship experiences on Christmas Eve was reinforced by creation of that large children's choir. The plan to change the Sunday morning schedule to include two services was timed to coincide with the organization of the high school youth choir that would sing at the first hour.

Too often new programs are launched completely independently of one another, and some die because of unanticipated competition, while others wither because of a lack of support. When new programs are designed to reinforce a central goal, the chances of destructive competition are reduced.

Four incidents in this narrative illustrate Jerry's "Affirm and Build" style of leadership. The most obvious to the reader was when he affirmed the doubting Board member who voted against changing to two services on Sunday morning. When that person moved that the whole idea be evaluated in May, Jerry affirmed both him and the idea of internal self-evaluation.

Earlier when Jerry arrived and saw that shabby, crowded, and badly lighted chancel, he did not waste time criticizing his predecessor or the trustees. Instead he affirmed those who wanted the remodeling and worked to build a new alliance that could turn the dream into reality.

By driving more than four hundred miles in one day to visit Mrs. Albert Porter, he not only made her know that while she was far away, she was not forgotten. That trip also was a powerful affirmation to those who saw themselves moving into a nursing home in the near future. If the new minister would drive two hundred miles to see Mrs. Porter, surely they would not be forgotten when the time came for them to move into a nursing home.

Perhaps most difficult of all, this new minister affirmed Ethel Powell, as she lay waiting for death to arrive, that it is all right for the dying to want to talk about death. Few can do that.

This account of one pastor's honeymoon year also illustrates the value of building on success. Jerry waited until after the new idea of two services on Christmas Eve was widely perceived as a success and he waited until the Sunday morning attendance had begun to climb before bringing in a specific proposal to change the Sunday morning schedule. He waited until Laura Miller, Eddie Heath's granddaughter, had organized an unexpectedly large number of children to practice for that early Christmas Eve Service before letting anyone place the idea of enlarging the chancel back on the agenda.

While to some this may appear to be a case study of a hyperactive pastor, an important lesson is the central importance of allies. The Reverend Jerry Buchanan is an initiating leader, but he always was seeking allies. Five types of allies can be identified in this story. The first are those Jerry enlisted. These include that group of longtime members who worked through the membership roll that evening soon after he arrived. That list also includes Mrs. Albert Porter who nurtured the grapevine, Laura Miller who organized two choirs, the three Vietnam veterans, and Lillian Zimmerman who told the children's story on Sunday morning.

A second list of allies includes those who had been identified as influential leaders by the members long before anyone at Trinity Church had ever heard of Jerry Buchanan. That list included Phil Stephenson and Eddie Heath.

A third group of allies were the various committees and the Board. Jerry did not bypass them. The worship committee, which had not met for three years, became a valuable ally. Jerry recognized that the larger the congregation, the more crucial the role of standing committees. If this congregation was to realize its potential, the standing committees had to become more active.

A fourth group of allies were the ad hoc committees organized to prepare for the two services on Christmas Eve, to carry out the proposal to remodel the chancel, to plan each of those special Sundays, and to carry out a stronger program that second summer. Jerry recognized that frequently ad hoc committees are more effective in implementing innovative ideas than are long-established groups and committees. Typically the ad hoc committee sees itself as being created to do rather than to debate why it cannot be done.

The fifth group of allies enlisted by Jerry were the self-identified losers. This list included Mrs. Elmer Wood, the director of the adult choir and the one Board member who in January voted against going to two services and in May reported, on behalf of the special evaluation committee, that the evidence suggested the new schedule be made permanent. This list also included the three Vietnam veterans and a couple of dozen other members who had dropped into relative inactivity long before Jerry appeared on the scene.

Another lesson from this account can be summarized in that bit of folk wisdom, "Most of us do our best thinking on the way home from the meeting." While he is an action-oriented individual, Jerry Buchanan tries to allow people to have a chance to reflect on their second thoughts. Many good ideas are rejected the first time they are presented. Some of us need time to talk ourselves into doing what needs to be done. Eddie Heath needed time, and some encouragement from his granddaughter, to talk himself into supporting the idea of remodeling the chancel. Several people needed time to talk themselves into believing that was a wise expenditure of money. While he waited until January before bringing it before the Board, for several months Jerry had been talking with various individuals and committees about the possibility of changing the schedule to two services on Sunday morning. Six months elapsed between the time when Jerry first suggested two services on Christmas Eve and the evening when that memorable experience occurred.

Jerry's seminary roommate and longtime friend, who had left the parish ministry to become a pastoral counselor, reflected on Jerry's approach to leadership, "If I were limited to one comment about Jerry, it would be that he is not an angry man. A remarkably large number of ministers are filled with partially suppressed anger. Some of them are superb preachers. Several of the most productive senior ministers I have met are very angry people. The two pricetags on their effectiveness are they usually are very hard to get along with and they make a lot of people feel guilty. That's not Jerry, however. Jerry is strongly goal oriented and he

NOW, EVERYONE, AT THE COUNT OF THREE, LET'S ALL MARK OUR CALENDARS!

we need ministers who will function in long time frames!

FRIAR TUCK

is persistent, but he's not angry. He loves people and he wouldn't know how to push that movitation button marked 'Guilt' if his life depended on it. I expect some of his parishioners criticize him for being too nonjudgmental, but that's their problem, not Jerry's. Jerry knows where he is going and he knows how to get there, but he'll be very careful not to step on anybody on the way."

Perhaps the most subtle point illustrated by Jerry's experiences in that first year is that he recognized the distinctive congregational culture of Trinity Church, he affirmed those traditions and values he could authentically affirm, but he was always willing to help reshape that culture, to create new traditions, and to lift up those values he believed in most strongly.

Finally, this account of a few episodes from the first year of a pastorate illustrates the value of a long time-frame. In addition to that central goal of increasing the proportion of members who gathered on Sunday morning to worship God, Jerry Buchanan functioned within a relatively long time-frame. He recognized that building a relationship with those three veterans of Vietnam could not be accomplished in one or two visits. He understood that Phil Stephenson and Eddie Heath needed both time and some face-saving reasons before they could reverse their position on remodeling that chancel. He knew that this congregation would need time before it would be ready to agree not to schedule the normal summer slump so he did not raise that issue the first summer. Jerry also recognized the long-term advantages of strengthening the committee system, of enlarging the program, of initiating new traditions, and of broadening the base of participation, even though many of the benefits would not be visible for several years.

The story of Jerry Buchanan's first year at Trinity Church also provides the introduction to a more detailed review of organizing principles and leadership concepts in a book that strongly advocates the concept of initiating and intentional leadership. Perhaps the best beginning point for that discussion is to examine the institutional context for leadership. This not only will help explain the nature of the tribe within which the Reverend Jerry Buchanan functioned, but also offers a broader context for looking at leadership.

TRIBES, MOVEMENTS, AND ORGANIZATIONS

"What you call a church council, we call the session in Presbyterian circles," explained Robert Burns, an elder at the Knox Presbyterian Church, to his neighbor. "Our session is composed of nine ruling elders plus our minister who is our teaching elder. Each of the nine lay elders chairs one of the standing committees in our church. For example, I chair the finance committee. When we meet together, we elders have responsibility for both the administrative and the spiritual oversight of the entire congregation."

"Sounds logical," observed the neighbor, "that's an ancient tribal organizing pattern. If it's worked elsewhere for thousands of years, it should work for you."

"What do you mean, 'tribal'? This is the Presbyterian way of organizing," questioned Elder Burns. "It's decent and orderly."

"Oh, nothing to be upset about," replied the neighbor. "I simply was observing that your system has ancient roots. The typical tribal system of government has three components. One is the family, the second is the clan, and the third is the tribe. The clan serves as the link between the family and the tribe. The tribe is ruled by elders, each one representing a particular clan—you call them committees—and the elders come together to make decisions on behalf of the entire tribe. Does your session meet around a campfire?"

"Only when we have our fall overnight officers' retreat," replied Mr. Burns with a smile.

* * * *

"One of the first things I learned after I arrived here was that if I wanted something to happen, I had to win the support of both the Nelsons and the Schumachers," explained the pastor of the 185-member Oak Grove Church. "Those are the two big family trees in this parish. About a fifth of the members are related to the Nelsons, but all of the Norwegians here identify with them. There are about five or six families that are interrelated with the Schumachers, but a lot of the members with a German ancestry identify with their point of view. While neither one is a majority, those two clans are very influential. My predecessor refused to play what he called 'church politics' and had a miserable time while he was here. I don't think of it as church politics, I see this parish as one big tribe composed of nearly sixty families. Some of the families identify with a particular clan and some with another clan. Nothing is going to happen if either the Nelsons or the Schumachers oppose it. My Dad calls it survival politics, but I call it human nature."

* * * *

"Susan over here represents our commission on nurture and outreach, Bill staffs education, Tom relates to music and youth, Florence is my secretary and manages the office, and I guess I represent the church council and the administration," explained the senior minister of the nine-hundred-member First Church to a visitor who was attending the regular Tuesday morning staff meeting.

"That's not quite accurate," interrupted Susan, looking at the senior minister. "While you may think of yourself as the chief administrator who also represents the council, you're really the tribal chief here, and we are your assistants."

"That may be true for the five of us," corrected Bill, who is both an associate minister and responsible for the Christian education program, "but from the congregational perspective you are both the tribal chief and the number one medicine man. While we're both ordained, Susan and I know we are only assistant medicine men in this tribe."

"What does that make me?" inquired Florence, who was in her twenty-seventh year on the staff at First Church.

"That's easy," replied Susan quickly. "You're the keeper of the tribal legends for this tribe."

"Yes, and you're also the beloved matriarch of this tribe," added Bill.

*   *   *   *

These three conversations identify a useful frame of reference for looking at congregational life and also provide a realistic context for an examination of leadership roles and styles. Most churches do resemble a tribe. While many of the members often say, "We're a big, loving family here in this church," that concept has two severe limitations. First, and most obvious, the vast majority of congregations are too large to be conceptualized as families. If one uses the Old Testament system of families, clans, tribes, and nations, perhaps 5 to 10 percent of all Protestant congregations on the North American continent could be described as extended families, and possibly as many as another 30 percent could be described as clans, but the majority resemble tribes consisting of several clans and many families. One or 2 percent are so large they resemble nations rather than tribes.

The use of the family as an analogy tends to understate the size and complexity, as well as limit the potential for numerical growth, of the typical Protestant church. It is a self-image with significant limitations for the future. Because of its self-limiting and exclusionary characteristics, it also can be a major barrier both to numerical growth and to reaching newcomers to the community.

More serious, conceptualizing a congregation as an extended family may enhance the feelings of caring and concern for one another, but it is a simplistic and misleading model for understanding the dynamics of the organizational life and for reflecting on leadership roles and responsibilities. This can be seen by looking briefly at the characteristics of tribes and relating these to congregational life.

What Is a Tribe?

The tribe has been the basic social unit for clusters of families on this planet for thousands of years. It represented the basic social unit among the nomads of Asia as well as among the natives of North and South America, Africa, and Australia. Throughout history tribes have displayed a number of similar characteristics that can help explain forms of human behavior within individual congregations and also in congregation-denomination relationships.

1. A high value is placed on kinship ties by blood. The man whose ancestors came from Germany, but who fell in love with and married the daughter of a couple who both came from Norway and who are members of a Norwegian Lutheran parish in Minnesota, soon discovered that while one can be adopted into a tribe, kinship ties are very powerful and tend to be both a cohesive force and an exclusionary dynamic.

2. Historically tribes have a strong interest in genealogy. It is a persistent thread in the Old Testament. This characteristic also surfaces very quickly if one reads the histories of congregations founded at least a hundred years ago, and it often shows up in the deliberations of the nominating committee or in the conversation at a wedding reception. Perhaps the clearest example in the ecclesiastical world is the continued power of the concept of apostolic succession.

3. The largest tribes have been built around the tenure of a highly influential and widely respected leader. The death of that leader does not automatically terminate that individual's influence. This characteristic can be identified today in dozens of large, independent congregations and in several radio or television ministries in which the son or son-in-law of the founding pastor is the heir apparent or successor.

4. As the years go by, the strength of the kinship ties may diminish as the distinctive identity of the tribe evolves from bloodlines and heritage to territory. Thus hundreds of what originally were Polish or Slovak or German or Norwegian or Swedish or Finnish or Scotch congregations gradually evolved during the first five decades of this century from nationality to geographical parishes. Historically this emphasis on kinship and territory are central threads of tribal identity. The same tendency can be seen in the claims to "our turf" by ethnic and racial gangs in the inner city and by adult Sunday school classes in big suburban churches. Turf reinforces tribal identity.

5. Some tribes experience substantial numerical growth and subdivide. This was the source of thousands of new churches in the first half of this century as a group of members left "Old First Church Downtown" to go out and colonize a new church several miles away. While less common, it still happens today, and scores of denominational leaders encourage it as one approach to new church development. The United Methodist Church has been using it with great effectiveness in Puerto Rico in recent years.

6. Historically the clan has been the link between the family and the tribe (Exod. 6:14-25). This pattern still can be seen in many rural congregations as well as in countless nationality churches. One of the many reasons attempts to create a replacement for the clan by organizing "parish units" or "zone systems" or "cottage meetings" often fail is that clans were bound together by kinship ties. In today's world, where the neighborhood no longer is a primary point of socialization, place of residence or territory no longer is an adequate substitute for kinship ties.

7. The members of the tribe speak the same language. This is part of the explanation for the failure of the hundreds of efforts to create multilingual congregations. Nations, not tribes, can be bilingual, but even the nation has difficulty when people do not speak the same language. Canadians have been very effective in illustrating that problem in recent years.

If *language* is defined more broadly, this also explains one of the reasons it has been difficult to develop congregations that cover a broad theological spectrum or are racially inclusive.

8. Tribal members normally obey and follow the same chief. This tribal characteristic explains (a) why so many churches have had difficulty with the concept of a co-pastorate, (b) why tensions occur in those congregations with a long tradition of one or two powerful lay leaders and a relatively powerless minister when a new minister comes along and secures more power than ever was granted a predecessor, and (c) why the group that leaves following a "church split" usually has one easily identifiable leader.

9. Thousands of tribes, especially the smaller tribes in Africa, never created the role of tribal chief. The tribe was ruled by a council of elders. The role of tribal chief was far more likely to exist in the Americas and in larger tribes.

The Protestant counterpart to that tribal characteristic can be seen in thousands of smaller congregations, as well as in some larger Lutheran, Reformed, Baptist, and Christian congregations, in which the council of ruling elders (or deacons) sees itself as the ruling group. The minister is the preacher, and perhaps also has a teaching role, as well as pastoral duties, but is not perceived as an influential leader. The ruling power is attached to the office of ruling elder, not to the pastoral office, and some of the elders see the pastor as an employee rather than as a leader.

One of the characteristics of the smaller tribes ruled by a council of elders was that the elders retained the right not to act. Although they sought and held tightly to the ruling office, they did not always rule. Sometimes nothing was done.

In today's ecclesiastical world this same tendency by organizations ruled by a committee or council, but without a chief executive officer, often produces great frustration among those activists who are convinced a ruling body must, by definition, rule. The tribal tradition may legitimatize inaction by the ruling elders.

10. The four most frequently followed organizing principles among tribes are (a) a common ancestry, (b) a common enemy, (c) a religious covenant, or (d) a long-tenured charismatic leader.

These same principles can be seen very clearly in the history of new church development. Several interrelated families came to Iowa from Norway and shortly thereafter organized their own Lutheran church even though a Swedish (or German) Lutheran congregation already existed in that community. In another community a group of members left the Baptist church to organize a new congregation in opposition to the leadership and/or what was being taught in the congregation they were leaving. Several couples, some of whom had no active church affiliation and some of whom were active church members but felt they were "not being fed spiritually" in their own church, met for weekly Bible study. Several months later they covenanted to organize a new congregation. The denomination sent out a personable, charming, extroverted, enthusiastic, energetic, and attractive minister to organize that new mission. In recent years the fourth of these principles has been followed by those denominations that seek to organize a new mission around the pastor.

11. Tribal customs and traditions become fixed, and gradually the tribe identifies these precedents as law. Presbyterians identify this as *The Book of Church Order* while Methodists refer to it as *The Discipline*. In most congregations, however, the vast majority of binding precedents, rules, traditions, and covenants never have been gathered together in written form, and frequently there is disagreement. Discovering these unwritten rules can be a painful experience for the newly arrived pastor.

12. In the smaller tribes a common custom was for the rulers of the several clans to come together to constitute the council of elders and to govern the tribe. This is still the custom in many rural congregations in which the death of an elder is more disruptive than the departure of a minister.

One contemporary version of this ancient tribal custom is the one-hundred-forty-year-long debate in the Southern Baptist Convention over whether deacons should be lay ministers or administrators who administer the affairs of the congregation. In some Baptist churches the elders rule while in others the minister is the tribal chief and the deacons serve as lay medicine men.

Another is the tradition in the Reformed Church in America and several other denominations that the primary role of the elders is to supervise the work of the pastor and to function as "enforcers" rather than as ministers.

A third contemporary expression of this tribal characteristic is the quarrel over, "Who's in charge here?" The pastor (tribal chief) or the governing board (council of elders)?

13. Historically one of the most common characteristics of the tribe as a social unit has been to drive out those who cannot or will not live up to tribal standards or conform to tribal customs and values. The ancient word for this is ostracism. The ecclesiastical word is excommunication. The issues may range from divorce to disagreements over biblical interpretation to language to challenges to authority. In each case, the normal tribal response is to drive out the dissenters. This has been one of the highly visible themes in the history of western Christianity and has been one of the leading sources of new denominations as well as of new congregations. This also has been the central theme of most of the great councils of the Christian church for the past nineteen hundred years beginning with the Council at Jerusalem (Acts 15:1-21) and including recent national conventions of the Southern Baptist Convention, The United Methodist Church, The Lutheran Church—Missouri Synod, and the Seventh-Day Adventist Church.

14. Tribal loyalties frequently are seen as a threat to the nation, and thus some leaders have felt forced to undercut tribal loyalties in order to encourage greater loyalty to the nation. David and Solomon represented this tendency. It also can be seen in the efforts in Africa during the third quarter of this century to form nations out of a predominantly tribal culture. This same characteristic has a long history in Methodism as senior ministers of large congregations are moved to a new appointment in order to reinforce loyalties to the denomination (nation) rather than to the congregation (tribe). This ancient tendency also was visible in the internal quarrel in The Lutheran Church—Missouri Synod during the 1970s in the demand that loyalty to the nation be superior to tribal (seminary, district) loyalties. More recently the Southern Baptist Convention has been playing the same game in the current conflict between tribal loyalties and denominational allegiance.

15. Tribes tend to flourish in an institutional setting in which there is an absence of strong central authority. This was part of the debate over the discontent in the 1780s with the Articles of Confederation and resulted in the Federal Convention of 1787 that produced a new constitution for the United States of America.

This may be one reason that the number of large congregations has increased dramatically in the Southern Baptist Convention, but that number has declined within The United Methodist Church and the Presbyterian Church (U.S.A.). This also may help explain the rapid increase in the number of very large independent or quasi-independent congregations in both the United States and Canada. A very important but almost neglected policy question is whether strong denominational ties and the emergence of very large congregations are incompatible goals.

16. Contemporary individualism and the ability to travel easily and freely beyond the boundaries of the tribal territory has undercut the traditional loyalties of the individual to both the tribe and the nation. This phenomenon can be seen very clearly among many of the native Americans who have left the Indian reservation, in the rural African tribes where many of the younger members have moved to the cities, among the Amish in Pennsylvania, among younger adults who may be fourth-generation members of the American Catholic Church, among the students who have left home to go to college five hundred miles away, and within the second and third generation of immigrant families to America from all parts of the world. The ecclesiastical term for this trend is the erosion of denominational loyalty, and it has become increasingly widespread during the past three decades.

17. Throughout the centuries tribes often measured time by the seasons of the year, by events and celebrations and births, weddings and deaths, rather than by the clock or calendar. That tribal tendency still is very powerful in many small rural churches. It may be a source of great frustration to the recent seminary graduate who attempts to teach that tribe the value of following the liturgical year, of beginning every service and meeting exactly at the appointed time and of contacting their pastor, if possible, only during the posted office hours.

18. One of the ancient responsibilities of tribes has been to "civilize" each new generation of members by teaching them to understand and honor tribal customs, traditions, and values.

Many parents see this as one of the primary responsibilities of the tribe and were dismayed when that "younger generation" born after World War II failed to accept and practice tribal teachings on courtship, marriage, divorce, dress codes, language, and deference to authority. A significant number of parents left the church because of its failure to socialize the children born after World War II into the ancient tribal customs.[1]

19. As the nation seeks to win the loyalty of the tribal members, the reasons for obeying the customs and laws change. The clan won loyalty and obedience on the basis of kinship ties, obligations to the family, and survival. These kinship obligations also were a powerful force in the tribe in gaining the loyalty and obedience of individuals even though the kinship ties might be remote. Sir Henry Maine, the founder of comparative jurisprudence, identified this sense of brotherhood, which was symbolized by the importance attached to genealogy, as one of the most important legal frictions in human history. This concept that everyone is related to everyone else encourages co-operation rather than war.

The importance of genealogy can be seen in the studies of tribal life, in the Daughters of the American Revolution, in defining one's social status in many of the newer and smaller Protestant denominations or even in some relatively very large denominations such as The Lutheran Church—Missouri Synod. Good bloodlines can make a difference.

When an attempt is made to win the loyalty of clan or tribal members to a larger unit such as the nation, a different organizing principle is needed. This has been illustrated most visibly in some of the new nations in Africa in which tribal loyalties are more powerful than allegiance to the nation. It also can be seen in many of the long-established and very large congregations in which a member's allegiance to an adult Sunday school class or to the choir or to the women's organization exceeds that person's loyalty to the congregation or to the pastor.

A sense of community obligation must replace the power of kinship ties to gain obedience to the customs, demands, and laws of the nation.

As the old cohesive forces, such as kinship ties and nationality identification, begin to erode, the congregation—and the denomination—must either replace those unifying factors or watch the erosion of loyalty and obedience to that tribe. One cohesive force is the community obligation called mission. When the members feel obligated to respond to a call to mission which is beyond the capability of any one member individually, cohesiveness, loyalty, and obedience are reinforced. World War II did this for the United States. A commitment to world mission has filled this need for many congregations. The more that tribe becomes infused with and expresses values that are sources of personal satisfaction for the individual members, the stronger the group identity.[2] This is part of the character formation of a new congregation, of a new denomination that is the product of a merger, or the happy transition of a congregation from one chapter of its history to a new era.

The ecclesiastical expression of this concept can be illustrated by the denominational loyalty of older members to the Evangelical Covenant Church or to the Seventh-Day Adventist or the American Lutheran Church or to the Cumberland Presbyterian Church where *both* kinship ties and a sense of community long have been very evident. By contrast, the feeling of denominational loyalty and obligation is much less powerful when both kinship ties and a sense of community obligation are absent. This can be seen today among some of the younger members who are newcomers to that denominational family, in some of the newer, big congregations on the west coast in the Baptist General Conference, in several denominations such as The United Methodist Church, in which the polity places the primary sense of community in the regional judicatory (a large tribe) rather than in the denomination (nation), and in some of those large, nation-size congregations where the sense of community is a central organizing principle and the denomination cannot match its attractiveness.

It also should be noted that the merger of denominations tends to erode denominational loyalties. Some members continue a strong sense of loyalty to the former denomination while others have a strong allegiance to a congregation but not to the new denomination that is a product of that merger. One result is that when these members move, they find it easy to change denominations.

The presence of this sense of community obligations makes it relatively easy to implement a huge capital funds campaign for missions in the Lutheran Church—Missouri Synod or in the American Lutheran Church. Its absence makes it far more difficult to implement a capital funds drive in the United Church of Christ or in The United Methodist Church, even though individual congregations in both of those denominations report remarkable success stories in capital fund campaigns.

20. In the mid-1950s the anthropologist Robert Redfield identified the conflict between what he described as the "little tradition" and the "big tradition."[3] Today the ecclesiastical expression of this concept can be seen in (a) those long-established adult Sunday school classes in which the members express great loyalty to that class (clan) but rarely attend the Sunday morning worship service for which the whole congregation (tribe) gathers, (b) the strong loyalty to their congregation felt by many Presbyterians, Disciples, Methodists, and Lutherans who are extremely discontented with denominational policies, decisions, and programs and would be very willing to see their congregation secede from the denomination, (c) the strong support by some denominational leaders for the National Council of Churches or the World Council of Churches, but the vigorous opposition by many members sitting in the tribal pews, and (d) the internal conflict felt by the young Amish farmer between adopting new aproaches to agriculture for economic survival versus leaving the farm and becoming a carpenter in order to adhere to the customs and laws of the Amish.

The emergence of these overlapping worlds often creates conflicts in the tribe.

Why Bother?

At this point the reader may feel overwhelmed by so many references to tribal characteristics and ask, "What does this have to do with leadership in the church?"

First of all, one of the characteristics of many effective leaders is the ability to look at a specific issue from a larger perspective or to "see the larger picture." The tribal analogy provides one such perspective.

Second, most leaders are reasonably comfortable and creative in responding when they are able to understand what is happening and why events are following that course. All of us, however, tend to be frustrated or immobilized or ineffective or to engage in counterproductive behavior when we are unable to understand what is happening or why. The tribal analogy helps to identify much of what is happening as normal and predictable behavior. That is simply the way tribes have always functioned.

Third, the tribal analogy helps one understand that many leadership roles are the result of tribal culture and may not be affected by such ecclesiastical factors as seminary education or ordination or polity or instructions from the denominational headquarters.

Fourth, a comparison of the worshiping congregation with the tribe helps to explain the value of symbols, customs, tenure, traditions, and legends in reinforcing identity and in conveying meaning.

Fifth, for those interested in church growth, the tribal analogy helps one understand why a substantial majority of all Protestant congregations have a natural and predictable tendency to be exclusionary and find it difficult to attract, receive, and assimilate new members, especially if they speak a different language, come from another nation, or represent a different culture. The stronger the tribal culture, the more difficult it is to fulfill the Great Commission. Several of the denominations which had until recently a strong northern European nationality and language heritage have illustrated this aspect of tribalism very clearly.

Sixth, many people believe that all congregations carrying the same denominational affiliation do, or at least should, offer the same religious culture. The large number of denominational mergers in the United States since 1950 has created the situation in hundreds of communities in which there are two church buildings, each now bearing the same denominational label, across the street from one another. The tribal analogy helps to explain why the two congregations may be very much unlike. Denominational mergers may have little effect on tribal cultures, especially if the local loyalties to that new denomination are relatively weak.

Seventh, for those in long-established and numerically growing congregations the differences between clan and tribe or between tribe and nation may help to explain some of the internal stresses produced by growth—including the enhanced leadership role for the pastor and the reduced influence of the council of elders in those very large congregations.

Eighth, for those in middle-sized and large congregations the tribal analogy helps one understand leadership roles. In the large congregation the pastor is not only the medicine man (shaman) or chief religious figure, but as time goes by often he is expected to assume the role of tribal chief and, after fifteen or twenty years, may even become the number one patriarch of that tribe. By contrast, in long-established smaller congregations, which usually experience short pastorates, the minister may function as the medicine man, but all leadership responsibilities are retained by the council of elders.

The differences in tribal customs on this issue of leadership and congregational self-government provide a useful context for understanding some of the difficulties encountered by the newly arrived pastor. In one case, for example, this minister had served for seven years in a congregation in which nearly all the ruling power was vested in a council of lay elders by the chief elder. The pastor was the chief religious figure, but a sixty-five-year-old layman had succeeded his father as the chief elder and the head of that tribe. No one questioned the fact that many important policy issues were decided either by the tribal chief acting unilaterally or in consultation with the other lay elders, but without the minister's being present.

After seven years in that tribal setting, the pastor accepted a call to a slightly larger congregation to follow a minister who had retired after a thirty-year pastorate, but was not moving out of the community. By the time this minister's retirement date had rolled around, he had changed the tribal customs so he was not only the number one religious figure in that parish, he also was understood to be the tribal chief and for his last decade or so had served as the patriarch of that tribe. The primary responsibility of the council of elders in that tribe was to affirm and support the suggestions and recommendations of the pastor.

Eighteen months later the new minister resigned. He felt frustrated over being called and paid to serve as the number one religious leader while being treated as the assistant medicine man or shaman. Most of the elders agreed that he was making a wise decision inasmuch as he appeared to be unwilling or unprepared to serve as the tribal chief and as the number one elder on the council. The departing minister felt he had been called to fill a vacancy that did not exist. The retired minister still cannot understand why the seminaries fail to train students to accept their rightful roles as tribal leaders.

Ninth, a brief examination of the social changes that have undermined the cohesion of the clan and the tribe also helps to explain part of the erosion of both congregational and denominational loyalties. This is a predictable phenomenon in a mobile society in which the old, cohesive forces have been discarded but not replaced by new and unifying values, goals, and visions.

Finally, and most important for this discussion, this review of some of the characteristics of tribal culture not only provides a larger context for looking at central organizing principles and leadership roles, it also illustrates the point that organizing principles both reflect and vary with the organizational context. This point can be seen more clearly by looking at movements which represent a substantially different form of collective behavior from that of the tribe.

What Is a Social Movement?

Christianity began with an individual who recruited followers, and it quickly evolved into a movement. Eventually the institutional expression of the faith acquired the characteristics and institutional paraphenalia of a formal organization. For many centuries the Christian church was an extraordinarily powerful organization in western civilization. It could force kings to come barefoot in sackcloth seeking forgiveness, and it set the moral tone for half the world.

As it grew into a powerful institution, it also sparked the creation of thousands of movements. Some were organized to reform the institution, others sought to restore it to its original role and mission, many were designed to recreate the New Testament church, and thousands more were formed to enable people to express their faith more meaningfully. Anyone concerned with the history of Christianity or with leadership in the church or with the concept of organizational principles cannot ignore the distinctive role of social and religious movements.

Movements, as an expression of collective behavior, can be located on a spectrum between individual behavior at one end and formal organizations with traditions, rules, and clearly defined criteria for membership at the other end. Such formal organizations dominate our culture today.

Innumerable approaches have been used to define the nature of a movement, whether it be religious, reform, protest, revolutionary, expressive, or social; and the literature in the field is immense.[4] Two different perspectives on movements are sufficient, however, to identify critical organizing concepts and the changing role of leadership.

The simplest, and one that overlaps the process for planned change described in a subsequent chapter, is chronological.

Movements frequently begin with unfocused discontent with the status quo. This may be a product of extreme deprivation or of the stress resulting from disagreements with the rulers of the organization or of a clash over priorities, values, and practices or of a concern for what the organization is neglecting or of a sense of powerlessness.

The Protestant Reformation; the civil rights movement of the 1960s; the women's suffrage movement of the early part of this century; the movement to ban drunken drivers from the nation's highways; the exodus of a large number of seminarians, professors, pastors, and lay persons from the Lutheran Church—Missouri Synod in the 1970s; the more recent emergence of the Mission Society for United Methodists; the antislavery movement of the nineteenth century; the prohibition movement in the early years of the twentieth century; the movement to organize labor in the 1870–1950 era; and the various caucuses in several denominations seeking a greater emphasis on the Holy Scriptures all began with the discontent with the status quo.

In the later months or years of this first stage leaders begin to emerge who usually are seen by protectors of the status quo as subversive, as agitators, or as traitors to their cause. The emergence of these highly visible leaders is usually accompanied by literature that identifies the basis for the discontent and is designed to enhance that discontent as well as to enlist adherents. The air is filled with what later is seen as unorganized talk. Mavericks often receive an unreserved welcome and often become short-term influential leaders. At this stage the movement may have many followers or adherents, but few if any members.

During this initial stage of the movement's life the focus usually is on a single issue, emotions run high, the agitators simply cannot comprehend the indifference of those who fail to agree this is the most urgent issue of the day. This pattern can be seen in the crusade by public health authorities of the last quarter of the nineteenth century to urge the cremation of the dead or in the prohibition movement of the first two decades of the twentieth century or in the civil rights movement of the 1960s or the feminist movement of the 1980s or the anti-nuclear-power drive of recent years or in the crusade against drunken drivers in the 1980s.

The first stage lifts up a single issue which is dramatized in various ways to serve as a specific rallying point and as the theme for enlisting new members. It always helps the organizational process if the cause can be identified with an "enemy," and this "we-they" concept becomes a strong polarizing force. For the leaders of the movement their cause is the most important issue in the world. At this stage the participants in the movement usually have relatively low needs on a social needs scale and tend to be strongly task oriented. The central focus is the issue, not winning friends or being identified as a "nice person."

Before the end of this stage is reached, however, at least a modest organizational structure usually is seen as necessary, but frequently widespread disdain is expressed toward any proposal for a more formal structure with offices. "Trust us!" is the response given to those who raise questions about accountability. With rare exceptions the emphasis is on enlisting individuals, not organizations, as allies in promoting that cause.

The second stage of a movement can be identified when the discontent is translated into operational goals, prophets begin to replace agitators, slogans begin to change from centering on the cause of the discontent to articulating the goals, many of the members find the continuity and meaning for their life to be in the movement rather than in themselves and their own personal background, the leaders express a crusading zeal seldom seen among the officials of long-established organizations, and the building of the social myth necessary to identify the central theme of this movement begins to take place. By this stage the movement also is more intentional about offering members and prospective new members a means of expressing their

3 5

commitment. Such expressions may range from picketing to attending a prayer meeting, to making a financial contribution, to fasting, to holding office, to stuffing envelopes, to handing out leaflets.

During this second stage opponents of the goals of the movement often strengthen it by self-defeating behavior. When the police turned fire hoses and police dogs on the civil rights demonstrators in Alabama in the 1960s, they unwittingly strengthened that movement and helped it win new adherents. Frequently tactical defeats turn into long-term strategic victories as the legalistic behavior of the opponents becomes counterproductive. Both leaders of the movement and the opponents see compromise as a dirty word and as an unacceptable tactic. Confrontational tactics flourish.

When the telephone rings in the crowded and cluttered headquarters, the person closest to it answers. Many callers are surprised when the current leader of the movement answers the telephone.

Casual visitors, reporters, and prospective members walk in off the street expecting to be able to talk to one of the prophets of the movement and often are successful.

A mailing list is developed, but it is not yet a productive source of either new adherents or financial support.

Many movements fade away during this second stage. Some dissolve when that central magnetic personality disappears from the scene. More than a few are co-opted by what was an earlier parallel movement but relatively early developed a greater degree of organizational sophistication and strength. Others never allow the prophets and reformers to replace the agitators and die from an overdose of ridicule. Some are wiped out by maladministration. A few commit suicide as the result of a devastating internal struggle over tactics or priorities.

Those that continue into the third stage of this evolutionary process usually are sustained in part by a high level of continued activity, in part by at least an occasional tactical victory, in part by the ability of the prophet or reformer to become an effective administrator, and in part by minimizing the internal discontent that could be divisive. Compromise begins to be perceived as a necessary tactic for maintaining harmony.

By the end of this second stage the original agitators often have been so successful in winning converts that they not only are replaced by the prophets, but the newcomers who are convinced the goals are attainable become a majority. The tactics appropriate for publicizing the vision are perceived by several of these newcomers as naïve or inadequate, and the reformers begin to replace the prophets in leadership roles.

During this second stage the social myth that was created earlier now is formalized as the ideology of the movement usually by an adherent who is a conceptualizer rather than an agitator. A few effective leaders of movements have served as agitators, conceptualizers, propogandists, and statesmen, but they are rare. Samuel Adams, Mahatma Gandhi, Martin Luther King, Jr., and Saul Alinsky might be included in this select group.

The program of the movement feeds the development of this ideology, but the ideology also makes it possible for the program to become more specific. Precise, measurable, and specific goals are articulated. Symbols, slogans, songs, buttons, signs, bumper stickers, and T-shirts are produced as part of the propaganda effort. The literature is still designed primarily as one-way communication, but financial contributions are sought and welcomed. The first annual meeting is planned and held. Public reports of that meeting are confined to relatively obscure periodicals.

The movement now is able to afford a payroll, and one of the first persons to be employed is a secretary, frequently someone with long service as a volunteer in the movement. The secretary not only answers the telephone but with the majority of calls is able to respond directly to the caller's needs without referring to anyone else.

The stronger the value orientation of the movement,[5] the more likely that by this stage it has attracted a variety of leaders including the original agitators, the propagandists, the conceptualizers (who can translate the discontent into goals for tomorrow), the organizers, the prophets, and the reformers. As time passes, these leaders come into conflict with one another because of these differences in values, tactics, and priorities. Some simply pass through very quickly and are soon forgotten while others are ostracized after a divisive battle, and a few eventually become bitter enemies of the movement.

Typically by the end of this stage the movement leaders become receptive to the possibility of enlisting as allies other organizations with parallel goals. Coalition building is identified as an attractive tactic. Certain individuals outside the movement are courted, not for what they can individually contribute to the movement, but because they represent a potential organizational ally or because their name on the letterhead symbolizes a broadening of the support group.

The third stage is marked by the evolution of the movement into a formal organization with carefully defined procedures for the selection of the official leaders, the preparation and underwriting of a budget, the creation of a membership roster with a system for enlisting and keeping in contact with new members, and by increased references to past experiences and traditions.

The organizational structure becomes more complex as the division of labor is made more explicit. The informality that marked stage two and the strong opposition to any formal organization that was a part of stage one are replaced by an appreciation for order. Norms for behavior are established, and even the untrained volunteers are asked to carry specialized responsibilities.

As the years go by, people begin to observe the anniversaries of momentous events of the past. What is now a computerized mailing list has become an important source of funding for the movement. Tenure, constituency, and seniority become as influential as rhetorical gifts and charisma in the selection of leaders. The national news media begin to publicize the movement, but the focus still is largely on individual leaders.

Sometime during the early years of this third stage the last of the prophets has been replaced in official leadership roles by the reformers, and the statesmen begin to emerge.

In the fourth stage of this evolutionary process what was once a movement is now clearly and firmly established as a formal organization. Some of the early and highly energetic disciples have become exhausted and have disappeared. Allegiance to the institution replaces the loyalty to the original leaders, many of whom are no longer on the scene. The statesmen and managers are now in control, and compromise is perceived as an essential tactic for the wise leader. The bureaucracy has replaced the earlier charismatic leadership and the ad hoc structure. The mavericks find the institutional freedom to be increasingly limited, and some leave. One writes a book about the movement, and it is published by one of the small presses.

At this fourth stage many of the leaders display a condescending disdain for those who favor the confrontational tactics that were so popular in the first stage of the movement's history. It is relatively easy to build a persuasive case for "working for reform from inside the system." Charges are made that the movement has been "co-opted by the establishment."

Close personal friends who were devoted allies years earlier now rarely see one another. One has accepted the need for the movement to evolve, and the other is still in stage one. Several of the prophets leave after an election in which their side loses. The national news media grant both respect and space to the organization. One of the official leaders is asked to serve on a presidential commission. The organization's headquarters is located in proper facilities at a respectable address, and the visitor who comes without an appointment is greeted by a receptionist who explains, "I'm sorry, but the person you want to see is in a meeting and won't be available before tomorrow."

When the telephone rings, the receptionist, who had no previous affiliation with the organization, answers it and refers the caller either to a subordinate staff person or to the personal secretary of the top leader.

Grants from foundations, denominations, corporations, and governmental agencies are sought to replace the diminishing income from that mailing list, and one staff person specializes in grantsmanship.

Organizational momentum often has replaced the original cause or sustained activity as the central organizing principle. The organization may continue and flourish with a new set of goals. A remarkable example of this is the March of Dimes, which was organized in the early 1930s to wipe out the crippling disease, poliomyelitis. That movement was given great impetus by the high visibility of President Franklin D. Roosevelt, who had been crippled by polio many years earlier. By the mid-1970s the number of reported cases of acute poliomyelitis had dropped from 33,300 in 1950 to 28,985 in 1955 to 3,190 in 1960 to 7 in 1974, but the March of Dimes marches on with remarkable organizational momentum and a new set of goals.[6]

What Are You Seeking to Change?

A second perspective for identifying the central characteristics of a social movement can be developed by combining two questions. Is this goal to change people or society? How much change is sought? This produces a fourfold set of categories.

The first is composed of those movements seeking a radical transformation of society. The civil rights movement, the peace movement, the movement for world government, the nineteenth century missionary movement to evangelize the world, the prohibition movement, the women's liberation movement, the world communist movement, and the Nazi movement in Germany in the late 1920s and early 1930s are examples of movements with radical transformational goals.

The second includes those movements seeking partial changes in society. The movement to keep drunken drivers off the highways, the antislavery movement of the seventeenth and eighteenth centuries, the contemporary prison reform movement, the school consolidation movement of the 1940s and 1950s in the United States, the current movement to organize women in the labor force, the single tax movement, and the public school reform movement of the 1980s.

The third consists of the movements seeking total change as individuals. The charismatic renewal movement of the 1960s and the revivalism of the nineteenth century are examples.

The fourth group is far more numerous and includes those movements seeking partial changes in individuals. The temperance movement of the last half of the eighteenth century and early nineteenth century, the birth control movement, the soil conservation movement, the marriage encounter movement, the world literacy movement, the movement to encourage smokers to become ex-smokers, the Sunday school movement of the nineteenth century, and Alcoholics Anonymous are examples.

Obviously both the tactics and the strategy will differ from one to another of these four types of movements. One result is that the expectations placed on leaders also will vary. The first of these four movements calls for leaders with a powerful ideological orientation who are able and willing to accept the role of a transformational leader, who enjoy working in opposition to the existing social structures and institutions, and who are not deterred by the threat of ostracism or martyrdom.

The second type of movement requires leaders who, by temperament, are reformers, not revolutionaries, who are patient and able to accept a long-term view of the process of change, who view compromise as a useful tactic in that long-term process, and who are comfortable working within the existing structures of society.

Leaders seeking total change in individuals require another distinctive set of gifts and skills, one of which is the ability to identify latent gifts. Another is patience. A third is persistence. A fourth is optimism about one's fellow human beings. A fifth is love. A sixth is a strong person-centered orientation.

Obviously the organizing principles used to rally people behind a revolutionary movement designed to radically change the world will be different from those used to produce partial changes in individuals.

The change agent seeking to transform the world often will challenge people with a vision of a new tomorrow. Martin Luther King, Jr.'s "I Have a Dream" speech at the Washington Monument in the summer of 1963 stands out as an illustration of such a challenge.

The effort to bring about partial change in people by making them sensitive to world hunger might be organized around visits with the poor residents of a rural county or watching a motion picture or a television documentary on world hunger or by serving as a volunteer in a food pantry in the inner city or by a visit to a landfill where a food processor is paying to be able to discard food that cannot be sold in grocery stores, but could be distributed by a food pantry.

The effort to convince state legislators to raise the drinking age to twenty-one might be organized around the stories of parents who experienced the death of a child by the carelessness of a drunken driver or around the highly rational statistical reports of insurance companies or around the testimony of highway patrol officers, or it might be the carrot-and-stick approach of reducing federal aid to highways for states that do not raise the drinking age to twenty-one. An interesting case study of the carrot-and-stick approach came when, after years of no progress on the issue, in 1984–86 several state legislatures began to adopt laws requiring the use of seat belts in cars when the automobile industry made that a high priority in their lobbying efforts.

The member of a charismatic Christian congregation seeking to bring radical change into the life of a neighbor or friend or relative may use that simple organizing principle of shared experiences. "Come with me to our prayer and praise service on Monday night. I know if you open yourself to the Spirit, God will come into your life in a way that you'll never be the same again. Why don't you come with me and share in this experience?"

The transformational movement that seeks to make changes in society often uses the "identify and organize against the enemy" principle. The enemy may be the devil, segregationists, capitalism, communism, socialism, war, booze, male chauvinism, the National Council of Churches, racial segregation, poverty, Jews, Christians, secular humanism, pornography, or the higher criticism in biblical interpretation.

This brief review of social movements seeks to emphasize (a) movements represent a different expression of collective behavior than do clans and tribes, (b) the context creates demands on leaders in terms of both role and style, (c) the evolutionary changes that mark the life cycle of a social movement are tremendously influential in changing the demands made on the leaders, (d) leaders whose gifts and skills make them highly relevant at one stage may cause them to be viewed as irrelevant or obsolete at a subsequent stage, (e) the organizing principles usually will reflect the stage of the movement and/or the nature of the change being sought, (f) some organizing principles are more appropriate with one kind of desired change than another, and (g) it helps to know whether you are working in a relatively uncomplex tribal setting or functioning as part of a movement or operating within the complex structure of a modern voluntary association.

The Other End of the Spectrum

A third aspect of collective behavior that sheds light on both leadership roles and on the subject of organizing principles is the formalized voluntary association.

Voluntary organizations differ from movements in many respects and call for a different set of qualities in the leadership, but before discussing those two distinctions it may be best to identify the nature of a formal voluntary organization or what some call human associations.

In a remarkably lucid chapter Lon Fuller points out that human associations can be described as falling along a spectrum.[7] At one end of the spectrum are those in which the central organizing principle is a shared commitment, often based on a common ideology. The Mayflower Compact is a great historical example of organizing around a shared commitment. An earlier one was the gathering of the twelve apostles around a shared commitment.

At the other end are those voluntary associations constituted around a core of commonly accepted legal principles. As a denomination the Southern Baptist Convention would be located near the shared commitment end of that spectrum, although one group of leaders wants to move it to the legal principle end of that spectrum, while the Presbyterian Church (U.S.A.) would be closer to the end labeled legal principles. While Lutheranism on the North American continent had its origins in churches organized around a shared commitment (and a common heritage), the design for the new Lutheran denomination to be created by the merger is much closer to the legal principle end of that spectrum. The Methodist–Evangelical United Brethren merger of 1968 and the Presbyterian "reunion" approved in 1983 demonstrated the difficulties inherent in any denominational merger designed from the legal principles end of this spectrum. The Lutheran mergers of 1960 and 1962 were based on a much greater emphasis on shared commitment.

Whether one is referring to the county medical association, the American Bar Association, a social club, a Protestant congregation, a private school, Presbyterianism, Little League baseball, or a community organization, it appears the natural tendency among voluntary organizations in the United States and Canada is to drift from the shared commitment end of that spectrum described by Fuller toward the legal principle end. Rules gradually supercede ideology.

Fuller observed what he identified as the "creeping legalism" that may undermine the principle of association by common aims. As a voluntary association moves toward the legal principle end of this spectrum, this shift in the basic organizing principle is reflected in (1) a greater reliance on precedents, rules, and quotas to define the duties of members and to determine their entitlements, (2) a greater emphasis on accountability in objective or measurable accomplishments or shortcomings which are the result of identifiable acts rather than on the more subjective assessments of character, personality, gifts, or motives, and (3) the formulation of clearly defined procedural criteria for allocating benefits, rewards, and punishments. Ministers in The United

Methodist Church may find it easy to translate those factors into how appointments are made in their annual conference. Measurable criteria such as tenure, seniority, age, salary level, support of conference apportionments, marital status, gender, responsibilities accepted in conference leadership role, and formal education may be perceived as more influential in the making of appointments than gifts, skills, experience, talent, and graces as the system moves toward the legal end of Fuller's spectrum.

Fuller also offers what he calls "laws" that apply to the interrelationships of these two principles of human associations.[8]

The first is the most obvious. Both of these organizing principles apply to nearly every voluntary association. Nearly every organization depends on both shared commitment and legal principles for cohesion, a sense of direction or purpose, and continuity. When disputes arise, some members may turn to a shared commitment as the basic reference point in resolving that dispute while others may turn to a specific bylaw or rule. The critical question in self-evaluation is to agree on which is the dominant principle in your congregation or denomination today. Next, does that represent a change from yesterday?

Most of Fuller's other laws are more subtle, but they do help one understand the institutional behavior of many religious institutions. For example, Fuller's fifth law states that as an organization moves toward the legal principle end of that spectrum, it not only can tolerate, it often needs, internal subgroups bound together by the principle of shared commitment. When the bonds holding a voluntary association together consist largely of organizational status and benefits, rather than the pursuit of a common goal, the members usually are granted greater discretion to pursue divergent aims and interests. In simple language that means that the caucus or the special interest group is more likely to emerge in the conference or synod or presbytery that is near the legal end of this spectrum.

This also is a partial explanation for both the existence and the value of those large adult Sunday school classes or bowling teams or prayer circles in the typical large Protestant congregation which also depends increasingly on a large quantity of rules, guidelines, job descriptions, titles, organizational structure, and procedures in order to function.

Finally, Fuller's concept provides a partial explanation for the natural and predictable emergence of a new missionary sending agency, The Mission Society for United Methodists, in a denomination which for several decades has been moving closer to the legal principle end of that spectrum.

Typically when an organization reaches the point that legal principles have become a major central organizing principle, it finds this may not be an effective means of mobilizing and allocating resources. The natural desire for what is seen as a more creative and effective use of time, human energy, and money often results in the creation of these new subgroups or adjunct societies organized around shared commitment or a clearly defined ideology. This almost invariably is accompanied by a sharp increase in the money contributed by the members for clearly designated special projects and a decrease or only modest increases in the amount given for the general support of the denominational agencies and causes.

Another example of the same pattern can be seen in the enlistment of ministers. In several denominations an increasing number of people are questioning the process for examining candidates for the ordained ministry, including the requirement they be examined in English and be graduates of a North American or European theological seminary. This can be seen as an unfair barrier to recently arrived ministers from Asia or Latin America. One response to that discontent is to organize a caucus or movement with a clearly stated ideological commitment to lift those institutional barriers and to utilize the gifts and skills of immigrant ministers. This new ideology immediately comes into conflict with firmly institutionalized rules and legal procedures.

Likewise, those who believe the rules, procedures, and criteria guiding the work of a denominational missions agency are resulting in an excessive emphasis on institutional maintenance with too few resources allocated to missions, outreach, and servicing the constituency naturally feel a compulsion to create a new organization around the shared commitment to a greater emphasis on missions. In a congregational context the expression of this same tendency can be seen in the group of five or six lay volunteers who believe a particular mission need was slighted in the unified budget (which is an expression of the drift toward legal principles) and so they organize a special appeal to raise additional money for this venture to which they shared a strong commitment.

The more dependent a congregation or a denomination becomes on legal principles to sustain that organization, the more likely new subgroups will emerge organized around a shared commitment to such goals as a stronger voice for blacks or a greater reliance on the Holy Scriptures or a larger allocation of funds for missions or a return to the day when that organization was organized around a shared commitment.

This generalization helps explain the emergence of Presbyterians United for Biblical Concerns and The Presbyterian Lay Committee, Inc., in the former United Presbyterian Church or the Good News movement in The United Methodist Church or the League of Christian Laymen within the Reformed Church in America or the Fellowship of Witness in the Episcopal Church or the Lutheran Evangelistic Movement among Lutherans or the Covenant Fellowship of Presbyterians in the former Presbyterian Church in the U.S.

These and similar renewal groups share several characteristics including (a) each began as a movement organized around a shared commitment, (b) the initiating leaders concluded that the formal leadership of the denomination was not responsive to their pleas, (c) leaders of the renewal movement felt frustrated by the bureaucratic structure (legal principles) of the national agencies of the denomination, and (d) many people perceived them as impatient agitators seeking to promote a particular ideology.

To place this concept in a larger context, the heavier the emphasis on legal principles in a voluntary organization, the greater the probability that dissenting movements will emerge. A common local church example is that in the face of growing opposition the greater the reliance the pastor places on legal principles to retain the office of minister of that congregation, the more likely this will reinforce the strength of the movement organized around the shared commitment of ousting that minister.

The modern army depends very heavily on legal principles, and it is a highly bureaucratic organization. Therefore it is not surprising to find that every modern army has a network of remarkably well developed informal organizations. These informal groups provide the mutual support, the flexibility, and the ability to adapt to a variety of personalities and situations.[9] This same phenomenon can be observed in the groups that form at the annual pastors' schools or in the coffee break taken every morning by the three secretaries and the bookkeeper in that large and remarkably well organized downtown church or in that group of three middle-level employees in the denominational headquarters who frequently each lunch together. Each fills the need for an informal organization that can provide mutual support for one another in a bureaucratic structure and also can respond with flexibility to special situations.

Effective leaders often display an intuitive understanding of the dynamics of this relationship between these two organizing principles and affirm the value of these informal groups organized around a shared commitment. The wise senior minister or the perceptive denominational executive recognizes these are important cogs in a large and complex structure, not enemies to be destroyed.

The less reflective and less effective leaders often impulsively view these movements, not as a natural and predictable organizational phenomenon, but as a personal threat, and sometimes label them as adversaries.

Fuller's fourth law helps to explain when these internal subgroups are most likely to be acceptable to the official leadership. Fuller observes that when the members are convinced their organization is being held together primarily by a shared commitment, the more likely the official leadership will be hostile toward any internal subgroup also organized around shared commitment. Thus when the professional staff of a national missions agency believe they share a common ideology and see that ideology as their central cohesive force, they naturally will tend to be hostile toward any new subgroups or movements also organized around a shared commitment to a particular ideology.

If that national denominational agency is located closer to the legal principles end of the spectrum, it natrually will tend to accept, and perhaps even encourage, the creation of these new unofficial subgroups or at least be relatively tolerant of them.

Thus the denominational bureaucrat who is primarily ideological and does not understand the basic nature of a formal voluntary association naturally will tend to be extremely intolerant of any groups that represent a different ideology.

Fuller's fourth law helps to explain the internal tensions that often arise when the new pastor replaces a predecessor who was at the other end of this spectrum. The new minister who is convinced that congregational life should be built around the same shared commitment may be intolerant of the closely knit prayer circle or that small group of self-identified charismatic Christians. Those who recall the tolerant stance of the predecessor toward these groups find it difficult to understand the new pastor's hostility.

From a denominational perspective this basic point can be illustrated by The Lutheran Church—Missouri Synod. During the 1950s and early 1960s, when it was organized and functioned as a voluntary organization located at the legal principles end of this spectrum, it could tolerate considerable diversity within the districts, the seminaries, and in the unofficial subgroups. A decade later, when the national structure was organized around a shared commitment to an ideology, it was much less tolerant of pluralism among the subgroups. This same phenomenon can be seen in the 1980s in the Southern Baptist Convention, in the Roman Catholic Church, and in The United Methodist Church. The "conservative" leadership in the Southern Baptist Convention has been seeking to change the common aims of that denomination, as expressed in missions, evangelism, and the Sunday school, into the "creeping legalism" identified by Fuller. Parallel, although less visible battles have been going on in the Roman Catholic Church under Pope John Paul II and in the highly legalistic quarrels taking place within The United Methodist Church in recent years. In each of these three religious bodies an increase in shared commitment to a particular ideology has produced less tolerance for pluralism. This generalization applies to both the ideological left and the ideological right. The existence of the subgroups creates competition for a limited resource, the loyalty to a particular ideology. Whenever a denomination, or a denominational agency, demands a high degree of loyalty to a particular ideology, rather than relying on legal principles as a continuing cohesive force, this increased competition for that scarce resource almost invariably creates tension, stress, and sometimes schism. The nineteenth century divisions among the Methodists, Presbyterians, and Baptists over slavery offer an historical illustration of this conflict over loyalties.

During the decades following the end of the Civil War, and especially since 1970, the states in the old Confederacy have experienced an erosion to the shared commitments and ideology of the nineteenth century and have moved increasingly toward the legal principle end of this spectrum. One result has been an increase in the tolerance level toward the Republican Party, history professors trained in northern universities, business leaders from the North, civil rights organizations, Lutherans and other religious bodies formerly concentrated almost entirely north of the Mason-Dixon line.

The conflict between these two organizing principles can be seen very clearly in the growing number of ecclesiastical battles being decided in the civil courts. One reason, of course, is the tremendous increase in litigation in American society and the willingness of the courts to intervene in cases they once would have avoided. Another is the predictable tendency of a voluntary association organized primarily around legal principles to turn to the civil courts for the adjudication of disputes. At the other end of this spectrum, many religious bodies such as the Church of the Brethren, the Seventh-Day Adventists and the Mennonite Church, who are organized around a shared commitment, often find it somewhere between difficult and impossible to resolve disputes through litigation.

The baking of a cake can be used to provide a simplistic analogy to describe the difference between the movement organized around a common ideology (or a shared commitment to a particular vision of what tomorrow should be) and the voluntary organization heavily dependent on legal principles for its cohesion, definition of purpose, and continuity. In the movement, the heart of the debate is over whether or not human beings should bake and eat cakes. The central organizing principles and the tactics will be similar regardless of whether the movement is for or against the baking of cakes.

If and when the movement favoring the baking of cakes prevails, natural institutional pressures will militate against dissolving the movement. One alterative is to seek a new issue, continue as a movement, and utilize the wisdom and skills gained in the earlier battles. Another alternative is to continue to focus on the values of cakes, to institutionalize, draw up a constitution, select permanent officers, hire a manager or two, encourage or require the old agitators and prophets either to change or to move on to a new cause, concentrate on preparing new cake recipes and inventing better ovens.

As this voluntary organization evolves from a cause-centered movement to an agency providing services to its constituency, its central attraction will change. Once it attracted adherents by rallying people around a particular ideology. Now it seeks to gain and retain the loyalty of its clientele by meeting their needs and being responsive to their demands.

With only modest adjustments this brief scenario describes the evolution of what once were independent or semiautonomous missionary-sending organizations into denominational agencies. It describes the evolution of several denominations as well as the first three decades of the life of thousands of new congregations. This scenario also can be applied to the YMCA, several dozen labor unions, the evolution of the Sunday school movement into denominational departments of Christian education, the March of Dimes, the birth control movement of the early years of the twentieth century, and a variety of organizations originally composed of farmers or teachers or physicians.

While this is getting into the theme of the next two chapters of this book, it should be noted here that the best leaders possess either an intuitive and/or a carefully thought-out conceptual framework that enables them to minimize the impact of "creeping legalism" on the voluntary association organized around a common commitment to a shared aim. One facet of this competence is to avoid the temptation to focus on personalities and to ignore the gradual undermining of that central organizing principle. This often takes the form of calling people back to the original purpose, rather than attacking those individuals who are seeking to push that voluntary association to the legal principles end of the spectrum. A simple example is the response of the pastor of the financially squeezed congregation to the plea, "Why don't we require that every member contribute at least $50 a year in order to keep his or her name on our membership roll?" Instead of attacking the person who proposed this, or ridiculing the whole concept, it may be wiser to change the discussion to the place of stewardship in a called-out community or to the need to focus on goals rather than means to an end.

One approach to understanding the differences between a social movement and a voluntary organization is to think in terms of the spectrum identified by Lon Fuller. A second is the evolutionary scenario described in these last few pages. A third is to focus on a few of the fundamental differences between a movement and a formalized voluntary association.

Four Basic Differences

Four of the most significant differences between a movement and a long-established formal organization such as a congregation, a political party, a professional association, a national denominational agency, a labor union, or an interchurch organization revolve around the two words *ideology* and *constituency*.

First, the typical movement, especially in its early stages, rallies adherents around an ideological stance. Ideology is an important factor in attracting and building up a following. Second, the movement, again especially in the early stages, does not have any obligation to its constituency. The movement's central obligation is to be faithful to its ideology. Third, the movement usually finds a clearly and precisely articulated ideological position to be a unifying force. It reinforces cohesion. Fourth, the movement's primary "product" usually is a vision of a better tomorrow reinforced by a strong ideological statement. Thus the brochure published by the movement usually emphasizes what is believed.

By contrast, the long-established formal institution that is close to the legal principles end of this spectrum has a constituency that expects some form of services or benefits from belonging to or supporting that organization. It prospers by servicing its clientele. This emphasis on service, rather than on ideology, becomes a central factor in retaining the old constituency and in attracting new supporters. The constituency soon believes it is entitled to receive services from this organization and the organization has an obligation to provide those services. If and when the organization that has been servicing its constituency begins to assume a strong ideological stance, this usually becomes a divisive, rather than a unifying, force. While the movement's primary product is that vision of a new tomorrow reinforced by an ideological position, the organization's primary product is service. Its brochure emphasizes what is done and downplays what is believed.

Since life is more a "both-and," rather than an "either-or," it is not surprising that many voluntary associations display several of the characteristics of a movement organized around a shared commitment to a common ideology as well as many of the characteristics of a long-established formal organization with rules, procedures, precedents, officers, and a range of services provided to its constituency.

The conflict produced by this ambiguity was illustrated by the Republican Party in the presidential election of 1964 and the Democratic Party in 1972 and again in 1984, by much of the political debate in Quebec in the late 1970s and early 1980s, by the confusion over the role and priorities of the National Council of the Churches of Christ in the U.S.A., by the evolutionary changes in the American labor movement, by the exodus of congregations from both the United Presbyterian Church and the Presbyterian Church in the

United States during the late 1970s and early 1980s, and by the debates in the 1980s within the Southern Baptist Convention and The United Methodist Church over whether national agencies in those denominations should specialize in serving the constituency or in reflecting a particular ideology.

The conflict in expectations produced by this set of differences also may turn out to be the determining factor in the Reverend Jerry Falwell's efforts to develop an extensive religious organization and also to spearhead an influential ideological movement on the American political scene.

One of the most common criticisms of Franklin D. Roosevelt was that he and his New Deal lacked a clear, coherent, and consistent ideology. That may have been one of the reasons for his extraordinarily long tenure as well as his success as a political leader.

One of the never ending debates on the American political scene is between those who argue that the primary obligation of a political party is to articulate an ideological point of view and those who are convinced its primary obligation is to elect the party's candidates to public office. A parallel is the debate within several Protestant denominations over whether staff members of a national denominational agency should be selected primarily to espouse a specific ideology or primarily to service the constituency.

In summary, while movements often are founded around the central organizing principle of a vision of a new tomorrow and an ideology that gives substance to that vision, formal voluntary organizations usually find that continuity rests on serving a constituency. It is difficult for the bureaucratic structure of a voluntary association to arouse the enthusiasm and support of volunteers for an ideology emanating from that bureaucracy. Movements based on a shared commitment are far more likely to arouse that enthusiastic support for an ideological position.

This generalization can be illustrated by the 1960s slogan that theological seminaries should be ecumenical, urban, and university related. Twenty-five years of responses to this ideological plea from a variety of bureaucratic structures have suggested it was not popular and certainly was not a response to the expressed needs of the constituency.

This ideological plea apparently was based on several assumptions. One was that theological seminaries should be graduate schools, not professional schools. In retrospect it now appears that the demand from the constituency was for theological seminaries that are primarily religious communities and secondarily professional schools. Pope John Paul II has made it clear that he wants American Catholic students for the priesthood to be taught by male Catholic priests, and especially not by female Protestant teachers, and that the teaching should occur in the context of a religious community rather than in a graduate school.

On the Protestant side of American Christianity it appears the big demand by the constituency has been for graduates from theological seminaries that resemble a religious community such as Gordon Conwell, Asbury, Oral Roberts, Concordia in St. Louis; Trinity in Deerfield, Illinois; Southwestern in Fort Worth; Bethel in St. Paul; Fuller and several other West Coast seminaries.

Those seminaries that have chosen to model themselves after a university graduate school of religion, rather than identify themselves as a community of faith, have been more successful in attracting scholars than in producing the graduates sought by the churches.[10]

Of those schools with a rapidly expanding enrollment, Oral Roberts Seminary in Tulsa may come the closest to fulfilling the goals of that ideological statement of the 1960s but it is interdenominational, not ecumenical, and while it is an integral part of a university, the location would not meet everyone's definition of urban.

Does that mean it is impossible for the leaders of a long-established formal organization to take and advocate a strong ideological position? Does it mean the pastor of the eight-year-old congregation or the staff of a denominational Christian education department or of an interchurch agency designed to provide services to churches cannot pursue an unpopular ideological position?

Not necessarily! The answer can be found in words such as priorities and balance. Scores of pastors have been forced to resign their pulpit because they articulated an unpopular ideology. Some were theologically too liberal, others were self-identified charismatic Christians, and many expressed a political or economic perspective that was unpopular. On the other hand, it is not uncommon to encounter a pastor who represents an unpopular ideological perspective, who makes no effort to conceal that ideological stance, but who is an exceptionally popular pastor. One explanation of this apparent inconsistency is that the minister who is an excellent preacher, a competent administrator, and a caring pastor earns the freedom to advocate an unpopular ideology. By contrast, the minister who displays only an average level of competence as a pastor, administrator, and preacher typically has substantially less freedom to advocate unpopular points of view.

A parallel can be seen in the national agencies of the various denominations. The Christian education department that provides a consistently high level of services to the churches and is responsive to their needs has far more freedom to advocate an unpopular point of view than does its counterpart which provides an inferior quality of services and is unresponsive to the needs of the churches.

It is not difficult to find examples of the freedom gained by "paying the rent on time." One is the freedom given to the editor-in-chief of *The Banner*, the weekly publication of the Christian Reformed Church, to advocate positions not popular with a great many of the readers. That freedom has been earned by the weekly publication of what is clearly an extraordinarily high quality denominational magazine.

A second example of the earned freedom of the staff of a long-established, formal denominational agency to advocate an unpopular ideology was the Home Mission Board of the Southern Baptist Convention when

Arthur Rutledge was the executive secretary and Walker Knight was the editor of the board's monthly magazine, *Home Missions*. These two men were able to provide prophetic, but often unpopular, leadership because of the exceptionally high quality services they provided to the constituency of that board.

The freedom to espouse an unpopular ideology from within the confines of a long-established voluntary organization that is being supported because it provides services to the constituency rarely is given. It must be earned!

In summary, the leaders of a movement typically are expected to articulate an ideology that may be unpopular with the majority of the general public, but the freedom to do that can be found in the nature of a movement. By contrast, the leader in the long-established voluntary organization usually is expected to specialize in providing services to the constituency and must earn the right to express an unpopular ideological point of view.

A significant number of new leaders of voluntary organizations are convinced they can gain that freedom by turning the calendar back and converting what is now a formal organization back into a movement. That rarely happens, and when it does, it often is accompanied by a loss of support from most of the constituency who were expecting service, not ideology, in return for their support.

The best and most effective leaders not only know who they are; they also know where they are. They also understand the basic principles of how to organize a collection of individuals into a cohesive and unified group with a common purpose, but that is the subject of another chapter.

Questions for Self-Evaluation

This discussion was designed primarily to provide a context for looking at leadership roles and styles and for an examination of basic organizing principles. It also can be used as the basis for reflecting on leadership responsibilities in your congregation. One means of doing that is to respond to a series of questions.

1. Does your congregation resemble a family, a clan, a tribe, or a nation?

If your congregation is really an extended family, what does this say to the leadership role of the minister? Can an outsider be more than a chaplain? Perhaps a marriage counselor and a good neighbor?

If your congregation resembles a clan that is dominated by two or three or four large family trees, does that mean the minister will be asked to serve as an arbitrator, as a spiritual leader, as a friend, but not as *the* leader?

If your congregation resembles a tribe, does that mean the various elders expect the minister to be the tribal chief as well as the shaman? Or is the role of tribal chief reserved for a lay person? Who is the patriarch? Are there more than one? How long after being established as the medicine man may the new minister be eligible to become the new tribal chief? Or did the former pastor retire from the role as medicine man but remain in the community and retain the role of tribal chief and/or patriarch? What is the relationship between the minister and the council of elders?

If your congregation resembles a nation of several tribes, what does that say to the role of the senior minister? Does each tribe, and perhaps even each clan, want someone who is "our pastor" to be part of the staff and/or "the pastor's cabinet"? Should the governing board be composed of individuals who represent the various clans and tribes? Or would it be better to have a smaller board with everyone on it expected to represent the entire nation rather than a particular clan or tribe? Who chooses these members of the board? What are the criteria? What does that say about their role?

After you have decided whether your congregation resembles a family, a clan, a tribe, or a nation, reflect on what this says to your efforts to reach and assimilate new members.

2. Does your congregation resemble a social movement built around a clearly defined ideology? Or does it come closer to resembling a formal voluntary association? If it is primarily a movement, how does it fit into the structure of your denomination? If today it resembles a voluntary association, is it at the legal principles end of Fuller's spectrum, or is it closer to the shared commitment end? Did it begin at one end but has moved toward the other end of that spectrum? If it has, what does this say to the leadership role of the minister?

3. What is the most useful conceptual framework for understanding the dynamics of life within your

denominational family? Is your denomination at the legal principles end of Fuller's spectrum or at the shared commitment end? Has it changed since the merger? If it has, what does this say to your congregation's relationships with the new denomination?

4. If you are interested in new church development, do you favor organizing new congregations *primarily* as movements that attract new members because of a clearly defined ideological stance? Or do you favor organizing new congregations *primarily* as voluntary associations designed to provide services to a constituency that will grow in numbers because of the attractiveness of those services?

After you have made your choice, ask yourself (a) what does this say to the role and the leadership characteristics you seek in the minister who will organize a new church, (b) what does this mean in terms of expectations placed on the first new members, and (c) how will this new congregation fit into your denominational family and relate to or compete with existing congregations from your denomination in this general community?

5. If you are on the committee searching for a new minister for a long-established congregation, are you looking for someone who will bring a strong ideological stance or for someone who will help your congregation serve its constituency more effectively? If you reply, "Both," which is the higher priority?

Are you looking for someone who will comprehend the role, be comfortable in it, and be competent to (a) be the chaplain for the family or (b) serve as the medicine man in a clan or (c) become the new chief of your tribe or (d) accept the role of chief executive of your nation-sized church?

6. If your primary interest in reading this book is on planned change, are you primarily interested in changing people or in changing all of society? Are you interested in modest changes? Or in radical transformations? What does your choice on these alternatives say to your choice of strategy and tactics? Or would you prefer to turn to the next chapter on basic organizing principles before thinking about planned change?

LEADERS KNOW
HOW TO ORGANIZE

"My cousin sent me a copy of the history of their church which they published as part of the celebration of the one hundredth anniversary of the founding of their congregation. As I read it, I discovered that the history was organized around real estate," commented a longtime member of the Magnolia Street Church. "The first chapter tells about the organization of the congregation in the 1890s and ends with the fire in 1903 that destroyed their first meeting place.

"The second chapter covers the 1903-1951 period. They built a new brick church following the fire, remodeled it once, added to it back in the 1920s, and remodeled it again after the end of World War II. That chapter ends with the vote in 1951 to relocate from near downtown, where they had been for nearly sixty years, to a large parcel of land on the west side of town. The third chapter tells about the three building programs they went through between 1952 and 1981. Not until the fourth and last chapter does the writer devote much space to program and ministry. That last chapter tells about all the organizations, groups, and programs in that church today.

"I might not have paid any attention to the outline," continued this person, "except last year one of our members wrote a very interesting history of our church. She organized it around the ministers who have served here. The first chapter covers the period from 1905 to 1917. It begins with the story of several laymen from old First Church downtown organizing a Sunday school outpost here in the spring of 1905. That fall the first minister arrived on the scene. That chapter ends with his departure to become a chaplain in the army in the first World War. The next chapter covers the period from 1917 to 1935, when the Reverend James Davis was the minister for eighteen years. The last page of that chapter has a brief reference to the minister who followed him in 1935, but only stayed for two years. The third chapter is about Dr. Frank Whitney, who was our minister from 1937 to 1962. I was confirmed while he was here, and I remember him very fondly. He retired after twenty-five years here. The fourth chapter has a couple of pages about the two ministers who followed Dr. Whitney, one lasted less than a year, and the second one left after about two years. Most of that chapter, however, is about the years when Bob Hanson was our pastor. He came in 1966 and left in 1981. A lot of us feel those were the best years in the whole history of this congregation, although some of the oldtimers would argue with that and claim the best years were back in the 1950s with Dr. Whitney. The last chapter covers the coming of the minister who is still here and the current program.

"I had always thought history was history until I compared these two booklets and saw how differently they were organized. In one the writer organized the book around buildings, and in the other the central theme is a series of pastorates," concluded this longtime member.

The reflections of this individual illustrate the two most widely followed themes for writing the history of a congregation. One followed a biographical theme while the other built an outline around real estate. Both, however, used a chronological approach as the primary means of organizing the material to be covered. A

Leaders know how to organize!

FRIAR TUCK.

small proportion of congregational histories are organized around the theme of mission and ministry while once in a great while one encounters the history of a congregation in which the author has chosen the ebb and flow of denominational life.[1]

More importantly, these comments introduce the concept of organizing principles. Each one of us needs some system of categories to help us comprehend reality. Julius Caesar wrote that Gaul was divided into three parts. Theological seminaries teach future preachers that a good sermon consists of three parts. The administration and faculty of the two-thousand student, four-year high school may use terms like freshmen, sophomores, juniors, and seniors to divide the student body into comprehensible units. The students may use terms such as jocks, blacks, straights, freaks, intellectuals, alcoholics, jerks, cowboys, socialites, rockers, mods, and druggies to accomplish the same basic goal. Every four years political observers divide the electorate into three categories—Democrats, Republicans, and independents—as they seek to analyze the election returns.

We all need a conceptual framework to help us divide this complex world up into smaller components that are easier to comprehend.[2] One ancient response is to look at this planet in terms of hemispheres, first the eastern hemisphere and the western hemisphere and more recently the northern hemisphere and the southern hemisphere. Now many prefer the political-economic terms of the first world, second world, and third world or the threefold division of the industrially developed countries, the industrially developing, and the industrially underdeveloped parts of the planet.

One side of the coin is how we divide up the world so we are more comfortable in trying to understand both the whole and the parts.

The other side of that coin, and the theme of this chapter, is on what can be done to bring together a collection of individuals, frequently people who previously had not known one another, and turn them into a cohesive and unified group? This concept can be illustrated first by looking at five common examples of the use of organizational principles that are common, but rarely identified as such.

The New Mission Becomes a Congregation

In the spring of 1925 several laypersons from First Church, with the vigorous encouragement of their minister, decided to start an outpost Sunday school on the west side of the city in a neighborhood in which scores of new single-family homes were being erected. The baby boom of the post-World War I era, when for the first time in American history the number of live births exceeded three million, stimulated this natural evangelistic urge. The effort was a success. Within a month the enrollment totaled over sixty children, and the leaders turned to their friends back at First Church for more volunteer help.

At this point the central organizing principles were (a) evangelism and (b) an outreach to children. Both are attractive principles that tend to win strong support from committed Christians.

The success of this initial effort encouraged the leaders at First Church to decide to sponsor a new congregation. The money was raised to purchase three residential lots as the site for a future building, and the young associate minister at First Church was assigned, on a half-time basis, to be the mission developer pastor. Four years later he was the full-time minister of a three-hundred member congregation that was meeting in its own new building on the property purchased and donated by the members at First Church. It was named the West Lawn Church.

Among the organizing principles used during these first years were (a) the attractiveness of the magnetic personality of this young minister, (b) the appeal to help pioneer the creation of a new congregation, (c) the imperative of the Great Commission (Matt. 28:19-20), (d) a call to sacrificial giving to help pay for the construction of that new building, (e) an opportunity for newcomers to the neighborhood to meet and make new friends, (f) a chance to express one's Christian commitment through the creation of a new congregation and a new house of worship, (g) the attraction of expanding the ministry with children, (h) denominational expansionism, and (i) the concern of some parents that their children be exposed to the teachings of the Christian faith.

By 1935 the second best organized facet of congregational life at West Lawn was the Sunday school. The recently arrived new minister had some reservations about the strength of and the loyalties engendered by the Sunday school—at times it appeared the tail was wagging the dog—but this pastor remained silent about those reservations and continued to support it.

When Women Organize Around Missions

The strongest and best organized aspect of this congregation's organizational life was the women's missionary society. It attracted many of the most competent and dedicated women in this new mission and every year raised large sums of money for foreign missions. One of the important sources of money was the dinner on the third Tuesday of every month with all the proceeds dedicated to missions.

Among the basic organizational principles that made this such a strong and cohesive group were (a) the commitment to bring the good news of Jesus Christ to every part of the world, (b) a sense of obligation to others—if we do not fulfill our commitment, Sister Florence or Brother Everett in Africa will not have any money to carry the gospel to the natives, (c) reinforcement of the cohesion among the members by that monthly shared experience of "putting on a dinner," (d) a sense of achievement through specific, challenging, yet attainable and measurable goals, (e) the competition and the reward of recognition for leading that region, on a per member basis, in the amount of money raised for missions, (f) inspiration of the annual missionary rally held at the regional level of the denomination, (g) the opportunity to express one's gifts of leadership and creativity through service to God, (h) the clear feeling of being needed—every woman was needed and made to feel needed at those monthly dinners, (i) periodic reports from the mission field and from denominational headquarters that the cause of Christ around the world was being advanced, (j) the inspiration of occasional visits from a missionary on furlough and this firsthand acquaintance with the missionaries being supported, (k) the personal satisfaction of learning and of having one's horizons broadened by the study program on world missions, and (l) the dedication, enthusiasm and hard work of Mrs. Betty Cook, who organized the society early in 1926, who served as the president for the first six years, and who by attitude and example was an inspiration to everyone.

A half century later this organization had experienced two changes of name as a result of denominational decisions, and the financial support of world missions had been incorporated into a unified budget of a national agency of the denomination. World missions no longer was the sole responsibility of the women of the denomination, and visits by missionaries on furlough were less frequent and much less exciting.

At its peak the women's organization at West Lawn Church numbered nearly three hundred very active members, and it included twelve circles that met monthly. The general meetings, held ten times a year, sometimes drew as many as one hundred fifty to two hundred if the program was especially attractive.

In 1986, sixty years after its founding, the women's organization at West Lawn Church included seventy more-or-less active and committed women, most of whom had been born during the first third of the twentieth century; the number of circles had shrunk to three, and the president was Betty Cook's sixty-one-year-old daughter. Those monthly dinners had been abandoned years ago, partly because of a widespread disdain of money-raising activities in the church, partly because the financial support of world missions was now incorporated into the unified budget at West Lawn, and partly because, "We just can't seem to find enough women willing to do all that work." Today monthly circle meetings have a threefold focus of study, fellowship, and mutual support. The biggest challenge every year seems to be to find women willing to accept a leadership role and specifically to find someone willing to serve as president of the organization.

The most common explanations one hears at West Lawn Church for the decline of the women's organization are, "Well, so many of today's women are employed outside the home, they don't have the time now," and "Women today have a different set of interests than the women of my generation had." A factual basis does exist for that excuse. As recently as 1960 only 31 percent of all married women in the United States, who were living with their husbands, were employed outside the home. By 1985, however, that proportion had climbed to 52 percent. It is widely assumed these women simply do not have time to be active in the church.

This can become a self-fulfilling prophecy. If most of the monthly general meetings and circles are scheduled for mornings or afternoons, this will reduce participation by women employed outside the home. If some of these monthly meetings are scheduled for the daytime and the rest in the evening, this will break the continuity—and discontinuity usually reduces both participation and frequency of attendance.

An opposite point of view is represented by a research study conducted by David A. DeVaus and reported in the March 1984 issue of the *Review of Religious Research*.[3] He found (a) women employed outside the home on a full-time basis were more likely to attend church regularly than men employed full-time, (b) there were no differences in church attendance patterns among women who were employed full-time and those who were not employed outside the home or those working part-time, but (c) men employed full-time were more likely to be regular church attenders than unemployed men or those working on a part-time basis. In brief, this study suggests that church attendance is not related to available time.

A second frequently heard explanation of the decline of women's organizations in the churches is, "Ever since women have become eligible to hold leadership positions and offices in the church that were formerly restricted to men, it has been increasingly difficult to interest them in the women's organization. The women's fellowship used to be the primary outlet for an expression of their gifts of creativity, leadership, organizational ability, and planning. Now that women are permitted to hold almost any leadership position in the church, the women's organization has become obsolete."

While this explanation undoubtedly is a factor, it can be only a minor consideration since scores of larger congregations also are experiencing a numerical decline in the women's organizations although fewer than 10 percent of the several hundred adult women members are functioning in offices formerly held by men. If in 1950 the congregation with 100 adult women could produce the leadership necessary for a strong women's organization, why is the congregation of 1985 with 600 adult women unable to produce the necessary leadership? Fewer than 10 percent of those women are now filling offices once restricted to men. The research of DeVaus mentioned earlier and that of Jon P. Alstron[4] challenge this social deprivation theory. Neither could find any evidence to support the thesis that women who cannot express their creativity or utilize their leadership skills elsewhere are more likely to be frequent church attenders.

A third explanation of what is clearly a numerical decline in women's organizations may be found in the dynamics of organizational life. The groups most likely to enlist new members are those (a) that are advancing a cause, (b) that feel a strong need to enlist additional members in order to fulfill their purpose or accomplish their task, (c) in which the organizational structure is a means-to-an-end and secondary to the task, (d) that challenge people with specific, meaningful, attainable, and measurable goals, (e) that have the benefit of strong and continuing leadership, (f) focus on a single issue, and (g) enlist people to help pioneer a new venture.

The groups that experience the greatest difficulty in enlisting new members tend to (a) be composed of people who have known one another for a long time, (b) display a strong past-orientation, (c) be highly relational, (d) be organized around study and/or fellowship as central values, (e) display a person-centered rather than task-centered orientation, (f) be ones in which the organizational structure appears to be more important than the task, and (g) if issue-centered, be concerned with a variety of issues.

Could it be that the shift away from missions as the primary reason for existence has undercut the women's organization? Are fellowship, mutual support, and study the best avenues for attracting new members to a long-established organization?

A fourth possible explanation for the declining participation in women's organizations in the churches also provides part of the context for looking at several interesting contemporary developments.

How are younger adults spending their discretionary time? That question has been researched repeatedly, and the evidence points to a decline in time spent in Scouting, service clubs, the PTA, lodges, political organizations, and other civic organizations. The big increases have been in jogging, bicycling, camping, membership in sport groups and health clubs, participation in professional societies, enrollment in night school classes and literary societies, canoeing, and Bible study. Instead of seeking fulfillment in an organizational or group context, today's Americans tend to focus more on their own personal needs and their own personal adaptation to the world. Instead of spending their discretionary time helping others, a large proportion of adults today are more concerned with their own needs and fulfillment.

Where Are Today's Women?

While there is no single answer to the question of where have the women gone who would be expected to be in the women's organizations in the churches today, some clues can be gained by looking at the contemporary scene.

The three big winners, in terms of how today's women spend their discretionary time, are (1) highly structured women's Bible study groups with trained leadership (Bible Study Fellowship may be the largest) that meet during the week, (2) personal health, including jogging, swimming, and aerobic dance classes, and (3) marital concerns, including the growing number of Mothers' Clubs, marriage enrichment and marriage encounter retreats, mutual support groups for the recently divorced, and single parent fellowships.

While the numbers are smaller than those engaged in Bible study or exercise classes or marital concerns groups, a good many of today's women spend some of their discretionary time in activities that involve far more people than was the pattern in 1950. These include the lobbies concerned with feminist issues, travel, membership in business and professional associations, night school classes, the care of an elderly parent who has survived an illness or accident that would have been fatal as recently as 1960, participation in groups that reinforce one's self-esteem, and a huge variety of short-term continuing education events and retreats.

Large numbers of women also are allocating their discretionary time to volunteering as tutors, visiting and caring for the growing numbers of shut-ins and residents of nursing homes (the number of Americans age seventy-five and over has nearly doubled since 1965), participating in amateur music and/or drama groups, working in daycare centers and as volunteers in the local hospital.

Despite the decline in numbers in the women's groups in thousands of churches in recent years, the history of these mission-centered and outreach-inspired organizations serves as a model of how to build a cohesive and closely knit cadre of dedicated Christians around a commitment to missions.

A less well known but extraordinarily influential example of organizing around a sense of mission is the Roman Catholic movement, Opus Dei. Founded in Spain in 1928, this high-demand movement has attracted thousands of Christians, especially in Africa, South America, and the Pacific rim. Among the crucial organizing principles are a high level of commitment by each adherent; a tremendous emphasis on outreach and service to others; a rigorous discipline that includes Communion, prayer, and Bible study every day; fasting and personal sacrifice; the strong opposition of an articulate group of liberal Catholics; and the vigorous support of Pope John Paul II.

An Ancient Organizing Principle

The Palestine Liberation Organization (PLO) re-emerged in 1967 and flourished during the 1970s and early 1980s. Its leader, Yasir Arafat, stood out on the global scene as the most highly visible symbol of that revolutionary movement for nearly two decades. Its strength, however, did not rest on military victories nor on advancing the cause of the Palestinians against Israel. Its life and prosperity rested on two basic organizing principles. The more visible was to identify and organize against the enemy, with the number one enemy being the nation of Israel. Second, it served as a dramatic and highly visible symbol of the legitimacy of the current political regimes in Syria, Libya, Saudi Arabia, and Iraq. Hostility to Israel was one means of sustaining the present governments in these nations. In simple terms the PLO was organized to hate the enemy and to serve as a common vehicle and as a symbol of several Arab nations to express their anti-Israel hatred. If Syria, Iraq, and Saudi Arabia had recognized Israel as a legitimate nation back in the late 1970s, the PLO probably would have collapsed, although the cause of the Palestinian refugees would not necessarily have been advanced. If Israel had chosen either to destroy or to make peace with the PLO, that revolutionary organization probably would have lost all its Arab support and would have disappeared from the scene. It could not have survived without an enemy to hate or without the allies who feared and hated the same enemy.[5]

This same basic organizing principle has been at the heart of thousands of movements throughout human history. Adolph Hitler used it to rally Germans behind him as he identified the Jews as the enemy. Ayatollah Khomeini used it very effectively in Iran for several years with the United States identified as the number one enemy. Mobilizing against the enemy has been the central organizing principle in the Catholic-Protestant conflict in Ireland. Senator Joseph McCarthy used it in Wisconsin to secure re-election to the United States Senate. It also has been the central organizing principle for the Klu Klux Klan. It was used in the United States to mobilize support for the war against Germany in 1917–1918 and again in the early 1940s to rally the nation in an all-out war against Germany and Japan. The book and the play *Mr. Roberts* is a classic illustration of organizing efforts in the 1950s and 1960s in Chicago and elsewhere. This organizational principle was at the heart of the prohibition movement as it rallied opposition to the demon rum. The same principle was used during the second half of this century to bring people together in opposition to the National Council of Churches. One writer uses that theme to describe the early decades of American Methodism—frontier Methodism was organized against the devil as the number one enemy.[6]

Identify a common enemy and rally the people against that enemy. That is one of the most ancient of organizing principles. It is a simple and effective organizing principle. It was used by those who feared Jesus, and it is used today to rally the opposition to drunken drivers. It was used by Jimmy Carter to gain election to the presidency of the United States in 1976 as he campaigned against the "insiders," and it was used by Ronald Reagan to defeat Mr. Carter in 1980.

This example of an ancient organizing principle illustrates the fact that the same organizing principle may be used by those we see as virtuous and also by those we identify as villains.

Before moving to a discussion of a fourth organizing principle, it should be noted that these first three can all be placed in the general category of organizing around a common aim. As was pointed out in the previous chapter, this is at the other end of the spectrum from the voluntary association organized around a legal compact. The organization of a new congregation, the creation of a lay movement designed to enlist Christians in mission and outreach, and the rallying of people together against a common enemy have more in common than might appear to be the case at first glance. One of the points of commonality is that all three may use similar techniques and tools in their organizational efforts.[7]

Rewards and Punishments

A fourth example of the use of organizational principles is illustrated by a literary fund created by Leo Tolstoy, Ivan Turgenev, and several other Russian writers in 1859. It was started to aid struggling young writers who displayed promise. More than a century later the fund still exists and is controlled by the eight-thousand-member union of writers in Russia. Today the fund is a source of special privileges and benefits that range from vacations on the Black Sea to food, housing, theater tickets, and health care. Access to these generous perquisites is limited to those who are loyal to the Soviet government and conform to communist doctrines. Political and ideological purity have replaced creativity and promise as a central organizing principle.

One of the basic organizing principles in the Soviet Union is access to privileges and perquisites denied the vast majority of citizens. The distribution of these special rewards is a means of strengthening the cohesion and loyalty of the military, the bureaucrats, the intellectuals, and the trade unions to the state. Disloyalty produces a punishment through the forfeiture of special privileges.

This carrot-and-stick organizing principle has been used by many churches which withhold the sacraments from the unfaithful, excommunicate the disloyal, and reward the faithful. The perquisites range from a pin for perfect attendance in Sunday school to the right to be buried from the church and in the church cemetery, to selection as a delegate with all expenses paid to the national convention that is held in a very attractive city, to honorary degrees, to the right to wear special garb, to generous gifts at retirement.

This organizing principle, based on a system of rewards and punishments, also is used by professional baseball and football teams, the sales departments of many corporations, prison administrators, school administrators and teachers, military organizations, and the leaders of political parties. A significant number of pastors contend it is an increasingly widely used principle in the process of ministerial placement in their denomination. In scores of cities and states it has been a critical tool in building what the opponents often describe as a "political machine."[8]

Organizing Principles for Large Groups

A fifth, and substantially different, organizing principle can be illustrated by comparing the chancel choir at Trinity Church with the one at Lakeview Church. Both congregations were founded in 1951, and each has between six hundred and seven hundred members.

Six years ago Lakeview Church hired Frank Burton, a music teacher in the junior high school, to direct the chancel choir. Frank graduated from the state university with a major in music and recently completed the work for a master's degree in directing. When Frank arrived on the scene that first September, he found he had inherited a choir of nineteen members. Six years later the typical Sunday finds between twenty-three and twenty-eight voices in the choir, and the reported choir membership is thirty-two. The choir members all like Frank. He is a good director and a warm and caring person. The minister, who suffered through Frank's predecessor for three years, is delighted with the increase in the size of the choir and finds Frank to be a very cooperative colleague. The congregation rejoices in the fact that the choir is larger today than at any time in the past. About ten minutes to eight at a Thursday evening choir rehearsal, Frank said to the members of the choir, "I guess everyone's here now, so we better take a few minutes to decide on the anthem we will sing on Mother's Day. I have two recommendations. One requires at least four or five tenors, and the other we can sing with only a couple. How many of you tenors plan to be here on Mother's Day?"

Two of the four tenors present raised their hands, and a third said, "I'll be here, and I'm pretty sure Mike will be, but I think Mark will be out of town that weekend." The fourth tenor replied, "That's six weeks from now. I haven't the faintest idea where in the world I'll be that Sunday."

"Well, just to be on the safe side, we better choose the second unless someone has a better idea," declared Frank. "Is that acceptable to you folks?"

Hearing no dissent, the director made the decision to begin practicing the anthem that required only two tenors.

Five years ago the choir director and the minister at Trinity Church became so unhappy with one another that the choir director resigned and left very suddenly. This had a negative impact on the chancel choir, which numbered twenty-three members at the time. A relatively new member of the congregation, Margaret Cole, applied to fill the vacancy and was hired with the understanding this might be a temporary position. Margaret, who was fifty-six years old when she took the position, dropped out of college after her second year to get married. She is the mother of six children, and her husband is an attorney. They moved here a little over five years ago when he changed employers. As a child, Margaret learned to play the piano, and she has sung in several choirs. Her first experience in directing came nine years ago when she served as the volunteer choir director in the 160-member congregation she and her family attended before moving here. Her only professional training consists of two summer workshops, a week-long event she attended seven years ago, and a two-week workshop she participated in two years after becoming the choir director at Trinity Church.

Within two years after she became choir director at Trinity, the choir was up to forty-two members and now, from September through May, only rarely are there fewer than sixty-five voices in the choir on Sunday morning. The chancel choir is on vacation during the summer, but Margaret has organized a men's and boys' chorus that sings in June, a coed choir of young adults that sings in July, and an intergenerational choir that provides an anthem for every Sunday in August. Several chancel choir members are represented in each of these three summer choirs.

This format not only gives the chancel choir a summer vacation after nine months of a rather rigorous schedule, but these three special choirs also serve as a training ground or entry point or confidence builder for several future members of the chancel choir. Summer visitors also are highly impressed by the thirty-voice men's and boys' chorus and the two dozen young adults in that July choir. The August intergenerational choir is more of a recreational group. While their vocal music may not be outstanding, it is obvious to any visitor that they enjoy what they are doing.

Why is the chancel choir at Trinity Church more than twice as large as the one at Lakeview? The minister at Trinity explains, "We sure were lucky the day Margaret offered to become our new choir director; she really knows how to attract people."

One person who is acquainted with both congregations declares, "Simple! It's the difference between a part-time choir director with a full-time job and a family, compared to the part-time choir director who doesn't have any other job, whose children are all grown, and whose husband is out of town a hundred days a year."

A choir member at Trinity who has been in the choir for twenty years reflects, "Margaret is never satisfied. She's great to work with, she makes us sing better than we know how, but she's always looking for a new challenge. Look at those three choirs she has organized for the summer. Until she came along, everyone was satisfied if we had a solo or a duet or maybe a quartet while the regular choir was on vacation."

A couple of people at Lakeview explained the difference very quickly, "It's really quite obvious. Trinity is blessed with a lot more members who have the gifts, experience, and dedication to be good choir members." Hardly anyone at either Lakeview or Trinity, however, placed much credence in that explanation—and they were right. As a general rule of thumb, a choir director can expect the potential number of members of the chancel choir to be equivalent to 7-12 percent of the confirmed membership, and typically it is about 10 percent.

Each of those explanations sounds plausible, but none represents the heart of the situation. The primary reason that Trinity's choir is twice the size of the one at Lakeview is simple to identify, but difficult to explain. It is the difference between the basic principles that are appropriate for middle-sized groups of seventeen to thirty or forty people and the organizing principles necessary to create a unified, cohesive, and large group of more than forty-five members.

Frank Burton, the choir director at Lakeview, spends the week working with junior high students, mostly in groups ranging in size from five to thirty-five. He is comfortable with the techniques and organizing principles appropriate for small and middle-sized groups. One result is a happy middle-sized choir of approximately twenty-five voices at Lakeview.

Why is the chancel choir at Trinity so large? While she has never had any formal training in large group dynamics, Margaret Cole intuitively knows how to build and maintain a large group of sixty to seventy participants. What does she do?

From interviews with members of the choir at Trinity, with the pastors, and with Margaret it soon became possible to identify several of the organizing principles she uses to build that big choir.

Before moving ino that subject, however, a word must be said about a concept that can be identified very simply as the "rule of forty." Throughout the course of human history it has been difficult to build and maintain cohesive and unified groups that include more than thirty-five to forty members. This generalization can be seen in the history of military organizations, service clubs, public school classrooms, Scouting, large business corporations, and professional sports. The infantry platoon and the third-grade classroom are two examples. Major league baseball teams may carry forty players on the winter roster, but only twenty-five in the summer. The United Methodist District Superintendent in the South is relatively comfortable with a district that includes thirty-five to forty preachers and feels sorry for the northern superintendent who has a district with fifty or sixty ministers.

There appears to be a natural and universal human tendency to express a need to subdivide the group into smaller units when the total exceeds forty. This dynamic is one of the reasons that church choirs tend to level off with thirty-five to forty voices, even if the congregation includes a thousand or more members. This is the barrier that placed a ceiling on the choir at Lakeview. This is the barrier that Margaret Cole had to eliminate to build a choir of more than forty or forty-five voices. What did she do? How did she circumvent the rule of forty?

While this should not be seen as a simple recipe for producing a large choir, a couple of hours of interviews brought to the surface a score of principles and techniques used by Margaret.

1. She did not simply invite people to join the choir. She asked them to make a commitment. Every year every choir member signed a covenant committing that person to regular attendance at both the Thursday evening rehearsal and on Sunday morning.

2. In many different ways, the covenant being only one, Margaret communicated high expectations. Difficult anthems were chosen intentionally. Margaret repeatedly declared, "The way to build a great choir is to expect a lot of people. That's also how you produce great people."

3. Every rehearsal began and ended exactly on schedule. The larger the group, the more important it is to adhere to the announced schedule.

4. Sometime before or during or after every rehearsal Margaret found a reason to call each person present by name. No one ever went home feeling, "Well, if I don't make it to rehearsal next week, no one will miss me."

5. From that very first rehearsal Margaret never saw the choir simply as one unit. She saw it as four sections of sopranos, altos, basses, and tenors. Each section had its own leader who to some extent also served as the pastor, the tribal chief, the captain, the shepherd, the coach, and the platoon leader for that section.

6. Whenever a choir member missed a rehearsal or was absent on Sunday morning, that person received a caring telephone call from the section leader or Margaret or both, expressing concern over that individual's absence and asking, "Is there anything I can do to be helpful?"

7. Margaret identified Violet Johnson, a fifty-six-year-old widow, as the person with the time and the skills to edit a choir newsletter which was published eight times a year and mailed to each choir member. The larger the group, the more important is systematic and continuing internal communication.

8. At least three members of the finance committee at Trinity church contended that Margaret is the most creative, aggressive, and persistent person they encounter each fall in the budget preparation process. In five years the choir budget tripled, but the complaints of the finance committee were offset by the growth of the choir.

9. Every October, Don and Barbara Wilson take individual photographs of each choir member, and these are reproduced in a twelve-page directory that is given to every choir member. The money for both the newsletter and the directory is in the choir budget.

10. Another battle that took three years to win was the installation of risers in the choir rehearsal room. One objection was the cost. Another was that this would reduce the flexibility in the use of the room. Margaret won that battle because she knew the larger the group, the more important frequent eye contact was between the leader and each member of that group. She also recognized that large groups, unlike small groups, usually place a high value on "having our own turf."

11. Margaret is blessed with a rich sense of humor, and every rehearsal is interrupted several times by laughter. Margaret knows (a) humor is contagious, (b) laughter is the lubricant that minimizes friction in a large group, and (c) laughter and boredom are incompatible feelings.

12. For a couple of weeks before Christmas and again for three weeks before Easter the chancel choir rehearses twice a week. One reason for this is to compensate for unavoidable absences. Another is that Margaret recognizes that the larger the group, the more important challenges are in reinforcing unity and cohesion.

13. While displaying a fairly strong task-orientation, Margaret is primarily a person-centered individual. She genuinely loves that choir, and she never hesitates to express her love for individual choir members. Every joy is celebrated, and every sorrow is shared. The members know Margaret cares, and several view the choir as "a big, but caring family." One soprano who lives alone declared, "I don't come on Thursday evening to rehearse. I come to be with my family."

14. As a mother of six, Margaret understands the concept of nurture. She does not simply organize, rehearse, and direct a large choir. She nurtures it. She mothers it. She loves it. She challenges it and she brags about it.

15. Margaret intuitively understood that the larger the size of the group, the higher the annual turnover rate. She recognized she would need six to ten replacements every year. Rather than bemoan that fact, she organized three distinctively different summer choirs. She knew some potential members did not volunteer because of a lack of self-confidence. Others could not or would not accept the commitment to that twice-a-week schedule for nine months. The summer choirs provide confidence building experiences for some and the opportunity for a short-term four- or five-week commitment for others who need that experience before they can make a long-term commitment. A single, never married member in his mid-twenties who lives alone, is a baseball fan, and sings in all three of the summer choirs explained, "The summer choirs are Margaret's farm clubs for the chancel choir."

16. While she does not have the technical competence to offer individual lessons, Margaret understands the need and helps some potential choir members secure lessons that enhance both their competence and their self-confidence. Margaret also never allows the occasions to arise when a person with a weak voice or a low level of self-confidence will have to carry part of an anthem alone.

17. The second week in October every choir member receives a schedule which includes the anthems for every Sunday through the following May. This has turned out to be one of her most frustration-producing responsibilities since the minister is reluctant to plan that far ahead, but Margaret realizes that the larger the group, the longer the time frame for planning. That also explains why she begins in February to plan and recruit for those three summer choirs.

18. Beginning in her first year, when four fellowship events were held for the chancel choir, Margaret has consistently emphasized the need for frequent social gatherings. She recognizes and affirms the value of these for what is primarily a task-oriented group and also as a means of helping new members become better acquainted with the oldtimers. During her fourth year these included a swim party, a Halloween party, a theater party, a New Year's party, a Valentine party, a bowling party, a Saturday afternoon volleyball

tournament, a birthday party for the minister for choir members only, and a surprise party for Margaret and her husband on their fortieth wedding anniversary.

19. As the wife of a man nearing retirement and a mother who now has survived six teenagers, Margaret is comfortable with people from different generations. The chancel choir at Trinity includes fourteen members in their late teens or early twenties and eleven who are past sixty. While this is not always a factor in organizing a large group, in a congregation the size of Trinity it would be hard to build a sixty-five-voice choir unless it were intergenerational.

20. By this time the reader will recognize that Margaret is not a weak personality filled with self-doubt and low self-esteem. That is true, but that is not the point.

Margaret understands that the larger the group, the greater the expectations the members place on the leader to accept an initiating role. She is willing to accept that role. Her style is a reflection of her gifts, personality, skills, experience, goals, values, responsibilities, age, and of the situation in which she finds herself. Most mature women could not replicate her style, but every leader can learn from studying the role she was given and how she fills that role.

Lest the reader be misled by that long discussion of Margaret Cole, this is not a lesson on how to create and maintain a large choir. This is a chapter on basic organizing principles, and this section represents an effort to identify several of the organizing principles that are appropriate with a large group of people. Usually that means a substantially different set of organizing principles than are used with small groups. A safe generalization is that most of the dynamics, principles, and techniques that are effective with small groups are often counterproductive when used with large groups of people.[9]

The primary thrust of this chapter is to lift up the importance of basic organizing principles in understanding the role and responsibilities of the effective leader. A secondary theme is to illustrate this abstract concept with examples that will be of interest to many leaders in the churches. It may be appropriate, however, to interrupt that sequence at this point and respond to three questions that are often raised when the subject of organizing principles is being discussed.

Three Questions

By this time the reader may have accumulated some qustions such as, "Aren't you really talking about motivation? What's the difference between organizing principles and just plain motivating people?" Or someone may ask, "Aren't you really describing how we can manipulate people to do what we want them to do? I'm not sure the church should be manipulating people." Perhaps most important of all, someone may ask, "Obviously there are many different organizing principles; how does a Christian decide which ones to use?" These are appropriate and complex questions.

In response to the first question, an argument can be made that motivation is a large and relatively inclusive term that embraces organizing principles as a subcategory, but these really are two different subjects. One can think of motivating individuals and organizing groups of people. For example, the United States Army operates an elaborate and expensive recruitment system designed to motivate young adults to enlist in the Army. The basic organizing principle it uses to create a sense of loyalty by these recruits to their military unit is called the Cohort program. Soldiers from the same region of the country are brought together to create a company-size unit of 120 persons, and they not only stay together for the entire enlistment period, they also remain with that same regiment. A regiment of 3,000 soldiers is sent overseas as a unit and returns as a unit. It is based in part on the British system of building organizational morale, developing a loyalty to the team, and strengthening the sense of bonding by keeping the soldiers together for their entire career. This is in sharp contrast with the morale-destroying system of sending in individual replacements and rotating individuals used during the Vietnam War.

The Cohort principle can be described very simply as "shared experiences while growing old together." It is a foundation for long-term marriages, hundreds of adult Sunday school classes, many high school youth groups, dozens of championship professional baseball and football teams, and many business partnerships.

The distinctive feature the Army has emphasized is that the collective memory goes back to exactly the same day since everyone joined that unit on the same day. It resembles the marriage of the couple, neither of whom had ever been married before, who are celebrating their fiftieth wedding anniversary. For both of them adulthood began on the same day, and they have grown old while sharing countless experiences.

While they overlap, motivation is not the same as organizing principles. This can be seen by looking at the synonyms or definitions of the two terms. Synonyms for *motivate* include induce, encourage, influence, stimulate, spur, incite, cause, and arouse. By contrast, *organizing* is defined as bringing together or combining the parts to constitute a harmonious whole. Another way of expressing the same thought is that Margaret Cole motivated dozens of people in the process of organizing and directing a large choir. The annual marathon race in New York City includes hundreds of highly motivated individuals, but it does not produce a tightly-knit, unified, and cohesive organization of participants. They begin at the exact same minute, and they share in the same experience, but a marathon is designed to produce winners and losers, not a cohesive and unified team.

An effective leader both knows how to motivate individuals and also how to create a closely bonded and unified group of people who share common goals and display a strong loyalty to that organization.

The Cohort principle is a means of creating a military unit that provides a supportive context so the leaders can motivate individual soldiers to take certain actions even at the risk of losing their own lives.

This leads into the second question and opens a highly emotional issue. Is this really only a lesson on how to manipulate people more effectively? For those who define the word *manipulate* with strongly negative values this is a serious issue. Frequently the word is used to describe the practice of causing people to act against their own self-interest or contrary to their values for the benefit of the one who is seeking to manipulate them.

Perhaps the best way to respond is to drop this highly charged word and shift to the more neutral concept of influencing other people's beliefs and behavior. By definition leaders seek to influence both beliefs and behavior. The twentieth chapter of Exodus is filled with admonitions designed to influence behavior, as is the Sermon on the Mount. The prophets of the Old Testament, John Calvin, John Wesley, Martin Luther, William Penn, and Martin Luther King, Jr., all sought to influence both belief and behavior. By definition leaders do seek to influence both the beliefs and the behavior pattern of others. Those unwilling to do this would be well advised to refuse any position of leadership in any organization or group.

This raises the most critical question of all. Which principles and techniques is the Christian leader free to use? While this is not a book on Christian ethics, a simple response to that issue is to utilize only those principles, techniques, and procedures that are compatible with your values and goals as a Christian, that are consistent with the role God has defined for your congregation, and that will support the direction you are convinced God has called your congregation to go in the days ahead.

This was the heart of the debate back in the 1960s over the churches' involvement in community organization efforts. Are the churches free to use that ancient and very effective organizing principle of identifying a common enemy and organizing the people against that enemy? The same issue came up again in early 1983 when the CBS television program "Sixty Minutes" and *The Readers' Digest* offered public criticisms of both the National Council of Churches and the World Council of Churches as well as of a couple of the supporting denominations. One response was to organize and attack the enemy. In both cases the same question was raised. Are Christians free to hate those they perceive to be the enemy? Or does the Christian ethic require one to love one's enemy?

Clearly the Christian leader is bound by some restrictions in the choice of organizing principles and techniques.[10] These restrictions include an acceptance of only those organizing principles that are consistent with the values of one who professes to be a follower of Jesus Christ and a rejection of some very effective organizing principles that are inconsistent with the teachings of our Lord. The Christian also is restricted in the choice of motivational techniques and in the definition of the purpose of a movement or organization designed to enlist Christians.

These ethical concerns must always influence the Christian leader's choice of organizing principles, but as was pointed out earlier, this is a book on leadership, not on Christian ethics. Therefore we can return to the theme of this chapter and examine three other common concerns which illustrate how the choice of organizing principles often determines the success or failure of a particular venture.

The Redevelopment of the Anglo Urban Church

Harry Stevens, a sixty-three-year-old leader at Grace Church, when asked about the future of what had become an ex-neighborhood church, replied, "When my wife and I moved here in 1956, this clearly was a stable, solid, middle-class neighborhood. This was a neighborhood church, and we averaged close to two hundred at worship and well over one hundred in the Sunday school. Most of the houses around here had been built sometime between 1915 and 1929. Our church was completed in 1923, and they added the educational wing two years before we joined.

"On Sunday morning we're now down to about forty or fifty people, most of them either bald or gray," he continued. "Our last minister left us four months ago, and we can't seem to find anyone to take his place. Through a series of bequests in recent years we've built up an endowment fund that is worth close to half a million dollars, so we're able to maintain the property and pay our bills. Money is not our problem. What we need is a bunch of new members. My wife and I bought a new house six miles west of here back in 1975, but we still drive in every Sunday. I really don't know why, since there are two churches out near us that are much closer, but we don't know anyone in either congregation. All of our close friends, except for our nextdoor neighbor, are members here. I guess that's why we drive back in two or three times a week.

"Twice we've had someone from denominational headquarters come out to study our situation and to talk with us," explained Mr. Stevens in response to a question about the neighborhood. "Both times they told us to adapt to meet the needs of a changing population in the neighborhood, but they couldn't tell us how to do it. The neighborhood immediately to the west of our property is increasingly Hispanic, blacks have bought most of the houses to the east of the church, south of us is almost all commercial now, and the interstate highway that was built twenty-five years ago cuts us off from anything on the north. The church is just two blocks from an interchange, so it's only a ten- or twelve-minute trip in for us, but we can't seem to persuade any of our neighbors to come in and join us. No one in our congregation speaks Spanish, so I don't see much hope in that direction. We've talked about getting a black pastor, but they are hard to find, and some of us are not sure that today blacks want to join a white church. Twenty years ago we heard a lot of talk about the racial integration of the churches, but today it's hard to find many success stories. Most of what were lifted up as models of racial integration have become all-black congregations as the whites fled to the suburbs. Four or five of our members have been arguing that we should become a tri-cultural church—Hispanic, black, and Anglo—but no one seems to know where to begin to pull that off.

"About eight years ago we got a new minister who seemed to be able to turn things around. Within a year after he arrived, attendance was up from sixty or seventy to over a hundred, and everybody was enthusiastic about the future. After a couple of years, however, he and his wife got a divorce, and he decided to leave the ministry. Each of the next two ministers got discouraged soon after they arrived, and neither stayed as long as three years.

"A couple of our longtime members have suggested we merge with the Westmoreland Church, that's a congregation we helped sponsor back in 1958," continued Mr. Stevens, as he began to describe alternative courses of action. "They're located about seven miles to the north. Someone else suggested we look for either a black or a Hispanic congregation that needs a building in this area, sell them our property for a fraction of its value, turn all our assets over to the denomination and disband. Most of our people really don't want to talk about closing or moving out of this building. They want to find a new minister and keep on as we have been. Maybe we could find a retired minister who would come and serve on a part-time basis. We have a nice house next to the church that's been kept in excellent condition. What do you think?"

What do you think this congregation should do? Disband or relocate or merge? Those are three of the alternatives that often receive serious consideration as an Anglo urban congregation discovers its traditional role has become obsolete. Sometimes it is the ex-neighborhood church, such as the one described here. Or it may be old First Church downtown that is experiencing a sharp decline in numbers. In several cities many of the congregations faced with these questions were founded a hundred years ago, more or less, as nationality parishes for the Swedes, Germans, and other immigrants coming to the United States from northern Europe.

In each of these situations the long-established Anglo congregation is faced with the necessity of either going out of business at that location or choosing a new role. Many deny those are the two basic choices and hang on for a surprisingly long time passively waiting for the miracle that will recreate yesterday.

It is not uncommon for several leaders in these urban Anglo congregations that are declining in numbers to seek a fourth alternative. This dream often consists of five components, (1) the future will represent a high degree of continuity with the past, (2) the children of members will grow up and continue as members when they become adults, thus closing that avenue of attrition, (3) no one will propose any course of action that will alienate some of the members and cause them to leave—everyone will make a serious effort to get along with everyone else, (4) by sheer effort, utmost determination, and complete cooperation as they work together, the members can reverse the numerical decline without abandoning any of the long-established traditions or altering the congregational culture, and (5) new members will come in and gladly accept, affirm, and identify with the values, goals, customs, and beliefs of that congregation. History is filled with the stories of people who dreamed that dream, but never saw it turn into reality.[11]

The concept of the redevelopment of urban Anglo congregations has been receiving a lot of attention for more than three decades. Out of that context it is possible to offer several comments on that process that also illustrate the importance of organizing principles, which is the central theme of this chapter.

Far and away the most popular advice from the experts has been to re-establish that church as a neighborhood congregation. If the members have moved to suburbia, the ideal course of action that frequently has been recommended has been to carve out a new ministry with the new residents of the neighborhood. Experience suggests four positive and at least a dozen negative dimensions to that counsel.

On the positive side, a few widely scattered examples demonstrate it can be done. This alternative reduces the need for already scarce offstreet parking, it often provides a reinforcement for a sense of community in that neighborhood, it results in the creation of a new role with a new constituency, and it simplifies the definition of that congregation's responsibility. Perhaps the most helpful note for the future is the emergence of what have been labeled "urban villages" in Los Angeles, New York, Atlanta, and other large cities. These renewed neighborhoods offer a bright future for scores of long-established urban congregations if the leaders in these numerically declining congregations are willing to identify a new constituency and to become responsive to the needs of this new constituency. Frequently the number one barrier is not age, race, social class, nationality, or language, but rather an unwillingness to move toward a more theologically conservative point on the theological spectrum and/or to change from a rational and intellectual approach to religion to a greater emphasis on an experiential expression of the faith.

On the negative side it must be noted that (1) the overwhelming majority of Anglo churches that have attempted it have been unable to mark the change, (2) language and cultural barriers make it difficult for the Anglo congregation to make Hispanics feel included, (3) many blacks find it insulting to be expected to surrender their unique religious subculture to fit into an Anglo religious tradition, (4) the middle and upper middle class Anglo congregations seeking to reach a new generation of Anglo residents often find that social class barriers are higher, stronger, and more divisive than racial or language or ethnic differences, (5) almost invariably Anglo congregations overlook the issue of power and control with the result that newcomers to the neighborhood perceive these well-intentioned efforts as a combination of paternalism, colonialism, and white guilt, (6) perhaps most serious of all, these efforts often are perceived by black or Hispanic or Asian ministers as a denial of the legitimacy of the black or Hispanic or Asian church and/or as an effort to cream off the best leaders from those churches to assuage the guilt of the Anglo congregation, (7) most of the long-established and denominationally related Anglo congregations in the cities of America pursue an intellectual approach to the faith while the Pentecostal, Holiness, and Adventist congregations that represent most of the success stories usually are new and emphasize an experiential approach to the faith, (8) the three most common products of the effort by the typical Anglo congregation to re-establish itself as a neighborhood church have been frustration, guilt, and passivity, and (9) content analysis of black preaching and of white preaching suggests black preachers are more likely to emphasize Old Testament texts and to stress visual imagery while white preachers tend to rely more on New Testament texts and to verbalize abstract concepts. (One result is that it is difficult to find a white preacher who can hold the attention of a black congregation for thirty or forty or fifty minutes. Another distinction is black preachers often expect an active response from those present while the typical white preacher is used to a more passive response.)

In addition to these nine negative factors, three other forces must be recognized as barriers to the redevelopment of the old Anglo congregation as a neighborhood church. The first is the theme of this book—leadership. Frequently the aggressive and creative leadership of the new pastor has been a crucial factor in those redeveloped urban churches that once again are neighborhood churches—and only rarely is the long-established Anglo church in the city able both to attract and to affirm that style of ministerial leadership.

Second, attempts to build a geographical parish consisting largely of blacks or Hispanics or Asians may represent an idealized expression of the parish church for Anglos, but it runs counter to the fact that the concept of a geographical parish is not a common characteristic of urban black or Hispanic or Asian congregations—the vast majority of these minority congregations gather people together with a different set of central organizing principles.

Third, and perhaps the most influential of all these factors is that the workplace has replaced the neighborhood as the primary point of socialization. In simple terms, the critical dynamic, the function of a neighborhood as a place to meet and make new friends, that was the cornerstone of creating neighborhood churches for several generations has been eroded by changes in our society. Today geography is only a minor factor in the choice of friends for most urbanites. This change in the role of the typical urban neighborhood may be the most widely neglected factor in the frequently heard advice to redevelop as a neighborhood church. Neighborhood institutions of all kinds are disappearing from the urban landscape.[12]

Rather than attempting the frustration-producing experience of seeking to re-establish itself as a geograpical parish, the Anglo congregation planning a new future for itself might be well advised to go back to a basic question. What is the common characteristic of those urban churches that are able to bring scores of people together to worship and praise God, to care for one another, and to implement the Great Commission?

If one looks back at the history of the Christian churches in urban America, it is easy to identify some of these central organizing principles by examining a half dozen case studies and seeking to identify basic organizing principles that run through all of them. Those concerned with the redevelopment of an urban Anglo congregation may want to identify the organizing principles that might apply to your church.

1. Immigrants come to the United States from Germany, Sweden, Scotland, Italy, Cuba, Korea, Hong Kong, or Colombia and either bring their own minister with them or send back to the home country for a pastor to come and organize a congregation. The central organizing principle is the combination of a common language, religious subculture, nationality, pioneering spirit, heritage, upward mobility, and initiating leadership.

2. Thousands of rural residents from Appalachia moved to Akron, Ohio, during World War I to work in the tire factories. Another generation moved north during and immediately after World War II to seek their fortune building tires. A preacher comes in and organizes a congregation that grows to include thousands of members. The central organizing principles of this process include a common religious subculture; a common heritage; shared values; a feeling of alienation from the ruling classes of Akron; a religious message with a distinctive ideological thrust that appeals to those who see themselves as strangers and sojourners with God in a land that others claim is not rightfully theirs (Lev. 25:23); a sense of satisfaction in being an essential and needed part of a church that is clearly a success story; a central and dominant role for a dynamic, imaginative, persistent, aggressive, and energetic minister; the reinforcement of a weekly radio—later television—program; the creation of an organizational structure that keeps track of every member and helps each one feel needed; an attractive and impressive building that was a useful rallying point while it was being constructed and subsequently served as a visible reminder that "we've made it here in this hostile environment"; the opposition or scorn of many of the leaders of the "establishment" churches; critical stories in the local newspaper that reassure those who are alienated from the local culture that they are in the right camp; and various other "enemies" who can be criticized or attacked whenever it is necessary to rally the people in a common cause.

3. In 1953 a delegation of eighty-five members from old First Church downtown was commissioned by that congregation to establish a new mission in a new residential development on the north side of the city. Twenty-five years later that new congregation is substantially larger in numbers than the mother church.

The central organizing principles in that effort included identifying a need not being met adequately by other churches; organizing a core of committed, venturesome, talented, self-confident, and creative people around the challenging, specific, attainable, measurable, visible, satisfying, and unifying goal of pioneering a

LEADERS KNOW HOW TO ORGANIZE

needed new congregation; the presence of an attractive, venturesome, energetic, extroverted, entrepreneurial-type personality as the first minister; and the support of denominational leaders as well as the people back at old First Church.

4. Against the advice of five of the seven pastors from that denomination in that part of the metropolis, the national staff of the denomination goes ahead with its plans to launch a new mission on the rural-urban fringe of a large metropolitan center.

Nine years later the new mission includes nearly five hundred new members, is experiencing a net growth of sixty members a year, and has just completed its second building program.

Why did it work when informed opinion advised against the venture? In retrospect it appears the most influential factors were (1) the attractiveness to newcomers of helping to pioneer and shape a new venture rather than attempting to fit into the traditions and customs of long-established congregations, (2) an attractive, energetic, extroverted, enthusiastic, optimistic, and personable pastor, (3) three families who were charter members and brought with them dedication, experience, skill, patience, and persistence and who are still extremely active leaders, (4) the resistance of many of the longtime residents of the area to this flood of new residents who were moving into the community as one expression of their upward mobility, (5) the choice of an accessible, attractive, and highly visible site for the meeting place, and (6) the categorical demand by the local school board that all new congregations must vacate their temporary quarters in a public school after a maximum of twenty-four months.

5. Shortly after celebrating its fiftieth anniversary, the leaders at Westminster Church began to realize their neighborhood had completed the change from an upper class white community into a middle class white-collar residential area and was about to move into the third stage of its evolution. A growing number of blacks, most of them teachers, dentists, physicians, attorneys, and self-employed entrepreneurs were moving into that section of the city.

Twenty years later Westminster Church had (a) experienced the retirement of its pastor of thirty years, (b) welcomed and two years later bid farewell to the successor to that long-term pastorate, (c) welcomed and four years later bid farewell to the successor to that two-year "unintentional interim" pastorate, (d) welcomed a new and personable minister who was and is completely committed to the goal of the racially integrated church and who is now in his eleventh year as a minister, (e) watched all but but a dozen of the younger white families with children at home move out of the neighborhood, (f) witnessed the local elementary school change from 98 percent Anglo to 60 percent black, 20 percent Anglo, and 20 percent Asian, (g) been disappointed to see the average attendance in the Sunday school drop from 175 to 40 and then level off at 65, (h) seen confirmed membership shrink from 735 to 225 white members, (i) grown to include 115 black members for a total membership of 340, (j) experienced an increase in the median age of the confirmed membership from 46 years to 59 years and had seen that figure gradually drop down to 47 years, (k) benefited from the experience and wisdom of more than a score of black couples who had spent twenty to thirty years in military service before retiring, had appreciated the racially integrated congregations they had worshiped with on several military posts, and who were determined to find and be active members of a racially integrated congregation on their re-entry into civilian life, (l) seen a disproportionately large number of its members serving as volunteer leaders in both regional and national agencies of that denomination, (m) been written up twice in the local metropolitan newspapers and once in the national denominational magazine as a model of how a long-established Anglo congregation had been able to be transformed into a growing racially integrated church, and (n) was attracting younger white couples who lived as far as twelve to fifteen miles from the building, but who wanted to be part of a racially integrated church.

Today Westminster Church stands out in that denomination as a model of how racial integration can be achieved in the church. Critics point out that while the membership is approximately 35 percent black, 60 percent Anglo, and 5 percent Asian, 80 percent of the children in the Sunday school are black or Asian while 75 percent of the active members of the women's association are Anglos, but in most respects it clearly is a racially integrated church.

How did it happen? Among the most influential factors were (a) a determined minister who was willing to lead those who wanted to follow down the road to racial integration, (b) a small cadre of Anglo allies eventually

63

GETTING THINGS DONE

reinforced by several blacks and Asians who were equally committed to that ideal of an inclusive congregation, (c) an infinite amount of patience by the current minister, (d) nearly all of the newcomers—Anglo, Asian, or black—being upwardly mobile individuals with an upper-middle-class orientation—their arrival meant raising, not lowering, the socio-educational–professional character of the congregation, (e) at least two dozen of the longtime Westminster members and the vast majority of the new members being vigorously dissatisfied with the high degree of racism that permeates American society and determined to prove that a racially integrated congregation not only can be an influential witness to Christ, but also can be a viable self-supporting and self-propagating congregation, and (f) lots of persistence.

6. St. Paul Lutheran was organized in 1875 as a German language congregation in a crossroads town of two hundred residents to serve the recent immigrants from the "old country" who were farmers and craftsmen. By 1925 it was the largest of the four churches in a town with three hundred residents and a four-teacher high school. The Roman Catholic parish drew people from a larger area but was slightly smaller in numbers. A small Methodist congregation and a tiny Baptist church completed the range of choices for those who wanted to go to church. In 1922, for the first time in its history, the confirmation class was conducted in English, and the German language service was dropped in 1939. By 1950, what was still primarily a working class parish of farmers and craftsmen numbered 271 baptized members. In 1957 the first houses in the community were constructed by three different families who sought to combine the joys of country living with the comfort of a city paycheck. In 1977 the recently arrived pastor commented to a visitor, "One-third of our six hundred baptized members are from longtime farm and working class families, one-third are descendents of those families who work in the city twenty miles away, and one-third are professionals and executives from the city who either come from a German Lutheran background or married into it, and who live just outside town on five-to-ten acre estates."

Seven years later, and eight years after the arrival of that new pastor, this 980-baptized-member congregation was moving from its century-old red brick building, with a cement block addition constructed largely with volunteer labor in 1961 on the original half-acre site, to a new $1.1 million building on a ten-acre parcel two miles to the east of the original meeting place.

Five of the seven members on the long-range planning committee that eventually recommended relocation were upper and upper-middle income professionals or executives who joined this parish in 1972 or later, as were six of the seven members of the building planning committee that planned the relocation effort. When the congregational meeting was held to vote on the recommendation to relocate, a total of 189 favorable votes were cast for relocation with 37 votes against it. Subsequently the pastor estimated that at least thirty of these negative votes were cast by persons who had joined before 1955 or by their adult children.

While there was substantial opposition to the relocation effort, the decision to do so was the result of (1) an aggressive and imaginative pastor who had a clear vision of what could be and was convinced that God was calling this parish to prepare for a new era in its history, (2) the disappearance by retirement or death from leadership positions of most of the leaders of the 1950s, (3) the upward mobility orientation of many of the children, but now adult members, of some of these longtime members, (4) the lack of interest by most of the newcomers in the traditions, customs, or culture of what, as recently as 1970, was clearly a *German* Lutheran parish, (5) the freely expressed doubts and reservations of many of the nonmember longtime residents of that community about the feasibility of such an ambitious effort, (6) the hearty support for this vision by a score of remarkably articulate, determined, analytical, highly skilled, and professionally trained laypersons, (7) the fact that the basic changes were from smaller to larger and from a working class parish to an upper-middle and upper class congregation, and (8) the timely interest expressed by a four-year-old Baptist congregation in purchasing the old property, but only if it would be available for their use within six months.

While these six examples do not cover the entire spectrum of congregations that have defined and accepted a new role, they do offer clues on the common ingredients in the organization of new congregations and the redevelopment of long-established churches. At least six of the following principles can be identified in each one of the case studies.

1. The congregation had the benefit of an aggressive, optimistic, persistent, dedicated, creative and future-oriented minister who was willing to accept the role as an initiating leader.

2. The minister enlisted and worked with influential lay allies.

3. These allies were enlisted as part of an effort to help pioneer a new creation, rather than to join, attempt to fit into, and conform to an old institution in an effort to recreate yesterday. Occasionally this approached the nature of a crusade. (A basic generalization about planned change from within an organization is that usually it is easier to enlist newcomers in helping to pioneer a new era rather than expecting them to fit into and adjust to the status quo.)

4. The process was reinforced by specific, attainable, measurable, satisfaction-producing, visible, and unifying goals. To paraphrase a famous book, each of these six congregations was value-driven, was goal-oriented, displayed a bias for action, exhibited basic entrepreneurial characteristics, and was able to manage ambiguity.[13]

5. Clearly defined rallying points helped to turn a collection of people into a cohesive and unified group.

6. Each congregation repeatedly benefited from one form or another of affirmation of its efforts. External affirmation was especially influential in developing the racially integrated congregation at Westminster.

7. In several cases the opposition of a clearly identified *external* "enemy" reinforced the sense of community and identity within the group.

8. The leadership represented a high degree of homogeneity in terms of social, economic, and educational characteristics.

9. Each example represented upward mobility for that congregation and for many of the members.

This last statement is the one that will disturb a great many readers, as well as this writer. The simplest means of explaining it is that it reflects the discrepancy between the teachings of Jesus and the nature of the New Testament churches. Repeatedly Jesus emphasized his concern for the poor, the oppressed, the downtrodden, the alienated, and the outcasts of society.

By contrast, the New Testament churches apparently attracted individuals who were dissatisfied with the ordinary social structures of that day, who were filled with hope, who were venturesome personalities willing to take risks, who were socially mobile and who were driven by a vision of a new day immediately ahead.[14]

Perhaps the two most disillusionary findings coming out of a study of Christian congregations in contemporary America are (a) they rarely can reach and include those who are completely without hope and (b) numerically growing congregations almost without exception also are churches that are moving up the social class scale. This is not a new insight. It has been emphasized repeatedly by those who have studied the upward mobility of such denominations as the Methodists, Nazarenes, Mormons, the Church of God of Anderson, Indiana, and many others.

This same generalization also can be illustrated by the tremendous difficulties encountered by the Christian Reformed Church, The United Methodist Church, and the Cumberland Presbyterian Church in reaching persons living on Indian reservations. By contrast, Presbyterians, Methodists, Southern Baptists, and others have been remarkably successful in reaching and including the recent immigrants from Cuba and from Asia and the Pacific rim who came to America filled with hope, with a determination to make it in their new home and to move very quickly into the upper dimensions of the American class structure.

Rarely, however, has this dynamic been considered when the subject is the redevelopment of long-established urban congregations. Rarely do those advising these congregations to "Serve your neighborhood!" add the advice necessary to help those churches to concurrently move down the social class scale while reaching upwardly mobile people *or* to retain longtime members while dropping in orientation one or two or more rungs on the social class ladder.

From a denominational perspective one implication is if the denominational leaders are serious about reaching lower and lower-middle class people, their efforts probably should be directed primarily at launching new congregations rather than urging long-established middle-class or upper-class congregations to identify, attract, serve, and assimilate people from the lowest third of the socio-educational-economic spectrum of society. These efforts, when they do appear to be successful, usually involve skimming off the upwardly mobile people from that lower class neighborhood.

Finally, when discussing the basic organizing principles to be followed in organizing a new congregation or in redeveloping the long-established Anglo urban church, four widely neglected lessons from history must be highlighted here.

First, what happens when the pastor leaves what is clearly a very promising situation and is followed by a new minister? In a small minority of such changes the successor comes in and continues without any changes in those organizing principles utilized by the predecessor, and the congregation continues to thrive. Far more often, the new minister arrives, either ignores or discards the organizing principles used by the predecessor and substitutes a new set, and everyone agrees the change in ministers was highly disruptive. All too frequently the new minister comes into what appeared to be a very promising situation, discards the organizing principles followed by the predecessor, does not substitute a new set of organizing principles, the situation collapses, and everyone begins the search to identify a scapegoat.

Second, what happens after four or five or more years of subsidizing the redevelopment of an urban congregation? How does the denomination discontinue that financial subsidy without creating an adversarial relationship between that congregation and the denomination? With rare exceptions the answer is that no one knows.

Some highly productive and mutually beneficial subsidies can be and have been granted for that transitional stage as the congregation concludes an era and outlines a new chapter in its history. If that denominational subsidy is extended for more than three or four years, however, it usually creates a dependency relationship that often degenerates into an adversarial relationship if and when the denomination seeks to terminate the financial aid. This is a natural product of subsidies in our society. They tend to be self-perpetuating. This can be seen in the subsidies granted to mailers of third class junk mail, truckers, theological seminaries, hospitals, farmers, river bargers, municipalities selling tax-exempt bonds, first-time home buyers, consumers of low-priced electric power, and hundreds of other beneficiaries of financial subsidies.

— FRIAR TUCK.

Dependent Churches become adversarial!

Therefore it is strongly urged that everyone involved in the redevelopment of urban churches agree that financial subsidies should be granted only on a short-term basis, preferably on a gradually descending scale.

Third, if the concept of recreating the long-established Anglo congregation as a geographic parish often has inherent shortcomings, what is a better strategy for the redevelopment of urban churches?

A brief and simplistic response to that highly complex question is to find a special niche. Identify people whose needs are not being met adequately by existing congregations and seek to fill that niche. This almost invariably means shifting to a nongeographical definition of the parish. Examples range from the congregation that has a special ministry with families that include a developmentally disabled child; to the hundred-year-old congregation in Brooklyn that has a growing ministry with young, urban professionals; to the church with a multi-faceted music program that now includes a dozen music groups; to hundreds that have built a new future around an Early Childhood Development Center and an expanded ministry with young parents; to the congregation that specializes in a ministry with the recently divorced. Find a niche and fill it! That can be a useful organizing principle for any urban church as it carves out a new role for itself in a new era of its ministry.

Finally, it may be helpful to examine those nine organizing principles derived from these six case studies and determine which ones may be useful in your effort to write a new chapter in the history of that urban Anglo congregation.

The Sunday Morning Fellowship Period

"The best change we've made in years has been adding a coffee and fellowship hour between Sunday school and worship," declared someone from the two-hundred-member St. Paul's Church. "We moved the Sunday school up to nine o'clock, the fellowship period begins around ten, worship is scheduled for ten-thirty, and it really works!"

"We tried the same thing after church, but our fellowship hall is downstairs," commented a layman from the four-hundred-member Pleasant Valley Church, "and we lost about 80 percent of the crowd. They simply won't walk down the stairs. They head straight for the exits right after the benediction."

"We've tried it, but we've not had much success, except for the adults who come early for Sunday school. We run our coffee time between Sunday school and worship, just as you do at St. Paul's, but only a few of our adults come to Sunday school, and we can't seem to persuade people to come half an hour early for fellowship," commented the minister from the seven-hundred-member Trinity Church. "About all we've accomplished is we clog up the halls with a big crowd about 10:58 when people are trying to get through to the sanctuary. There really is not much fellowship, and I'm about ready to drop the whole thing."

This conversation illustrates three of the problems congregational leaders frequently encounter as they plan a Sunday morning fellowship period. The goals are commendable. That twenty- to forty-minute period of time is intended to encourage members to become better acquainted with one another, to greet the first-time visitor with a warm and friendly atmosphre, to stimulate the caring impulses that are a natural part of a Christian fellowship, to make sure everyone, whether it be a stranger or the member who attends only rarely, is greeted and made to feel welcome and to facilitate the working of that internal communications network often referred to simply as "the grapevine." In addition, in many churches, that period is a productive time for the youth to sell tickets to their spaghetti supper, for the women to sign people up to work in the bazaar, for the Christian education committee to continue their never-ending search for new Sunday school teachers, and for the trustees to enlist volunteers for next Saturday's workday on the building.

This conversation also offers an excellent example of the concept of basic organizing principles and of how the principles followed influence the outcome.

A common question is, "Should we schedule this period before or after worship?" For those congregations with a large adult Sunday school or with two worship experiences on Sunday morning, the best answer usually is immediately before the last worship service of the morning. That, however, usually produces two objections. "One of the primary reasons for the fellowship period is to provide a warm and friendly greeting to first-time visitors. Most of them don't arrive until a few minutes before worship so that won't work!" The second is, "Most of our adult members don't come to Sunday school, and many of them won't come early simply for a cup of coffee."

If these objections fit your congregation, it may be wise to move the Sunday morning schedule up a half an hour and plan the fellowship period for after worship. Most people do find it easier to linger an extra fifteen or twenty minutes—and for some an extra forty or fifty minutes—than to arrive early.

A second issue is the lack of an attractive room on the same level with the sanctuary that is easy to find. The ideal arrangement, as one congregation in Wisconsin has demonstrated, it so design the building so everyone leaving the nave walks through the fellowship area on the way to claim their coats or to reach a convenient exit. In that congregation nearly every attender, including the first-time visitors, stays for twenty to fifty minutes after worship.

If you are faced with the difficulty either of using an inconvenient room for the fellowship period or of enticing people to come early, it may be useful to reflect on alternative means of increasing participation.

The first step is to post a redundant set of signs that direct people to the appropriate place and also state the time. The signs should be designed to be easily understood by a first-time visitor, and it may be useful to provide a space for insertion of a card highlighting this week's special attraction. The second most useful step is to provide nametags for everyone. The third step, if space permits, is to offer the convenience of the appropriate number of lightweight, easy-to-move, comfortable individual chairs that *do not fold* (stacking chairs are acceptable). Fourth, always offer people a choice of at least four beverages. Fifth, secure one gregarious volunteer host and one extroverted volunteer hostess every week who will encourage everyone to wear a nametag, welcome strangers, and introduce those who do not appear to be well acquainted to the more sociable members.

After you have implemented those five basic steps, choose five more ways of strengthening that fellowship period from this list: (1) encourage groups and organizations, such as adult classes, the choir, the women's organization, or the youth fellowship to set up tables or booths to enlist volunteers or sell tickets or secure reservations or sell merchandise, (2) post on one wall a changing variety of conversation starters such as posters, maps, charts, 11 x 14-inch and larger photographs, clippings, and announcements, (3) schedule one or two action events every week such as a six- or seven-minute musical performance by a violinist or a vocal group or a brass quartet or a puppet show or a juggler or a mime or a color slide exhibit or a clown ministry by teenagers or a conversationlist who will discuss a publicized-in-advance topic, (4) if you expect more than fifty at any one time, provide food as well as a choice of beverage and use two widely separated tables for refreshments (people who are eating both attract other people and create clusters that block traffic), (5) legitimitize the concept that many adults simply like to sit and watch people, (6) if space permits, create a couple of attractive right-angle corners of furniture that encourage informal, ad hoc, small group conversation, (7) recognize the tendency that while standing, people tend to cluster in the center of an open space and/or in traffic lanes, but while seated they prefer to be on the edge of the room, and arrange the furniture accordingly, (8) accept the fact that women prefer slightly more space between one another than do men, (9) plan one low-key activity every week in one corner of an adjacent room that will attract and interest younger children, (10) define a corner with its own refreshment table for teenagers, (11) provide an occasional opportunity for upcoming special programs or events to be publicized, and (12) perhaps use another wall for a three- or four-week exhibit by a painter, photographer, weaver, or hobbyist. (This last item might include a collection of presidential campaign buttons or postage stamps or coins or souvenir spoons.)

In other words, if that fellowship period fails on its own to attract a satisfactory number of participants, ask someone to accept responsibility for making it a planned and attractive event that will encourage people to return next week.

The third common problem with the fellowship period is a result of differences in the size of congregations. In the congregation with fewer than a hundred at worship, it may be adequate to simply announce it and provide the refreshments. Most of the people will come.

In middle-sized congregations that average between one hundred and two hundred at Sunday morning worship, fewer than one-half of the attenders may participate in the fellowship period unless the location is exceptionally attractive or unless it is carefully planned. Usually it will be necessary to plan it more carefully and to have someone in charge of the design for the week, as well as someone else responsible for the refreshments, to increase that number of participants.

In big congregations the fellowship period rarely attracts more than a minority of the attenders unless either (a) it is held in a room through which nearly everyone passes to enter or leave the sanctuary and/or (b) every week it is a carefully planned event with a variety of attractive features—and that means someone in charge with additional volunteer assistance.

Finally, three comments should be made about the factor of the time zone. First, as a general rule, the farther west one travels on this continent, the more likely that people will be going to church earlier. In North Carolina the general pattern appears to be that people prefer to begin Sunday morning worship at 10:30 or 11:00 A.M. while in California scores of congregations have their largest attendance at the 8:30 or 9:00 A.M. service.

Second, the National Football League games and other television programs make it more difficult for churches in the West to keep people past 11:30 A.M. than is the case in the East.

Third, churches located in the eastern end of any time zone usually find people more responsive to an early hour in the winter than do congregations in the western end of the same time zone. Thus the congregation meeting in the eastern end of a time zone east of the Mississippi may find people willing to linger for the fellowship period after worship (except in the Southeast where a high priority is to beat the Baptists to the cafeteria), while in Kansas, Nebraska, the Dakotas, and the Pacific Coast it may be wise to plan a much earlier fellowship period.

What are the organizing principles that you follow in planning that Sunday morning fellowship period in your church?

The Fifth-Grade Sunday School Class

"For years we've had a big drop in our Sunday school attendance after fourth grade," complained Harriet Thompson, one of the longtime leaders in the Sunday church school at the Woodlawn Church as she finished her second cup of coffee on Saturday noon. The occasion was the annual regional workshop on Christian education sponsored by the denomination. Harriet was eating lunch with two acquaintances from other churches, and the three were sharing their frustrations, none of which had been mentioned during the morning session.

"We have the same problem, except it doesn't hit us until after the fifth grade," commented Marty Lawson, from Trinity Church. "Several years ago our public school system was reorganized so that now the elementary schools run through fifth grade; the sixth-, seventh-, and eighth-graders are in what are called middle schools; and the high school is for ninth through twelfth grades. Ever since they put that change into effect, we've experienced a big dropout rate as the kids enter middle school. I guess that when they're ready for middle school, they think they're too old for Sunday school."

"We do pretty well keeping the girls interested," observed Mickey Rogers from North Church, "but we can't seem to be able to hold the boys. In third grade we have almost as many boys as girls, but by sixth or seventh grade on the typical Sunday the girls will outnumber the boys by a two-to-one margin."

At a table thirty feet away another conversation was taking place.

"We moved here last December," commented Martha Daley, a relatively new, but very active member in South Hill Church. "I was sure we were going to have a problem getting Jimmy to go to Sunday school. He had hated it in the church we were in back in Pennsylvania; you know how fifth-grade boys are. In addition, he was really upset when my husband was transferred and we had to move three months after the school year had begun. He didn't want to leave all his friends behind and start new in a strange school. I didn't blame him. By December most of the kids have built their friendship circles for that year, and it's hard for someone new to come in and be able to make new friends. So, before we moved, we told Jimmy that we expected him to go to Sunday school for the first three Sundays after we moved and if he still didn't like it, we wouldn't force him to go anymore after that."

"What happened?" asked Mike Verhoef, a longtime leader in the Christian education program at South Hill. "I see Jimmy every Sunday. He's in Sunday school every week, and he seems to be enjoying it."

"My husband had to be at work here in early October, and we bought a house here about that time. He went ahead and moved, but Jimmy, the younger two kids, and I stayed back in Pennsylvania until we could find a buyer for our house there," continued Mrs. Daley. "By the time the kids and I moved, the first week in December, my husband had visited five or six different churches and suggested we attend three of them before making a choice. All three are about the same distance from our house. We decided to come to South Hill the first Sunday after we moved, visit another one the Sunday before Christmas, and go to the third the Sunday after Christmas.

"Well, to make a long story short, we never got to the other two," concluded Martha. "As we were driving home after church that first Sunday at South Hill, Jimmy was just bubbling over with enthusiasm about what they were doing in Sunday school, and he couldn't wait for the next Sunday to come so he could go back. As it turned out, the fifth-and-sixth-grade class at South Hill was making a videotape on the story of the birth of Jesus. The boy who had been playing the role of Joseph had fallen off his bicycle and broken his leg on Friday.

They said he was about the same height as Jimmy, so they asked Jimmy to take his place. They planned to complete the story the following Sunday so it could be shown to anyone who wanted to come early on Christmas Eve to see it. At the end of that second Sunday Jimmy was fully assimilated into that class, and he met two of his closest friends in that class."

"We had a similar experience when we moved here two years ago," commented Hazel Burton. "We also moved in the fall after school had started, and our daughter, Laura, who was ten at the time, also hated the idea of moving, leaving all her friends behind, and starting new in a strange school several weeks after school had opened up again in the fall. She was opposed to everything, including going to Sunday school. We moved in on a Tuesday, she started school on Wednesday, and on Thursday, shortly after she got home from school, she got a telephone call from the fifth-grade Sunday school teacher at First Church inviting her to come to that teacher's house for a slumber party on Friday night. There were eight girls at the party, and I guess they didn't sleep much. Laura got home a little before noon on Saturday, ate a bite or two of lunch, and went to her room to take a nap. When she got up at about four o'clock, she told me all about the slumber party and how she could hardly wait until Sunday morning to go to Sunday school and see all her new friends again."

"How did that Sunday school teacher know that you folks had moved here?" questioned Mike Verhoef.

"Oh, our next-door neighbor is a member of First Church," replied Martha. "She dropped in to welcome us as we were moving in and brought us a casserole and a pie for our supper. We discovered later that she went home and immediately called her minister. Two hours later she brought him over to meet us. They both stayed for an hour helping us unpack. A day or two later the minister told Mrs. Hakken, the Sunday school teacher, about Laura, and she invited Laura to the slumber party."

On the surface it appears these are simply two conversations about the children's division in the Sunday church school. Actually, however, these are conversations about basic organizing principles, cohort theory, initiating leadership, the assimilation of newcomers, group dynamics, and other esoteric subjects. The lessons illustrated by these two conversations can be discussed best within the context of the larger question, "What organizing principles can we utilize to encourage attendance in our fifth-and-sixth-grade Sunday school classes?"

The first lesson in organizing principles is that the typical promotion system used in the public schools creates problems when applied to the Sunday school. The public school has the coercive power of the law to force children to attend. Only the highly legalistic churches have an equivalent motivating force to make people attend. Those congregations organized as voluntary associations must use a different set of organizing principles to encourage attendance.

Cohort theory suggests that the most effective means of building a closely knit, cohesive, and unified group is to bring all the members together on the first day and keep them together as one unit year after year. It is highly disruptive to the sense of unity in a group to attempt to introduce newcomers into the group long after that original group was formed. Promoting fourth-graders into a fifth-and-sixth-grade class after those children have completed fourth grade is a predictable way of creating dropouts. The public schools can use the coercive power of the law to reduce the number of dropouts. The voluntary association does not possess that coercive power and is really left with four or five alternatives. One is to build a class at age five, or perhaps of five-year-olds and six-year-olds and keep that class together for the next dozen years.

A second alternative is to adopt the promotion system used by the public schools and accept the dropout rate as a deplorable fact of life.

A third alternative is to focus on a series of community building experiences that will help the recently promoted fourth-graders gain a sense of belonging when they come into that fifth-and-sixth-grade class and also will help the children who enter during the school year gain a sense of belonging.

A fourth alternative is to use the concept of rewards and punishments as the basic organizing principle to encourage attendance. This has been and still is a widely utilized organizing principle in thousands of Sunday schools.

A fifth alternative is to adopt the concept of modeling as the primary organizing principle. An immense quantity of research over the past quarter century suggests that children are greatly influenced by what they see adults do. Examples include cigarette smoking, the use of alcoholic beverages, reading, teenage pregnancies, child abuse, church attendance, the choice of a vocation, and the probability of divorce. In each case children tend to follow the path of their parents or other influential adults.

Dozens of churches utilize this principle in encouraging children to attend Sunday school. The first step in building a strong children's division in the Sunday school is to create a strong adult program with adult males constituting a majority of the attenders (men tend to model behavior while women tend to model beliefs), to make these adult classes highly visible to children (opening exercises and/or a small one-room building facilitate this), and to encourage the adults and the minister to talk frequently and favorably about their Sunday school experiences.

A second lesson to be gleaned from these conversations was illustrated by Jimmy Daley's experience. The unwilling Jimmy became an enthusaistic member of that fifth-and-sixth-grade Sunday school class at South Hill Church. Jimmy illustrates the old adage, "You know you belong when you know you are needed." He was needed to take the role of the boy with the broken leg. A more common example of this is the congregation engaged in a building program that depends largely on volunteer labor. When the volunteers go home after a long evening's work, each one leaves feeling, "I know I belong here because I am needed." This includes the skilled craftsman who just moved into the community a week earlier and really had not yet decided which church to join.

Jimmy's experience also illustrates the concept of the unfinished task. People are more likely to return when they feel they have left an unfinished task behind from the previous visit. A parish pastor in the United Church of Canada uses this concept in the presentation of the children's sermon. Each Sunday morning he uses the first half of that brief period to complete the unfinished children's sermon from the previous week. He begins by holding up the line drawing or cartoon he had drawn the previous week to illustrate that message. After completing that story, he introduces the new drawing he has prepared to illustrate the new children's sermon. Just as he reaches an exciting point in that story, he announces, "Sorry, our time is up. We'll finish this next Sunday." The hand-drawn cartoon makes it easy for everyone to recall the first half of the story when next Sunday rolls around. The videotape the fifth- and sixth-graders were making at South Hill Church also stands as an example of the unfinished task.

Another basic organizing principle was illustrated by the slumber party Laura Burton attended. One of the problems facing the leaders in the National Guard and in the Army Reserves is to build a cohesive, closely knit, and unified organization out of a collection of civilians who hold civilian jobs and are distracted from their military obligations by other interests, hobbies, and friends. The task is further complicated by a relatively high turnover rate among the troops. One of the most effective organizing principles utilized by the National Guard and the Reserves is the weekend encampment or the two-week summer maneuvers. Spending a weekend together or living together for two weeks during the summer both reinforces cohesion and integrates newcomers into that group. The equivalent organizing principle for a Sunday school class is a slumber party or summer camp or a weekend retreat. For the class of young adults it is a weekend ski trip, for the eighth-grade confirmation class it is a three-day canoe trip, and for the high school youth choir it is a spring trip. Each experience reinforces the cohesion of the group.

This same basic organizing principle was explained in these words by the superintendent of the Sunday school at Community Church. "Last year we kept a careful record of the attendance in the fifth-and-sixth-grade class. That's the only class that has a party every month. It also is our biggest class. We found that the attendance for the Sunday morning following the party on Friday evening or Saturday was the peak for that month. The typical pattern was twenty-eight or twenty-nine or thirty the Sunday right after the party. It then generally declined until there were about twenty-two or twenty-three in attendance on the Sunday before the next party. The kids come from several different school districts, and the class is taught by a team of three teachers. I suggested to the teachers the parties were a means of gluing the class back together again."

Three additional significant lessons were illustrated by Jimmy Daley's experience. The first Sunday when he agreed to substitute for the boy with a broken leg, he not only knew he was needed, he also knew that if he did not return the following Sunday, he would be missed. This organizing priniple helps to explain why it is easier for one soprano to be absent from the adult choir rehearsal than it is for the shortstop to miss a practice session for the church softball team or for a member of the handbell choir to skip a rehearsal. You are more likely to make the extra effort to be present if you know you will be letting the team down by your absence.

Filling the role of Joseph in presenting the Christmas story, playing shortstop on the church softball team, and being a member of the handbell choir also have another point of commonality that is especially significant in reaching boys and men. Each role calls for an expression of creative gifts without a substantial dependency on verbal skills. Many fifth-and-sixth-grade Sunday school classes are organized to place a premium on verbal skills. A predictable result is that (a) the girls will excel, and (b) the boys will avoid any situation which makes them feel inferior to girls. Many male members will volunteer to help put a new roof on the building or to lay a new sidewalk or to help serve a pancake breakfast, but they will not volunteer to teach a Sunday school class or to be members of a book circle. How do you ask males to express their creative skills?

Finally, while it was not mentioned earlier, both Jimmy and Laura benefited from the continuity of the teachers and the continuity of meeting in the same room week after week. One means of increasing the sense of belonging and cohesion is to minimize the frequency of changes in leadership. This is one of several arguments for long pastorates, for encouraging Sunday school teachers to teach the same group several years, and for building in continuity in the adult leadership of youth groups—and, as the U.S. Army discovered in Vietnam, for not changing company commanders every six months. Rotation in office for administrative leaders has more merit than rotation in office for program leaders.

Likewise the continuity of the group is reinforced by meeting in the same room week after week. The importance of the attachment to a familiar place is one of the most widely neglected concepts in church planning. That organizing principle is illustrated by the habit many people have of sitting in the same chair at the dinner table, in the same pew on Sunday morning, and in the same seat on the bus. Group cohesion is reinforced by meeting in the same physical setting whenever possible. The generalization also applies to the third-and-fourth-grade Sunday school class, the weekend camping experience, the adult choir rehearsal, the monthly meeting of the governing board, staff meetings in the large church, and the special Thanksgiving service held every year.

The impact of a different organizing principle that often is useful when working with adults can be illustrated by reflecting on one more case study.

"Perhaps the most unusual group here is the Century Club," commented the Sunday school superintendent at the Hilltop Church. "It began as an adult Sunday school class back in the early 1950s. The entrance requirement was that the combined ages of the husband and wife had to be at least one hundred years. For a good many years it was the strongest class in the church, and many of our most influential leaders came out of that class. From the very beginning they developed the tradition of a big social evening on the third Saturday of every month. They eat together, sing, tell stories, and play games. For several years that event also served as an entry point for new members to join that class. About three years ago, when we remodeled the building, they were forced out of their room and they decided not to meet on Sunday morning until after the remodeling had been completed and they could return to their room. Well, to make a long story short, the remodeling took more than a year, and during that time their teacher retired and moved to New Mexico. When the time came for them to resume their Sunday morning classes, they decided they weren't interested and told us we could use their old room for a new class. We did need the space and accepted their offer. They continue to meet for a social evening every month, but none of them attends an adult class. They still refer to themselves as the adult class, but they never meet on Sunday morning!"

In simple terms the central organizing principle that has held this group together for so many years can be described as a friendship-building process. It is widely used in thousands of churches. The seven common characteristics of this process are (1) food, (2) music, (3) humor and laughter, (4) informal fellowship, (5) a structure of schedule that provides a sense of movement or progression in the event, (6) a dependable and regularly scheduled meeting date and time, and (7) perhaps most critical of all, a leader or a leadership team that accepts the responsbility for planning and overseeing this type of event.

Frequently three or four or five of these guidelines are combined in a single experience. The friendship-building process also is a frequently used organizing principle by workers with youth,[15] by some choir directors, in creating circles in the women's organization, and in summer camp experiences. The most common objection to its use is that the dynamics of that process tend to limit the size of a high school youth group to five to ten regular participants, the adult choir to ten to fifteen voices, and the circle to eight to fifteen monthly attenders. The reason is simple. Very few of us can "keep up" with more than five to seven close personal friends.

This extended discussion of organizing principles is included on the assumption that leaders need both to understand the concept and to be able to utilize the principles. An even more fundamental assumption, however, is that by definition leaders do accept the responsibility to lead, but that is the subject for another chapter.

LEADERS DO LEAD!

To the surprise and delight of the denominational leaders who had planned it, nearly four hundred people showed up for the all-day regional workshop on Christian education at Redeemer Church. The section on teaching adults attracted forty-one laypersons and six pastors. The leader began by listing five approaches to biblical interpretation on a sheet of newsprint and asked each member of the group to copy these and individually rank them in order of usefulness in teaching a Bible study class with adults. "Place a five opposite what you believe to be the most useful approach and a one opposite the approach you believe to be least useful."

After a few minutes of silence the leader asked, "Now who gave a five to the first approach on the list, and would you explain to the rest of us why you gave that a five?"

For the next forty minutes four of the six ministers and one exceptionally well read layperson dominated the discussion. Finally with great frustration, one layperson burst out, "We've wasted almost this whole period playing the old game of 'My point of view is right and your perspective is wrong.' When are we going to get to the subject posted on the door? I came for some help, not to listen to a few people argue their biases!"

In a defensive tone of voice the leader replied that he did not believe he had any special or unique competence, and that he preferred to draw out the experiences and wisdom of the group.

"If that's true," inquired the frustrated layperson, "why didn't you explain in the publicity that this was to be a bull session rather than to advertise it as a class on how to teach an adult class?"

"I didn't know when we started what direction we would go," responded the leader. "I wanted to be open to your concerns and to where you are. I simply do not believe that I have a right to manipulate the discussion to reflect my own point of view. That is manipulation, and I'm a facilitator, not a manipulator! I came to facilitate our discussion, not to tell you how to conduct an adult class."

* * * *

It was the Thursday evening before the next-to-last Sunday of the six-week building fund drive to raise $100,000 at Grace Church. The design of the campaign called for every household to be visited during the final two weeks and for the members to bring their pledge cards to the worship service on the last Sunday of the campaign. The drive had generated tremendous enthusiasm, and the volunteer callers had been working very hard at completing their assignments.

After the committee had gathered for this meeting, the person chairing the group announced, "We have a problem. It's both a delightful problem and a complex ethical issue. As you know, a lot of our members already have turned in their pledge cards, even though our plan doesn't call for the pledges to be received for another ten days. Two hours ago I learned that nearly half of our members have turned in their cards, and we now have $103,000 in pledges toward our $100,000 target. In other words, we already have surpassed our goal!"

"That's not a problem!" exclaimed a member of the committee. "That's a cause for celebration!"

"I agree we should rejoice," offered the pastor, "but what do we tell the folks this Sunday? Should we tell them that we have achieved the goal and that if they haven't pledged yet, they need not bother? What do we say to our people this coming Sunday morning? Do we tell them the truth, that we already have passed our goal? Or do we not mention the amount we've already received in pledges?"

"There are seven people in this room," commented Harry MacPherson. "We all now know that we've exceeded the original goal. I doubt if keeping this a secret is on the list of alternatives. The architect's estimate is the new addition will cost approximately $250,000. We had planned to raise $100,000 in cash and pledges and borrow $152,000 on a ten-year mortgage. I suggest that next Sunday morning we simply tell our people that if everyone cooperates and gives generously, we can reverse those figures—we can raise $150,000 in cash and pledges and borrow only $100,000."

"I'm afraid I would have to oppose that," objected Jack Barrett. "I believe we made a commitment to our people when we went into this that we needed $100,000 in pledges. We have the $100,000 now, and I believe we are obligated to tell the people next Sunday that we have exceeded our original goal. If that means some who haven't pledged yet won't pledge, that's between them and their conscience. I simply cannot be a party to any scheme by which we seek to manipulate people by withholding information."

"But that's not fair to those who have made the pledges that enabled us to exceed our goal. When they made their pledges, they had no idea of what the sum of all pledges to date was," argued another member of the committee. "What you're suggesting is we provide information to those who haven't pledged yet that was not available to those who made their pledges early."

While this interchange was taking place at one end of the table, the person chairing the committee, the pastor, and Harry MacPherson were engaged in a whispered conversation at the other end of the table.

"Harry has offered to make an announcement next Sunday that will take into account all our views," announced the chairperson. "Since it is Harry's turn to speak on behalf of our committee, I believe we should trust him to say what is appropriate. Unless someone objects, we'll let Harry prepare his own speech."

"That seems to be fair," declared another individual. "When I spoke to the congregation two weeks ago, no one told me what to say. I believe it's only fair to give Harry the same privilege."

"Just be sure, Harry, to tell the folks that we've passed the goal," urged Jack Barrett. "I still believe we have to be completely honest with our people."

* * * *

These two incidents illustrate a number of issues facing those who accept the responsibility of leadership. Several of these issues can be summarized by terms such as fairness, dissent, creativity, manipulation, freedom, full disclosure, trust, responsibility, honesty, and initiative. Some of the issues are more difficult to define than others.

Both of these incidents illustrate the fact that a leader does not have the choice of a neutral course of action. Every leader has to make choices on role, on style, on information that will be shared, on information that will be withheld, and on values that will be reinforced.

The leader or facilitator at the workshop on teaching adults made several arbitrary and unilateral decisions. The first, and probably least defensible, was to attempt to follow a small group discussion format with a large group of forty-seven participants. Some would call that an uninformed or ignorant decision while others might term it irresponsible or stupid. A more accurate term would be counterproductive or manipulative. The leader declared he wanted to be open to the concerns of those present and then used a pedagogical technique that is almost guaranteed to produce complete silence from the vast majority of those present.

The second unilateral decision was to begin by asking people to rank a series of abstract concepts—the five approaches to biblical interpretation—and to defend that ranking. In a room with forty-one laypersons and six ministers that is a guaranteed means of intimidating the majority of the laypersons present.

The third, and to many of those present the most objectionable unilateral decision made in advance by the person in charge, was to refuse to accept the leadership role. It appeared to those present that he had accepted the responsiblity for leading a session on teaching adults, that he had made a series of unilateral decisions during that introductory period on the pedagogical style he wanted to follow, and then had claimed that he did not want to set the direction or lead the group.

For some of those present the experience illustrated how one person can manipulate people so as to turn a crowd of forty-seven eager, smiling, enthusiastic, and receptive students filled with anticipation into a collection of surly, resentful, bitter, disillusioned, and angry individuals—all in less than an hour!

The clearest illustration of outright manipulation of the group by the self-identified facilitator came when, rather than asking the group what they wanted to discuss, he chose the topic of five approaches to biblical interpretation as the opening that set the tone for what followed. Instead of beginning with the advertised topic of teaching adults, he chose to go down a road in which the debate would be largely on biblical interpretation rather than on pedagogy.

This particular leader identified himself as a facilitator, but functioned in a highly manipulative role, while denying that behavior pattern—a point we will return to shortly.

The debate in the building fund committee meeting at Grace Church also raised the issue of manipulation. Should we manipulate the responses of those who have not yet pledged by telling them their pledge is not necessary, or should we seek to manipulate them into making a more positive response by withholding facts?

That discussion also raised the increasingly troubling and divisive issue of fairness. How can we be fair with all the people? A consistent, undiscriminating, and comprehensive effort to be fair to everyone ultimately means it is difficult to be fair with anyone. When a company has to lay off employees, who should be laid off first? Those with the least seniority, many of whom are women who were late entrants into the labor force or blacks who were discriminated against in earlier employment practices? Or should they be retained and employees with more seniority be laid off first? Do quotas designed to produce fair treatment for some result in the unfair treatment of others?[1] In the congregation in which 55 percent of the members, age eighteen and over, are women, and on the typical Sunday morning 65 to 70 percent of the adults present for worship are female, what proportion of the governing board should be women?

If irreconcilable differences arise between the senior minister, who arrived three years ago, and the associate minister, who has been on the staff for nine years, who should be asked to resign? How much time should be given that person between that decision and the date of departure? What is the fair way to resolve this situation? What are the criteria that can be followed to maximize fairness?

A third issue that creates frustration among leaders that was illustrated at Grace Church is how to respond to dissent. Jack Barrett held a position that apparently was not shared by the majority. Should his dissenting opinion be ignored? Should his dissent force the majority to seek a new course of action that would receive unanimous support? When he left that meeting, Jack did not know how his dissent would be handled. Only after he had heard Harry MacPherson's remarks the following Sunday was he able to determine whether or not he had been heard and heeded.

Do Leaders Manipulate?

For many, however, the central issue raised by both episodes is the issue of manipulation. Does a Christian have the right to manipulate people in a manner designed to make others respond in a way the leader desires?

One of the reasons that this is such an emotion-laden issue is the language. Words such as manipulate, propagandize, maneuver, wangle, trick, machinate, rig, juggle, influence, indoctrinate, or brainwash tend to evoke negative images and feelings. That happens, at least in part, because these words are powerful value terms and arouse strong reactions based on one's values.

If the language is changed to avoid the use of these value-laden words, the issues can be presented in a different light. Do leaders intentionally and deliberately seek to influence the beliefs and behavior patterns of others? For some, including this writer, that not only is the central issue, it also is a definition of leadership. By definition, leaders guide, give direction, and choose among alternative courses of action. By definition, leadership exists in a social setting that includes other people.[2] Leaders do not exist in complete isolation from other people. One of the more frequent complaints by the laity about their pastor is, "Our minister probably should have been a professor rather than a pastor. He likes to read and to study and to work on sermons, but he really doesn't like to be around people. Now our former pastor was a wonderful leader, and when he was here, things really got done in this parish! He gave us wonderful leadership." Scholarship and leadership are not incompatible attributes—look at Theodore Roosevelt—but they are different traits. Scholarship can exist in isolation from people, but leadership happens only in the context of a social setting with people.

To return to the opening illustration in this chapter, the person leading that class on teaching adults accepted the role of leadership for that hour, he took several unilateral actions that determined how that hour would be spent (or in the view of many, how it was wasted), he did influence the behavior of many in the class, and for most he also influenced their degree of participation, their feelings, and their evaluation of the hour, but apparently he refused to accept the *responsibilities* that accompanied that role.

Six Central Characteristics

This brings us to six of the central characteristics of leadership. The first, and most important, is that responsible and effective leaders accept that role. Good leaders are drawn only from among persons who are willing to lead. (But not all willing leaders turn out to be good leaders!) All the great presidents of the United

Good leaders accept that role!

States, all the great military commanders, all the great bishops, and all the great Sunday school teachers were persons who were willing to accept the mantle of leadership. Many were reluctant, others were frightened, but all accepted the role. The late Harry S. Truman is an excellent example of a reluctant but effective leader. It also should be noted that some of the great leaders of history were eager to accept that role.

A second characteristic of effective leaders is their willingness to influence the beliefs and behavior patterns of others. This list includes Moses, Jesus, Julius Caesar, Charlemange, John Calvin, Martin Luther, Thomas Jefferson, John Wesley, Napoleon Bonaparte, William Lyon MacKenzie, Abraham Lincoln, Michael Joseph Savage, Sir Wilfrid Laurier, Frances E. Willard, Susan B. Anthony, Margaret Sanger, Eleanor Roosevelt, Winston Churchill, John Curin, John L. Lewis, Martin Luther King, Jr., and Barbara Jordan.

The qualifications on this issue that some like to call manipulation can be summarized by four questions. Are you seeking to influence the beliefs and behavior of others in a manner that is consistent with your value system? Is your approach consistent with the goals that have been adopted by this organization or group? Is your approach consistent with the motives, goals, values, and needs of the followers? Do the followers have an opportunity to participate in the formulation of those goals, the design of the strategy, the selection of the leader(s), and the definition of priorities?

For some of those who are concerned about manipulation, this last question is crucial. For them the leadership spectrum has manipulation at one end and participation at the other. Those who see manipulation and participation as opposite poles on the spectrum may be troubled by the opening illustration in this chapter. The leader assigned to that class clearly had a goal of encouraging the participation of those present. Is it fair to state that he manipulated the situation in the hopes of achieving the active participation of those present? Or was he simply inept, and he unintentionally created a counterproductive process? Does participation occur spontaneously? Or does leadership help to create an environment that encourages participation? Is that manipulation? Do incompetent leaders unknowingly manipulate others?

For the Christian this places severe limitations on both style and tactics.

The most obvious limitation for the Christian is the obligation to treat other persons, not as things, but as God's creations. This Christian leader also must act within the constraints of what is appropriate in a Christian community.[3]

A third central characteristic of leadership is that it does not occur in isolation. Effective leaders function in a complex social setting that not only includes other people, but almost invariably includes conflict over priorities, over the allocation of scarce resources, over goals, and over what is contemporary reality. That was the theme of the second chapter. In addition, that social setting frequently includes competition among several clientele for that leader's time. The pastor who is attending a denominational meeting two hundred miles from home that is scheduled to adjourn at 5:00 P.M. wonders, "Should I leave early so I can attend our church council meeting that begins at 7:30 this evening, or should I leave even earlier, stop and see Florence who had surgery this morning and be late to the council meeting, or should I stay until this committee adjourns at 5:00 P.M. and, if I skip supper, get home by 9:30 so I can say 'Goodnight' to the kids before they go to sleep?" The social setting places conflicting demands on those who accept the role of being a leader. The greater the responsibilities that go with a leadership role, the more complex is that social setting and the greater the competition among the demands placed on that leader's time and energy. That is one reason why being president of the United States is a more complex responsibility than being governor of South Dakota. It is one reason why a bishop's job is more complex than that of the pastor of a two-hundred-fifty member rural church. That also explains why it is easier to write a book on leadership than it is to function as a leader.

The fourth of these central characteristics of leadership is power. Many people in the church regard power as a necessary evil in society. A variety of means have been devised to limit the power of any one leader. These include a limitation in tenure, rotation in offices, restricting individuals in the number of offices they may hold at one time, mandatory retirement at a certain age, dividing authority among various officers and committees, popular elections of leaders, the term call for pastors used by some denominations, limiting the size of the staff, establishing competing agencies, and budget controls. This fear of power is the basic reason that the United States has a two-house legislature, an executive branch, and a judicial system. Leadership is an exercise in the use of power.[4]

Fifth, all leaders have a vision, or at least some sense of the direction they want to go. This vision or goal provides the basic criterion against which leaders estimate the probable consequences of a particular course of action. Some leaders are far more effective than others in enlisting adherents who will help turn that vision into reality, but by definition every leader possesses a dream or vision of the world that could be.

The last of these six central characteristics of leadership can be summarized by the word *evaluation*. Every leader is being evaluated by the followers.

Traditionally the basic yardstick for the evaluation of leaders has been accomplishments. Presidents, corporation executives, university administrators, governors, mayors, and, to a lesser extent, pastors are evaluated by their followers on the basis of whether or not goals were achieved and promises were fulfilled.

In recent years, however, an increasing emphasis is being placed on the style and personality of the leader. Ronald Reagan was re-elected president of the United States, despite the fact that he did not fulfill his pledge to balance the federal budget. When choosing a new minister, many parishioners give a greater weight to style than to competence, and a growing number of church-shoppers pick a church on the basis of the pastor's style rather than because of the denominational label.

For some, style has replaced performance as the most important criterion in the evaluation of a leader. A bishop may be affirmed, not on the basis of performance, but rather because that bishop is an easily approachable and highly democratic leader in contrast to an extremely autocratic and aloof predecessor.[5] The evaluation of the pastor by the youth in the congregation often is based more on style than on competence or performance.

In a pluralistic society some will evaluate the leader primarily on the basis of performance while others will place a far greater weight on style and personality. What is the *primary* criterion you use in evaluating leaders?[6] Style or performance?

These six central characteristics provide the context for looking at the issue of leadership roles and styles, but before moving to that subject it may be useful to look first at the overlapping subjects of the congregational setting and culture. The congregational culture does influence the definition of role and frequently determines what will be an unacceptable style. The congregational culture is half the story in any effort to create a good congregation-pastor match in the ministerial placement process.

Leaders, Cultures, and Values

On a November Sunday in 1948, the seventy-year-old John Haynes Holmes, one of the great liberal preachers of the twentieth century, announced his retirement after thirty-six years as the senior minister of the Community Church of New York. He added this decision was not as difficult as it might have been, since his junior colleague, the thirty-four-year-old Donald Harrington, had proved his competence while serving as the associate minister and could take over and carry on the work.

The next day Dr. Holmes summoned Harrington to Holmes' office on a matter of great urgency. When Harrington arrived, he found Dr. Holmes and Judge Dominick F. Pachella, who was president of the congregation, waiting for his arrival. Judge Pachella was one of the most influential leaders of the congregation, a former chairman of the governing board, and for many years the president of the congregation. Every Sunday morning the judge arrived early to greet his minister. He helped Holmes take off his coat and put on his robe before the service and to take off his robe and put on his coat after the service. The judge was a confidant as well as a close personal friend of Dr. Holmes. When Harrington arrived in the office, Holmes explained, "Don, Judge Pachella has come to tell me that he thinks I overreached my authority yesterday when I said, after anouncing my resignation, that I felt easy in heart because you were at hand and well trained to succeed me. Only the congregation, he says, has that right to choose my successor. Furthermore, he believes you are too young and too immature to be our senior minister and that we need an older and more seasoned man. I wanted you to be present to hear my reply."

The stunned Harrington listened as Holmes turned to the judge and said, "I am sorry, Judge, but if this is your view, there is nothing for you to do but to resign at once." Judge Pachella immediately replied, "You have my resignation, Dr. Holmes."

Harrington thanked Dr. Holmes for his confidence, agreed with the judge that it would be necessary for the congregation to elect him to succeed Holmes as senior minister, and pleaded with the judge not to resign. Several weeks later Harrington was elected senior minister, the judge became one of his closest friends and soon was helping the new senior minister don his coat after the morning service. The night the judge died, Harrington sat with him and closed his eyes at the end. Thirty-four years following this incident, the Reverend Doctor Donald S. Harrington retired as the senior minister of that congregation.[7]

For three decades the Baltimore Orioles have been the winningest team in major league baseball. Every fall, whether they are needed or not, the Orioles summon the most promising prospects from their minor league farm clubs to spend September with the major league team. The purpose is to build in a sense of cohesion and continuity. The following spring those rookies can participate when the players reminisce about the previous fall's pennant race. They were there and they have shared in that experience. The general manager of another team commented, "The amazing thing about that organization is that it has been consistently good with different owners, different general managers, different scouting directors. It must be a baton of production, a torch that keeps getting handed on from one regime to the next."[8]

These two stories illustrate the importance of the context for leadership. The larger setting influences what happens. In the business world this is now identified as the corporate culture. In the churches this may be described simply as "tradition" or as "the way we have always done things around here."

The congregational culture at the Community Church of New York enabled Dr. Holmes to demand the resignation of the judge in what struck the young Reverend Donald Harrington as an imperious manner. The culture provided the setting that enabled the judge to resign without being offended. The continuity of that institution and of its ministerial leadership (Holmes and Harrington served that congregation for a combined period of seventy-five years) made it easy for the judge to transfer his allegiance from Holmes, who was much older, to Harrington, who was much younger. The continuity of one baseball club's organizational culture meant that few were surprised when Joe Altobelli won both the American League pennant and the World Series the first year he succeeded Earl Weaver as the manager.

The most important single element of any corporate, congregational, or denominational culture, however, is the value system. At the Community Church of New York in the 1940s, a central value was the freedom of a prophetic pulpit. This widely shared value enabled Dr. Holmes to identify his successor before the congregation was even aware of his retirement. That value took precedence over congregational autonomy, participatory democracy, or "following the proper procedures." The central value of the Baltimore Orioles organization is winning. If that central value were economy, they would not bring up so many minor league players every September.

The values of any organization control priorities, provide the foundation for formulating goals, and set the tone and direction of the organization. This can be illustrated by a common experience among hundreds of middle-sized and larger congregations. The pastor proposes that the Sunday morning schedule be changed from 9:30 Sunday school and 10:45 worship to 8:30 worship, 9:45 Sunday school and a second worship experience at 11:00 A.M. The heart of the pastor's argument is church growth. Offering two *different* worship services with two different choirs at two different hours has proved to be one of the most effective means of increasing church attendance by 15 to 40 percent.

Among the arguments marshalled to defeat this proposal are (a) the building is too large, it rarely is filled now with only one service, (b) it would split the congregation into two factions—the early service crowd and the eleven o'clock people, (c) who would want to sing in that second choir and who would direct it? (d) it would adversely affect the Sunday school, (e) those coming to the eleven o'clock service would get out too late to beat the Baptists and the Methodists to the cafeterias, (f) it already is difficult to enlist enough ushers with only one service, and (g) we are too far west in the time zone to expect people to come to the church at 8:30 in the morning during the winter. Each of these points represents a strongly held value ranging from the importance of keeping the building happy by filling it at least once a week to the priority of fellowship and intimacy over evangelism. If the most strongly held and widely shared value of that congregation were to reach more people with the good news of Jesus Christ and to bring more people together to worship God, it would have been relatively easy to adopt the proposed schedule.

Uncertainty about values has divided the Democratic Party for at least twenty years, immobilized the missionary outreach of The United Methodist Church, produced a serious internal division within the Southern Baptist Convention, inhibited the aggressive new approach to evangelism and church growth that was launched in the United Church of Christ in 1980, complicated the merger discussions for the creation of a new Lutheran Church in the United States, blocked the proposed merger of the Christian Church (Disciples of Christ) with the United Church of Christ, split The Lutheran Church—Missouri Synod back in the late 1960s and 1970s, and has caused literally millions of persons reared in a Roman Catholic home to join a Protestant congregation.

Shared values in a congregation may range from a free pulpit to a central emphasis on the sanctity of marriage and the value of the family as expressed by The Church of Jesus Christ of Latter-day Saints (Mormons), to the importance of the Sunday school among Southern Baptists, to church growth in the Church of the Nazarene, but even there that is not the universal number one value.

Other values that frequently are a central component of a congregation's culture include a high commitment to world missions, greeting and warmly welcoming every visitor, building a large endowment fund, caring for one another, preserving the building in excellent condition, not disrupting traditional schedules and procedures, paying all bills on time, "taking care of our wonderful minister," perpetuating nationality or ethnic customs, keeping control over policy in the hands of a few trusted oldtimers, and building the chancel choir primarily on the basis of excellence in vocal music rather than on a broad participation base.

These examples are cited to illustrate a vital dimension of any organizational culture. Ideally these strongly held and wisely shared values are not only consistent with the basic purpose of that organization, they also are compatible with its future role. Frequently, however, the most strongly held and influential values (a) represent a means-to-an-end concern or (b) are incompatible with a redefinition of role. This point can be illustrated by two more examples.

Trinity Church was founded in 1921 and completed its new building in 1924. Thirty years later the members voted to relocate to a new residential area seven miles to the west. The relocation was completed in 1956, the second unit of the new building was constructed in 1959, and the long-awaited third unit, the new sanctuary, finally was completed in 1984. Current plans for expansion of the ministry and outreach by organizing an early-childhood development center that would include a weekday preschool program have been stymied by fears that the additional use would damage those beautiful Sunday school rooms and tear up the lovely lawn on the east side of the building.

The relocation effort was driven by the triple values of institutional survival, the desire to continue to reach and win "our kind of people," and the dream of a modern, new meeting house closer to where the members lived. The folks who were "our kind of people" in the 1950s are now too old to bear children today, but they are still present in sufficient numbers that the absence of members of child bearing age is not yet seen as a threat to institutional survival. The values that fueled the relocation effort, designed to reach and serve the young parents of the 1950s and early 1960s, now block the effort to reach and serve the young parents of thirty years later.

Bethel Church was established in 1927 in a solid upper-middle class neighborhood populated largely by persons employed by the state government or the university. For nearly forty years it continued as a neighborhood church. On a typical Sunday in 1965 nearly one-third of the 120 to 140 worshipers walked to church. The twin values of "neighborhood oriented" and "family centered" still are frequently articulated. In the mid-1960s, however, as the university continued to expand, many of the larger homes on the two nearby streets were rezoned and remodeled into rooming houses. Subsequently several of the houses on the larger parcels of land were demolished, and three-story apartment buildings were constructed.

Today nearly 80 percent of the people living within one mile of Bethel Church are university undergraduates, graduate students, or junior faculty. Most of the remaining 20 percent are elderly couples or widows.

Currently the congregation is immobilized as the leaders seek to plan for the years ahead. One group places a high value on seeking to re-establish this church's role as a congregation composed of and serving university faculty and administrators and upper-level civil servants in the state government. They are convinced this means relocation of the meeting place. Another group wants to place the highest priority on its role as a neighborhood church and argues that relocation would be a betrayal of all that Bethel Church has stood for over the years, urging that the focus of any evangelistic outreach be on reaching students and younger faculty members, many of whom are passing through on one- or two-year appointments.

A third group also opposes the relocation proposal as inconsistent with Bethel's history and urges that the most important value to be reinforced is an emphasis on the family. They demand that the program be centered around reaching and serving parents with young children, regardless of where the parents live. They are willing to give generously to remodel the building and hire the staff necessary to make this possible.

No one group comes close to representing a majority of the membership. Each defines the traditions, the history, and the culture of Bethel Church in a way that will reinforce those values that undergird their point of view. Forty years ago all three values were compatible. Today it appears this congregation can reinforce any one of these values only by discarding one or both of the other values.

Leaders operate within the culture of that organization, they are influenced by that culture, and they would be stupid to ignore that culture; but leaders also determine the culture. Instead of simply reacting to the culture, leaders can and should help to shape it. This is best done by supporting, shaping, and helping to redefine that culture.[9]

If we can return to the first chapter, Jerry Buchanan recognized that the congregational culture placed a high value on (a) pastoral care of the elderly—so he drove two hundred miles each way to call on Mrs. Albert Porter, (b) the power of Phil Stephenson and Eddie Heath—so he affirmed their influence and enlisted them as allies, (c) a ministry to the dying—so Jerry regularly called on the dying Ethel Powell, and (d) the tradition of a Christmas Eve service—so he suggested making Christmas Eve an even bigger event than it had been before.

The congregational culture at Trinity Church accepted as natural, inevitable, and acceptable the idea of the summer slump. This was unacceptable to Jerry so he reshaped the culture by not scheduling the summer slump during his second year. Likewise a central tradition at Trinity was only one worship service on Sunday morning. Jerry could not accept that since it clashed with his value system. He enlisted allies and changed the culture to include two services on Sunday morning.

Instead of ignoring the congregational culture Jerry Buchanan recognized it as a powerful force, affirmed what he could authentically affirm, built on those components of the congregational tradition that he could endorse, and reshaped the culture. He did not do it alone. He enlisted allies. He trusted those allies. Some of his allies came from the subculture of Trinity Church—the three Vietnam veterans, Laura Miller, and Mrs. Elmer Wood were examples.

As he functioned within the congregational culture he inherited, Jerry recognized that culture was based on values, traditions, rites and rituals, an informal communication network often referred to as "the grapevine," a community context or environment which reinforced certain values and traditions, a variety of informal rules and policies, some highly visible heroes such as Phil Stephenson and Eddie Heath, a few underdogs such as Elmer Wood and his wife, and the denominational affiliation.

In another congregation the number one hero might have been a predecessor, or a critical component of the culture might have been the social status of the members or a magnificent meeting place or one family tree. The culture of one congregation is never identical with that of another.

Instead of being controlled by the congregational culture, Jerry Buchanan reshaped it. Among the reasons he was able to do that, ten stand out. First, and most important, he was willing to accept a leadership role. Second, he had a vision of what could be, and he was willing to promote that vision. This meant he chose the proactive stance of a leader rather than a reactive manager. Third, he recognized the values of allies.

Fourth, he "paid his rent" and *earned* the right to be an initiating leader by doing more as a pastor to individuals than anyone really expected—three examples are Mrs. Porter, Ethel Powell, and the three Vietnam veterans. Part of the power Jerry exercised came from holding the position of pastor, but much of his power influence was earned. Fifth, he was willing to speak first and to set the agenda for a meeting. That was one way he exercised the power of leadership.

Sixth, he recognized that people need time to reflect on new ideas before they can accept them. Jerry recognized that when people are pressured to respond prematurely or when they are surprised, they tend to respond negatively.

Seventh, as a responsible leader Jerry understood that one of his obligations was to foresee the probable consequence of any proposed change. Robert Greenleaf describes this as the ability to "foresee the unforeseeable" and identifies foresight as the central ethic of leadership.[10]

Eighth, and from a tactical perspective this was of crucial importance, Jerry knew he was not functioning in isolation. Whenever he came in with a new idea that challenged existing traditions or that might evoke instant opposition or that meant a change in the congregational culture at Trinity Church, Jerry always placed that issue within the context of values and a long-term goal. He did not argue change versus tradition. He argued

good leaders
do <u>not</u> work
in isolation!

—FRIAR TUCK.

that every proposed change was a reinforcement of existing values and was compatible with the culture of that congregation. Usually these values could be summarized by such terms as goals, Word and Sacrament, reaching more people, doing more for the children, and bigger crowds at the traditional rituals.

A ninth characteristic of Jerry's leadership carries us back to the opening theme of this chapter. He was willing, and often eager, to influence the beliefs and behavior of people. Once in awhile he would be charged with being a superb manipulator, and he always took that as a compliment.

Finally, from even before he arrived on the scene at Trinity Church Jerry knew that he, like every minister, would be the subject of a never-ending evaluation of his ministry by the people. Instead of protesting that only

God had a right to evaluate his ministry and his faithfulness, Jerry made sure that positive responses to his ministry were fed into that continuing evaluation process. He did this by being faithful to his pastoral responsibilities. He did this by enlisting allies. He did this by repeatedly and clearly stating his values and goals as a pastor. He did this by strengthening the internal communication system at Trinity Church. Most important of all, he did this by recognizing that the option of a neutral, value free, and non-involved role in that continuing evaluation process is not available to any pastor.

Good leaders do lead. They do not allow the corporate culture to control them. How they lead is the subject of another chapter.

TYPE, ROLE, AND STYLE

"I'm confused," confessed the thirty-year-old associate pastor to the fifty-three-year-old senior minister at the 835-member Westminster Church. "In seminary I was taught that a minister should be an enabler, although no one ever fully explained what that meant. After I graduated, I spent four years in a small rural congregation and soon discovered that Carl Dudley was right. The small church wants their minister to be a lover.[1] During that first pastorate, I spent a week in a group dynamics workshop where I was taught that a minister should avoid any autocratic tendencies and seek to function as a democratic leader.

"For the past two years I've enjoyed serving with you here at Westminster, and this really is a wonderful church, but I'm puzzled by your leadership style," continued the associate. "This place seems to break all the rules I've been taught about leadership in the church. If you'll pardon my speaking so bluntly, I simply don't see you as a democratic leader. From my perspective you're pretty autocratic. At times you make important decisions unilaterally without even consulting the official leadership. At the same time, you're immensely popular with the members, the church has doubled in size since you came eleven years ago, no one seems to question what's going on here, and by every criteria I can think of this as a healthy and vital church. How come?"

"I'm not quite sure what you're getting at," replied the senior minister, "but you're right, the people here do place a great deal of trust in me and my leadership. One reason is that I've been here eleven years, and that gives me some clout. Another is that well over two-thirds of today's members joined since I came, and the folks who didn't like me or my leadership style left a good many years ago or never joined. I guess a third factor is that when I came, the leaders all said the number one priority was church growth. We paid off a mortgage that was worrying everyone, built a new sanctuary, and have that almost paid for. Finally, you have to recognize that we have a lot of high-powered business and professional leaders here, and they expect me to be the chief executive officer."

"It seems to me you've left out the two most important factors that account for your popularity here. One is your unbelievable ability to call everyone, including all the children, by name and the other is that you must hug at least a couple of hundred people every week. Maybe the folks here really want a loving dictator," interrupted the associate.

"Well, I don't think I deserve being called a dictator," replied the senior minister somewhat defensively, "but I do love the people, and I think I've earned their respect. I am somewhat directive in my leadership approach, but I don't apologize for that. In a big church someone has to point the way, and I'm willing to do that."

"Thanks for letting me bend your ear," said the associate, "but I'm still a little confused. This congregation violates all the rules I've been taught about the need for more democracy in the church today, but it's still growing and no one seems to be particularly unhappy about what I still see as anything but a democratic approach as to how decisions are made here."

One reason this conversation did not clarify the associate minister's confusion is that it rambled all over the conceptual landscape without distinguishing among four different facets of the subject under discussion. The obvious one is the impact of the size of the congregation on the leadership role of the pastor. The basic generalization on that point is that the larger the congregation, the more likely the members will expect the senior minister to be an initiating leader.[2]

The other three facets of the conversation that are relevant to this discussion can be identified by the words *type*, *role*, and *style*. The associate minister was speaking from a conceptual framework that distinguished a democratic *type* of leader from the authoritarian or laissez-faire type of leader. The senior minister responded from a conceptual framework that emphasized the leadership *role* of the pastor of a large church. The associate minister then shifted the focus to praise the senior pastor's *style* in which he repeatedly affirmed people by calling each one correctly by name and by hugging many of them.

Before moving into a discussion of roles and styles, it may be useful to take brief trips down two sideroads. The first goes back to the emergence of some concepts and categories that are still very influential in contemporary thinking about leadership. The second sideroad consists of a brief discussion of political philosophy.

Who Wants to Be Called an Authoritarian Leader?

Fifty years ago one of the most influential studies of leadership qualities was undertaken by Kurt Lewin and Ronald Lippit.[3] This experiment was concerned with the results of two contrasting types of leadership. In this experiment the authoritarian leaders were trained to take complete charge of the group, set policy for the group, formulate the goals, dictate all procedures to be followed, and direct the entire procedure.

By contrast the democratic leaders were trained to encourage broad participation and to involve the members of the group in all decision making. While the authoritarian groups were more productive, there was less tension and hostility and more cohesion in the democratic groups.

A few years later Lippit and R. K. White reported on an experiment contrasting democratic, authoritarian, and laissez-faire leadership.[4] One of their conclusions was that laissez faire is not the same as democratic. They also pointed out that when an autocratic leader was followed by either a democratic or a laissez-faire leader, the group usually displayed an initial outburst of hostile and disruptive behavior.

One result of these and similar experiments has been the offering of group dynamics experiences to train people in the democratic approach to leadership. One critique of the sensitivity labs and other experiences that were supposed to develop democratic leaders is that in fact these were courses in the laissez-faire type of leadership.[5] This critique suggested that in the typical experience the teacher functioned as a nondirective and "ambiguous authority figure" who, by modeling a behavior pattern of placing the entire initiative for direction and content on the members of the group, actually was teaching a laissez-faire approach to leadership.

In his review of the research on democratic and autocratic patterns of behavior, Stodgill concluded that "satisfaction with democratic leadership tends to be highest in small, interaction-oriented groups. Members are better satisfied with autocratic leadership in large, task-oriented groups."[6]

This conclusion came as no surprise to senior ministers of big churches who earlier had served in much smaller congregations. As was pointed out earlier, the basic generalization is that as the size of the membership increases, the people place greater expectations on the pastor to be an initiating leader. One of the greatest sources of satisfaction among the members of smaller congregations is a pastor who listens and loves. One of the greatest sources of dissatisfaction among the leaders of larger congregations is a pastor who refuses to accept the role of an initiating leader.

The big boost to this concept of three basic types of leadership—democratic, authoritarian, and laissez faire—came with the publication of *The Human Side of Enterprise* by Douglas MacGregor in 1960.[7] In this widely read and discussed book the author identified and labeled two sharply different approaches to leadership. The traditional approach, which MacGregor argued was based on the assumption that the typical human being is lazy, prefers to avoid responsibility, dislikes work, must be directed by a superior, and can be motivated only by rewards and punishments, was labeled Theory X.

By contrast, MacGregor proposed a radically different approach to leadership which he called Theory Y. This approach assumes that the vast majority of people find satisfaction and fulfillment in meaningful work, have the capacity to accept and fulfill responsibility, are naturally creative, and can be motivated most effectively by active involvement in the planning and decision making that is a part of the world of work.

This "human relations" approach to management flourished in the business world well into the 1960s, but no longer is as influential as it once was.[8] Despite the gradual drift away from the human relations approach to leadership in the business world, it continued to be an influential school of thought in the churches and seminaries through the 1970s and, to a limited degree, in the early 1980s. One way of describing this change is that in the middle of this century the human relations specialists began to replace the efficiency experts who had monopolized the scene during the first few decades of this century. Instead of focusing on efficiency and production, the emphasis changed to an unprecedented (in the business world) concern with interpersonal relationships, communication, and the dynamics of the small group. In recent years the focus has shifted to an examination of the institutional context for leadership, the quality of the outcome or performance, the tremendous differences between small groups and large-scale enterprises, a growing interest in fostering creativity and innovation, and a much greater emphasis on results.

One of the unfortunate products of the research mentioned here and of the wide circulation of MacGregor's book among church leaders, and the primary reason for the trip down this sideroad, was that these terms came into common usage as the basic categories for describing types of pastoral leadership. Obviously very few ministers want to be identified as authoritarian leaders, and others are not sure exactly what the term *laissez faire* means. These value-laden terms naturally cause most pastors to reject all suggestions that might cause them to be identified as anything but democratic leaders.

While it is true the English root for the term *authoritarian* is *author*, and this suggests a positive and productive connotation, in popular usage authoritarianism usually is perceived as repressive, dictatorial, or domineering. If one turns to a Latin word for authority, *auctor*, that term traditionally has referred to the guarantees authority can offer to others about the value of what they do.[9] In our day and culture, and especially since the early 1960s, authority has become a dirty word, and no one wants to be identified as an authoritarian type leader.

An alternative offered by the human relations school is the laissez-faire leader. This is the leader who does not intervene, who allows everyone to do as he or she pleases, and who is highly nondirective. While this has in fact become the operational style for too many pastors, it too is an unattractive label.

In effect, Lewin and Lippit loaded their nomenclature with value-laden words that made the choice of being a democratic leader the only defensible self-identification.

For another perspective on this issue it may be useful to turn to that famous sociologist, Max Weber, who described three types of authority—traditional, legal-rational, and charismatic. Most pastors recognize the traditional authority that is a part of the office they hold as pastor of that congregation. In some religious bodies, such as Roman Catholic, Episcopal, Anglican, and Lutheran, that office traditionally has carried a large amount of authority. In others, such as Christian, Baptist, Brethren, and Quaker, the office of pastor does not have a long tradition of great authority.

In several denominations the authority of the pastor is based more on a legal-rational foundation than on tradition. The Presbyterians and the Methodists both have provided a strong legal foundation for the leadership role of the minister. While the charismatic basis for pastoral authority exists in the mainline denominational churches, it must be claimed and demonstrated by each new holder of the office. The very large independent or nondenominational churches, since they often are largely without either a traditional or a legal-rational foundation for defining the authority of the pastor, are where one is most likely to encounter the charismatic (using Weber's definition of that term) pastoral leader.

Perhaps the most important contribution by Weber is that he identified authority with legitimacy. Weber argued that people will not obey those they believe do not have a legitimate basis for their leadership role. Weber was convinced that when people voluntarily obeyed their rulers, that meant a sense of authority was present in that culture or society. When people had to be coerced to follow their designated leaders, that was a signal that the people did not believe those leaders had legitimate authority.

From this observer's perspective there is no question but that the concept of being a democratic-style leader has great appeal to ministers who see it as the preferred alternative to being perceived as an authoritarian pastor. That illustrates a major thesis of this chapter. The definition of categories, and the labels affixed to those categories, has a tremendous impact on the choices people make.

Since the widespread use of these three types (democratic, authoritarian, and laissez faire) still affects thinking in the churches about leadership, it may be useful to review briefly the findings of more recent research on this subject.

Subsequent research using these three definitions of leadership types suggests that the initial praise for a democratic approach to leadership may have been somewhat exaggerated. Perhaps the most significant findings have been (1) much of what was labeled as a democratic approach to leadership in the training programs offered by many group dynamics labs actually was much closer to a highly nondirective laissez-faire style, (2) the group's expectations of the leader often may be more decisive than the style of the leader in determining the group's satisfaction with that leader and in the group's performance, (3) when an autocratic

Proactive Leadership

HELLO! IS THERE ANYONE HERE ... REALLY?

ZZZZZ

LAISSEZ-FAIRE

Those unwilling to lead could be left for dead!

—FRIAR TUCK

leader is followed by a democratic or laissez-faire leader, the group often does display an initial outburst of hostility and negative behavior, (4) the smaller the size of the group and the greater the emphasis on interpersonal relationships, the greater the satisfaction expressed by the group toward the democratic leader while the larger the size of the group and the greater the emphasis on tasks, the more comfortable the group tends to be with an authoritarian-style leader and the more uncomfortable with a permissive or laissez-faire leader, (5) group production and/or group cohesion are not higher under the more permissive nondirective leader than under the more directive leader and often are lower, (6) the more directive style is necessary for infusing and reinforcing values in an organization—and the values, not the task, produce loyalty, cohesiveness, and commitment, and (7) Douglas MacGregor's concept of Theory X and Theory Y leaders as mutually exclusive is both overly simplistic and a misreading of reality—effective leaders can be both highly authoritarian when the occasion demands as well as very person-centered and very open on other occasions.[10]

When translated into operational terms, these findings suggest that a pastor should realize that (1) the expectations of the congregation will have a great influence on the members' satisfaction or dissatisfaction with a minister's leadership role and style, (2) those expectations often have been shaped by the leadership role and style of a long-term predecessor who may not be the current pastor's immediate predecessor, (3) the larger the size of the congregation, the more likely the members will expect a more directive approach from the pastor, (4) the pastor who places a high value on congregational renewal and/or infusing other values into that congregation probably will find a directive approach to leadership more effective than a laissez-faire or democratic style—only in times of a widely perceived crisis is it possible to secure reform by a majority vote, (5) the pastor who decides to introduce a different approach to ministerial leadership into a long-established congregation should recognize this may be difficult, time consuming, frustration producing, and may require retraining or replacing much of the inherited leadership, and (6) perhaps most important of all, it might be wise to discard such value-laden terms as *democratic, authoritarian,* and *laissez faire* when discussing leadership in the churches and to introduce a more useful set of categories; and that is the point of this chapter, but before discussing that, it is necessary to take a trip down one other side road.

How Do You Define Democratic?

"The three things I'm committed to as a parish pastor are that Jesus Christ is Lord and Savior, the centrality of the worshiping congregation, and a democratic approach to leadership," explained the fifty-eight-year-old senior minister to his recently arrived associate minister.

"I can't argue with those," responded the associate, "but Jesus was not really a democratic leader, was he?"

"No, I guess not," replied the senior minister, "but I don't pretend to be Jesus Christ. I'm just an ordinary human being who is convinced I've been called by God to be a parish pastor. When I say I want to function as a democratic leader, I mean I want all the people to be involved in the planning and decision making. I don't believe in that old concept of 'Herr Pastor' running the church like a dictator."

"I'm not sure I know what you mean when you talk about all the people being involved in the planning and decision making," persisted the associate. "Do you really mean all? This is an eleven-hundred-member congregation. Do you expect all of them to come to monthly congregational meetings to plan and make decisions? I was told in seminary that about the only time you can expect a big crowd at a congregational meeting in a large church is when there is a proposal to fire the minister."

"Well, if you want me to be more precise," replied the senior minister somewhat impatiently, "I guess what I really mean is I see this as a representative democracy in which the people select those who will represent them on the Board and on committees. My basic point, however, is that I want the people to feel that each one of them has as much authority and responsibility as anyone on the staff. I simply don't believe in this idea that the staff should run the church!"

"Do you have a system for rotation in office here?" inquired the new associate.

"Yes, everyone is elected for either a two-year or a three-year term of office, and the maximum for anyone is two consecutive terms. That rule was adopted long before I came here."

"Let's see," reflected the associate. "You've been the senior minister here for sixteen years now, don't you think that gives you an edge over those laypeople who are in their second or third or fourth year in a particular office? People do sort themselves out by seniority, you know."

The bigger the church the more directive the pastor must be!

FIRST CHURCH

NOW HEAR THIS...

FRIAR TUCK

"You've got a point there," conceded the senior minister, "but that's a trade-off. I strongly believe in long pastorates in large churches, and you can't always have it both ways."

"I know," agreed the associate. "I spent my first three years out of seminary serving a 140-member church where all the leaders had been members for at least twenty years and all but two were at least thirty years older than I was. I know how it feels to be at the bottom of the seniority list. I can't help but wonder if you don't underrate the impact your age and tenure here have on your role as the senior minister.

"Although I've only been here three weeks," continued the associate, raising another issue, "my impression is that you work at your job sixty to seventy hours a week and, with perhaps the exception of Bill Thomas and Isabel Lawrence, none of the other leaders puts in more than ten or twelve hours a week in this church. Don't you think that gives you a lot of power around here?"

"You've raised some things I'll have to think about," admitted the senior minister, "but I want to return to my philosophy of leadership. My basic point is that I want broad-based congregational support for any major course of action that we choose to follow here. In simple terms, I want our people to be involved; I do not want to be seen as an authoritarian leader who makes all the decisions!"

"I can't quarrel with that," agreed the new associate. "Every minister wants all the members to be involved, but I still have two questions. You say you want broad-based congregational support for any new course of action we choose to follow here. Does that mean 90 percent or 60 percent or 51 percent or 30 percent or 10 percent? In an 1100-member church 10 percent means 110. Do you mean we need at least 110 supporters for every new program? How about if I offer a Tuesday evening Bible study class and only thirty show up? That is less than 3 percent. Do we cancel it? Or do we go ahead with it if thirty display their approval by participating and 1070 remain indifferent?

"My second question goes back to your point that you follow a democratic approach to leadership. I'm still not sure what you mean by that. Do you mean the majority rules? Or do you mean participatory democracy? Or do you mean you lead with the consent of the members? Or do you mean the initiative always rests with the laity, and the staff responds to their initiative? My dad was a city manager for thirty years, and one of the issues city managers were always wrestling with was whether they should see themselves simply as administrators and respond to and carry out the directions of the city council or whether they should be initiating leaders who identified issues, brought them to the attention of the city council, and made recommendations on what they saw as the appropriate policy. A lot of them were fired because they were perceived as being too aggressive in their leadership, and others were fired because they chose a reactive rather than a proactive stance. What's your definition of a democratic leader?"

Those who have a deep interest in the issue of democracy in the churches may want to read Alexis de Tocqueville's *Democracy in America*. This one-hundred-fifty-year-old classic provides a good introduction to the difference between the European and the American definitions of that term. Europeans, who were reacting against an aristocratic society, saw in democracy the abolition of inequalities. In western Europe the choice has been perceived as between egalitarianism or totalitarianism. By contrast, Americans, since we perceive ourselves as having been born equal, tend to define democracy as the protection of individual rights. Thus in American Protestantism a democratic approach to congregational self-government often tends to emphasize the rights of every member including the right to have a voice in every decision.

This view naturally produces a conflict with those who begin with a New Testament definition of the nature of the church which (a) affirms an elite (I Cor. 12), (b) emphasizes the obligations of the members to that called-out community, and (c) says very little about protecting the rights of the individual. Tocqueville pointed out that in a civilized world, individuals have reciprocal obligations to one another. An excessive emphasis on protecting the rights of the individual, Tocqueville argued, would close the door to truth, beauty, and the good. This can be seen in American society today as the emphasis on individual rights has eroded the value placed on excellence.

The operational implications of how democracy is defined can be illustrated by two contemporary examples. The merger negotiations to create a new Lutheran denomination placed a great emphasis on egalitarianism in selecting the membership of the various committees working on the merger.

By contrast, several ministers in The United Methodist Church have either threatened or have taken legal action in the civil courts against denominational executives or agencies on the assumption that a democratic system of church government must protect the rights of the individuals. It may not be irrelevant to point out the different historical roots of Lutheranism and Methodism. One comes from a Germanic heritage and the other from origins in England.

What trade-offs are you willing to make in order to implement a particular definition of democracy in your congregation or denomination? The trade-offs are real and inescapable!

The conversation that opened this chapter, the lack of universal agreement on the definition of a democratic leader, and the trade-offs that come with democracy introduce one of the most complicated issues facing leaders of congregations with more than 150 to 200 members. The goal of a participatory democracy appears to be relatively easy to attain in the congregation with thirty or fifty or sixty members, especially if full participation is limited to adult males—but is that really a participatory democracy if women and children are barred from the decision-making process? This has been demonstrated for decades in thousands of small congregations, especially those that came from an Anabaptist tradition and emphasize the ministry of the laity. It is far more difficult to implement a participatory democracy system of congregational self-government when the membership reaches one hundred and nearly impossible if the membership exceeds two hundred. The larger the size of the congregation, the higher the proportion of members who simply will refuse to invest their time and energy in attending ten or fifteen congregational meetings every year. Likewise the greater the emphasis on participatory democracy, the greater the probability that the natural and inevitable distrust by the members of the leaders will lead to a "split" as some of the members walk out to form a new congregation.

One response to this can be found in those churches that devote considerable resources to developing and maintaining a system of representative democracy. The larger the congregation, however, the more likely that a nominating committee rather than "the people" selects the officers who will function as volunteer leaders. Instead of functioning as a truly representative democracy, the system of congregational self-government drifts in a direction that it becomes vulnerable to charges of elitism.

Another response in the middle-sized and large congregations is to define democracy as an elaborate system of committees with a series of checks and balances that limit the authority of any one committee. Major decisions, such as approval of the budget, adding new positions to the staff, alterations to the real estate, and the formal election of officers, can be made only at congregational meetings at which all voting members have a voice.

In those denominatons in which ministers are called by congregational vote, rather than assigned by a bishop, the claim frequently is heard, "We really have a democratic system of church government since every member has a vote in the calling of our pastor." That claim has more substance to it in those congregations in which the minister is called for a two- or three-year term and must be "recalled" in order to continue than it has in those congregations in which the pastor receives a lifetime call. It is not unusual, for example, to find a minister who received a lifetime call to a parish fifteen or more years ago, but only 30 percent or less of today's members had a vote in that decision.

In several denominations that profess a democratic system of congregational self-government that claim is based on the premise that the ultimate decision-making power rests in the members, not in the minister and not in the denomination. That is one of the classic definitions of democracy, but the operational implementation varies from those churches in which the control is vested in a majority vote of the membership to those in which the majority vote of one committee is automatically approved unless it is rejected by an appeal to a vote of the entire congregation. In these churches the congregation may dismiss the minister, disaffiliate from the denomination, dispose of the real estate as the members see fit, and allocate the financial resources by a simple majority vote at a congregational meeting. In others, which have developed an indirect constitutional democracy system of church government in contrast to the direct democracy, the charter members may severely limit the actions of future generations of members.

The lack of a constitution, or the self-identified freedom to ignore that constitution, opens the door to what historically has been called the tyranny of the majority. This fear of majority rule has been expressed by political philosophers from opposite ends of the spectrum, ranging from Friedrich Hayek to Walter Lippman. One writer has contended that the basic danger of a free government is that it will perish by vote of the people and cites the experience of Rome in the age of Augustus, the control of Florence by the Medici, the disappearance of the First French Republic with the acceptance of Napoleon as a dictator, the rise of Hitler in Germany, and the coming to power of Mussolini in Italy.[11] Even a constitution does not guarantee the perpetuation of democracy. This has been experienced by both the Protestant congregations and denominations as a majority of those present and voting have taken that religious organization down a road that a majority of members probably did not want to travel.

While the concept of functioning as a democratic leader in a democratically governed church has great appeal, it is easier to articulate that vision than it is to implement it.

One of the most painful experiences that may be encountered by the self-identified democratic parish leader is due in part to this danger of the tyranny of the majority that is inherent in the democratic process. A second, but less widely recognized factor, is that, with the exception of a relatively few congregations at the high-demand end of the voluntary-church–high-demand-church spectrum, the vast majority of Protestant congregations function as voluntary associations in the decision-making process.[12]

Three of the characteristics of these voluntary associations are that (1) the right of withdrawal or of nonparticipation is a jealously guarded right, (2) the possibility of control's being seized by a small group of very determined individuals is an ever present fact, (3) as was pointed out earlier, the greater the emphasis on participatory democracy, the more likely the distrust between followers and leaders will become divisive. (This last point is illustrated by the fact that schisms tend to be more common in those denominations in which the polity provides for a wide dispersal of authority and a strong emphasis on democracy.)

A common local church scenario involves the pastor who resists being forced to accept a highly directive role, works hard to include as many people as possible in the decision-making process, sets up a system that will involve a wide range of members, and watches in growing frustration as two or three determined leaders seize control and easily convert that participatory system into a means of achieving their ends. The pastor is convinced a majority of the members do not agree with what is being done, but the system does not include a clearly defined process of accountability. The number of pastors who have experienced this is legion.

The moral is that a truly democratic decision-making process includes the procedures and sanctions that require everyone to play by the same rules. The lack of an official and carefully designed organizational structure is not the most productive setting for democracy. Rather it is often a fertile seedbed for anarchy, schisms, or the seizure of power by a few. Those who take seriously the doctrine of original sin will understand this more easily than those who believe in the perfectability of human beings.

The voluntary association that seeks to function as a participatory democracy must both have a constitution that protects the rights of minorities and also be a member of a larger body that has the authority to enforce adherence to that constitution and, if necessary, to expel those who gained leadership offices but do not feel obligated to act in accordance with that constitution. This is one reason why "takeovers" tend to be far more frequent among independent churches and those that follow a nonconnectional polity.

The vulnerability of democratic institutions is only one of the hazards facing those who seek to be democratic leaders in churches. After being involved in parish consultations with hundreds of congregations in which the pastor sought to be identified as a democratic leader, it appears to this observer this approach is vulnerable to several pitfalls.

The first, and the easiest to define, is that the vast majority of church members are in congregations organized on the hierarchical pyramid that can be traced back seventeen hundred years to Cyprian, the bishop of Carthage. That usually means the pastor who seeks to function as a democratic leader may have to radically revise the basic organizational structure in order to create a democratic setting. This is not a serious problem in some Friends meetings, but it is a major undertaking in Episcopal, Presbyterian, Methodist, Lutheran, Anglican, and several other traditions. In several denominations such a reorganization would not be permitted by the rules of that denomination.

Furthermore, in many traditions, the recommended or required structure for congregational self-government is a representative system, not a participatory democracy. To change this usually means not only revising the structure, but also retraining the leaders to be comfortable in a radically different system or replacing many of the inherited leaders.

Another facet of this issue is that in the vast majority of congregations the current organizational structure was not designed to provide a basis for democratic decision making, but rather to get the work done. This usually means the heart of the structure is a series of functional committees (worship, missions, evangelism, finances, education, property, personnel) plus a central governing board. The basic structure was designed with the primary focus on getting the work done, not on how the decision would be made and certainly not around a goal of enhancing interpersonal relationships!

In most congregations a decision to change all of that in order to encourage a more democratic approach to decision making would be a sizeable undertaking and almost certain to encounter considerable resistance.

Perhaps the most subtle pitfall, and one that is encountered very frequently, is the distinction between the obligation of the effective democratic leader and the temptation to drift into a laissez-faire approach. As was pointed out by Bradford, Gibb, and Benne,[13] this is a thin line, and frequently what is identified as a democratic approach in fact closely resembles the laissez-faire approach. This appears to be the path followed by some self-styled enablers who actually function in a highly laissez-faire leadership style.

Another problem is that the New Testament does not provide a model of participatory democracy for congregational self-government. Paul made it very clear that God has appointed leaders because of their gifts, not in response to a popular mandate (I Cor. 12:27-28). One of the classic accounts in the Old Testament makes it clear that majority rule should not always prevail, but that at times the minority report should carry the day (Num. 14).

What for many is the most frustration-producing dimension of participatory democracy is that it tends to repel the people that organization was designed to attract and serve. Examples of this include the high school youth group organized around the question, "Now, kids, what do you want to do?"[14] as well as the national Democratic Party in the presidential elections of 1972 and 1984, and the United Mine Workers in the late 1970s.

Others are discouraged by the tendency that the greater the emphasis on participatory democracy in defining the mission and the role of a congregation, the greater the probability the top priorities will be on institutional maintenance and care of the members rather than on outreach, missions, and witness. This tendency simply reaffirms the validity of the doctrine of sin.

Finally, as both the biblical narrative and the history of American Christianity illustrate repeatedly, when asked to choose between the status quo and change or between tomorrow and yesterday, the majority usually chooses the status quo or yesterday.

How much emphasis do you really want to place on democracy in your congregation? In your denomination? As you respond, it may help if you explain what you mean by *democratic* and offer a New Testament foundation for the operational expression of that concept.

In many congregations and regional judicatories a more productive debate will focus on the question of whether we are seeking a manager or a leader.

Administrative Manager or Initiating Leader?

"This is the second time I've raised this question in three years now, but I believe we've reached the point where we need to go to two services on Sunday morning," urged Everett Hughes, a member of the board at Bethany Church, who also was an usher. "Last Sunday we had to set up chairs again for nearly a dozen people. If we continue to grow, we must either build or go to two services."

"I know you set up chairs, but there was room for a dozen more people in the front pews, and I expect there were some empty places behind me," argued a longtime member. "I don't see any point in splitting our congregation into two factions until we have to, so let's not talk about two services until every pew is filled for at least three consecutive Sundays!"

"This really is a matter for the worship committee to decide," urged the Reverend Harold Mack gently. In his nine years as pastor at Bethany, Pastor Mack had seen the average attendance at worship fluctuate between 135 and 160 in a building designed to seat 185. For the second time in nine years attendance was now averaging approximately 155. Six years ago, after it had peaked at 160, it gradually drifted back to 140 three years later. When no one objected, the question of two services was referred to the worship committee, and that was the last anyone on the council heard of that issue.

A half hour later another member of the council raised a different issue. "As you recall, three months ago the youth council called our attention to the fact that attendance in the senior high youth group was down to six or eight, and the junior high group is averaging about nine or ten. It is now their recommendation that we merge the two groups into one. They want our response to their recommendation."

As this matter was being presented, all eyes gradually turned to watch Pastor Mack to discern his response. "Ever since I came to serve as your pastor, I have urged that we trust our committees. It seems to me that if this is the recommendation of the youth council, we have no choice but to support it." Within seconds a motion was made, seconded, and adopted to approve the recommendation of the youth council.

The last item on the agenda that evening was a letter signed by five women asking that the ladies' restroom be repaired. Their complaint was that it was difficult to keep clean and that one of the toilets leaked and water frequently was standing on the floor. At the pastor's suggestion, and without any discussion, this letter was referred to the trustees.

Eighty-seven minutes after this monthly meeting of the church council had convened, the benediction was pronounced, and the meeting was adjourned. As he circled out of his way a few blocks to drop off his friend, Tracy Hughes, Ray Bennett commented, "Our pastor may not be the best preacher in the world, but he's an excellent administrator! I can remember back twelve, fifteen years ago when Reverend Harrison was here, our council meetings rarely were over before eleven o'clock. It's a real pleasure to come in, work through the agenda, and in a hour and a half or less be on our way home."

"Well, since I have to get up at six every morning to go to work, I can't complain about getting home at a decent hour," replied Tracy, "but I'm a little concerned that we didn't take time to go into the policy implications of a couple of those issues. We've been on a plateau in size ever since we joined Bethany eight years ago. Oh, we go up and down a little, but we really haven't grown significantly while this end of the county has experienced a 30 percent increase in population during the past decade. For example, I don't think we can grow until we either go to two services on Sunday morning or enlarge the sanctuary. That's a policy issue this council should discuss rather than simply passing the buck to the worship committee. It also seems to me that the decision to merge the two youth groups is really a decision to cutback on youth programming. Finally, I can't understand why someone didn't raise the issue of the women's restroom before now. That must really repel any first-time visitor who would go in there."

"Well, here's where you live," replied Ray Bennett as he turned into the Hughes' driveway. "See you in church."

* * * *

"The other day one of the younger women in the congregation came to me to complain that we asked only husband-wife couples with young children to light the Advent candles," commented a member of Central Church at the February Board meeting. "I told her I thought her complaint should be directed to the worship committee, but when she insisted, I agreed to bring it up tonight at our Board meeting. She told me she thought that next December we should ask at least one single parent and one childless couple to light those candles."

"I can't agree with her," declared a veteran member who was serving his third hitch on the Board. "We're a family church, we stand for the integrity of the family, and I believe we should use only couples with young children to light the candles."

"I agree with you," added a third member of the Board, "but she does have a right to have her complaint heard by the proper committee. I suggest we make a note of it and refer it to the worship committee."

"No, that's an important issue, and I believe we need to discuss it in terms of the broader policy ramifications before we refer it to any committee," declared the Reverend Jack Carlson, senior minister of this 1100-member congregation. "You haven't told us the name of the person who made the complaint, but it could be she is raising a question of how this church discriminates against single adults."

* * * *

"According to my calculations, based on our offerings for the first eight months of this year and on our record for the last four months of last year, I expect we will end the year with approximately $18,000 in unpaid bills," announced the treasurer to the September meeting of the church council at Trinity Church. "This is my seventh year as the treasurer, and we've always been able to pay all our bills before the end of the year, but I'm afraid this year will be an exception."

"I warned you a year ago when we approved that huge increase in our budget this would happen," declared a fiscally conservative member of the council. "The rest of you agreed the money was there if we only asked for it. I told you we were going to have hard times this year. Should we ask the finance committee to have a special financial campaign just before we have our regular every-member canvass?"

"That's for the finance committee to decide," suggested a third member of the council. "Let's refer this to them and ask them to take appropriate action. They may decide it would be wise to get a short-term loan from the bank and catch up next spring. Things are a little tight right now for a lot of our people."

"I agree we may want to refer this to the finance committee," observed the Reverend Andrew Lance, the thirty-nine-year-old pastor of this 387-member congregation, "but there are a couple of policy issues we need to discuss here in the council before we make a referral. The first is are we willing to accept the psychological implications of ending the year with a deficit? When I learned about this last Friday, I checked with our previous treasurer, and he said in his nine years as treasurer we had never ended the year with a deficit. The second is whether we should decide to direct the finance committee to undertake a special financial campaign as soon as possible in order to eliminate this deficit before we ask our people to make a pledge for next year? I think we're really faced with two questions on this issue. First, what's the best way to raise $18,000 between now and the end of the year? Second, when is the best time to do that? As the church council here, we have an obligation to deal with both of those questions."

These three brief accounts illustrate one of the most significant distinctions in leadership. This is the difference between functioning as an efficient administrator of what is perceived as a small-scale and relatively simple organization versus providing the institutional leadership required by a large and complex enterprise. It appears from this account that the first pastor, Harold Mack, saw himself as the manager of a small and uncomplex congregation at Bethany and was primarily concerned with the smooth and efficient management of that organization. By contrast, both Jack Carlson at Central Church and Andrew Lance at Trinity Church identified questions about values and the significant long-term policy implications on what others saw as relatively simple issues.

In a small and remarkably lucid book that has become a classic since it was first published three decades ago, Philip Selznick identifies this distinction and its implications for leaders. Selznick argues that the basic difference between the manager of an organization and the leader of an institution is that the leader has both the ability and the willingness to recognize the difference between routine or short-term questions and those critical decisions that have long-term implications for that institution and its mission or purpose. Unlike the human relations specialists, Selznick contends that an effective leader must focus on the values, identity or character, and goals of the institution.[15]

Selznick places great emphasis on the value of elites and of the leader's ability to recognize and protect the elites that create and infuse values into that institution. He also lifts up the value of goals as a means of enabling an institution to be what it is called to be. When the goals are formulated from a managerial perspective, the organization may easily become totally absorbed in routine housekeeping tasks and begin to drift.

These last two abstractions can be illustrated very simply. At one time the women's organization in several denominations was built around the central goal of world missions. In tens of thousands of congregations the women's organization became the number one advocate of such values as missions, missionary education, social justice, and outreach. In the best sense of the word it became an elite. Those pastors who saw themselves as managers of a smooth running and efficient organization often attempted to integrate the women's organization into the total program of that congregation and/or saw it as a problem and tried to minimize its role. By contrast those pastors who identified themselves as responsible leaders of a large, complex, and pluralistic institution (any long-established congregation with more than one hundred fifty to two hundred active members qualifies as a large and complex institution for this discussion) typically saw the women's organization as an essential infuser of values while affirming it and protecting it from its critics. A parallel story could be told about the adult Sunday school in many congregations.

The distinction between setting goals from a managerial perspective versus from a larger perspective can be illustrated by another incident. Mrs. Violet Harrison, a forty-three-year-old widow with two teenage children, approached the Council at St. Paul Church with a request to use four rooms on the first floor of the educational wing for a weekday nursery school she was planning to open the following September. Although she was not a member, Mrs. Harrison was known to five members of the Council. They knew her as an honest, capable, inner-directed, responsible, aggressive, talented, creative, and personable woman with obvious entrepreneurial skills. She had been left with limited economic resources when her husband died three years earlier, so the Council was sympathetic. She offered to pay for all the out-of-pocket costs such as utilities the first year as well as the full costs of staffing and operating the nursery school. She stated that she hoped by the end of the second year, she would be able to pay rent for use of the space, but she was hoping the Council would see this as a needed community service program and would be willing to house it without full rent charges for at least the first two years.

"HERE TO ETERNITY" BIBLE STUDY

True leaders intervene
to point out the pivotal
in the church's routine !!
—FRIAR TUCK

When one of the members of the Council asked if she planned to teach the children about Jesus and the Christian faith, Mrs. Harrison was categorical in her response. "No, we expect to serve children from different religious backgrounds including some from homes where neither parent is a member of any religious organization. Therefore, we cannot be a sectarian school. Furthermore, I do not believe I have any right to impose any particular religious teachings on these young and impressionable children. We want to be able to offer a value-free educational experience. When I talked with your pastor earlier, I explained we would come in early on Monday morning and remove any religious pictures or symbols from the walls of the rooms and the corridor, but we'll put them back up before we leave Friday afternoon."

After a brief discussion, with most of that time devoted to questions about the church's legal liability and Mrs. Harrison's insurance coverage, and after assurance that the nursery would provide its own janitorial services, the Council voted to approve the request for a two-year contract, but made it clear any extension would require review and even negotiations. After the meeting one member of the Council reflected, "Although I don't see anything wrong with our decision and I think it may be a useful community service, there is no such thing as a value-free educational experience!"

Five years later the nursery school was widely accepted as a success story, the members at St. Paul Church saw it as a community service, and the leaders added it to their bragging list as they boasted about how this congregation served its community and about the "busy building." This story has parallels in hundreds of congregations, and it illustrates four aspects of the distinction between the response by the manager(s) of an organization and that of the leader(s) of institutions which have a clearly defined sense of mission based on firmly established values and expressed in operational goals.

First, and perhaps least significant, this was a reactive decision. Mrs. Harrison, not one of the members of this congregation, initiated the proposal for a weekday nursery school. She, not the members of the Council, had the vision of what could be.

Second, going back to Selznick's central thesis, this was largely perceived as a routine issue, not as a critical or long-term decision. Once permission has been granted to Mrs. Harrison to use those four rooms, the burden of changing that arrangement almost invariably will fall on those who may want to terminate that use of those rooms. Usually it is difficult to alter the status quo, and a new status quo included Mrs. Harrison's nursery school.

Third, and perhaps most significant, for the most part the members of the Council perceived this as a "community service program" and identified for themselves the role of a landlord negotiating with a prospective tenant. A good argument can be made that responsible leaders of a mission-centered church would have conceptualized the proposed nursery school as one component of a larger package of ministries with families that include preschool children.[16] By letting the tenant initiate and manage this new program, that made it easy for the elected officials at St. Paul to abandon a creative or initiating responsibility and retreat into the more passive role of responding to external initiatives. Experience has demonstrated that simply responding to external requests makes it easy for any institution to drift into a posture where it is without either role or goals.[17] Once a congregation retreats into this passive stance, it is difficult to change it.[18]

Finally, this incident illustrates the point that leaders of mission-centered institutions know how to ask the right questions. These are the questions that deal with purpose, values, mission, role, and goals. By contrast, managers more concerned with order and efficiency tend to ask housekeeping questions.

Among the other distinctions between the manager who concentrates on the routine or short-term dimensions of a question and the more proactive, assertive, and initiating leader who can identify and respond to critical questions are these: (1) the leader functions in a longer time frame, (2) the leader understands and accepts the responsibility for asking the right questions, (3) the leader has a clearly defined and determined commitment to reinforce specific values in that organization,[19] (4) the leader appreciates the distinctive contributions of elites,[20] (5) the leader understands the mission or reason for existence of that organization, designs the administrative structure to accomplish that mission, and is able and willing to turn that design into reality,[21] (6) the leader understands the value of allies and coalitions (see chapter seven), and (7) the leader encourages rather than smothers creativity.

It would be a serious misreading of reality, however, to suggest one is either a manager or a leader. A better concept is that the manager sees leadership basically as managing a smoothly running and efficient organization. The leader, as the term is used here, may or may not be an excellent manager, and excellent managers may not be effective leaders. The distinctive contributions of the leader are felt on those occasions, frequently less than half a dozen times a year, when that leader identifies what others see as a routine issue as really being a critical or pivotal decision that may shape the future of the entire organization. It really matters little whether the style of the leader is democratic or authoritarian as long as that pivotal issue is identified in terms of its long-range impact on that institution. By definition, of course, the laissez-faire type leader would not intervene in the decision-making process by highlighting that critical issue.

Most of what has been discussed in this chapter was illustrated in the prologue in the story of the Reverend Jerry Buchanan's first year as the pastor at Trinity Church. Jerry is an example of a minister who was able and willing to lift up for the Board's consideration what he saw as critical long-term issues that would shape the future of Trinity Church.

Jerry also illustrates how a minister can be both a good pastor (remember his visits to the dying Ethel Powell and to the three alienated Vietnam veterans) and also function as an assertive, proactive, and initiating leader.

One of the parallels between a good pastor and an effective manager comes out of studies on managerial leadership. Despite the emphasis in business schools on long-range planning, the studies of how effective managers actually spend their time suggest they do not plan their schedule in advance in much detail.

Instead, they spend a huge portion of their time reacting to others, and the typical day is interrupted with a variety of unrelated, brief, and frequently disjointed conversations.[22] In the best-selling book ever published on business, the authors make a big point of what they describe as "hands-on, value driven" leadership.[23]

Many pastors can identify both with the amount of time consumed reacting to others and responding to interruptions as well as to the "hands-on" concept. The parish expression of that are the unexpected telephone calls, unscheduled visitors, the unforeseen interruptions from conversations, and unanticipated crises that consume a large chunk of the typical day. When a member dies or someone goes into the hospital for unexpected major surgery, the schedule has to be adjusted to accommodate those surprises. That may produce considerable frustration, but often is the mark of a good pastor as well as of the effective manager.

As was pointed out earlier, the effective leader functions in a conceptual framework that includes a much longer time frame and tends to be much more proactive. The pastor who has adopted a managerial model of leadership and is about to move to a new parish may decide, "I think I'll wait until I'm on the scene for several months and hear what the people have to say before I make any suggestions about the future." The pastor who has decided to follow a more proactive leadership model might decide, "On the basis of what I know about that congregation, I believe I'll spend the first year getting acquainted with the people, identifying allies, and laying the groundwork for some changes that obviously must be made during the next four or five years." Both, however, take advantage of chance encounters.

Recent years have brought a deluge of studies and research that lift up the influence of the initiating leader, as contrasted with the more traditional administrator in a variety of settings. An impressive portion of that research has been directed toward determining what creates a productive learning environment in a public school. Repeatedly these reports stress (a) the importance of the principal as a proactive, assertive, initiating, and transformational leader and (b) the impact of leaders projecting high expectations of both teachers and students.[24] Likewise, Baptists, both black and white, as well as many other denominational leaders and observers of the local church scene are once again emphasizng the role of the minister as an initiating and assertive leader, rather than as simply an administrator who has primary responsibilities as a preacher, pastor, and priest.[25] The demand for initiating, proactive, and assertive leaders in the church appears to be growing. As you reflect on your leadership responsibilities, what categories or terms will you choose to describe your approach? What values are reflected in your categories and terms? Are you comfortable with them? Or do you want to look at leadership from a different conceptual framework?

Alternative Categories

Rather than continuing to use a conceptual framework for looking at different approaches to leadership—one that utilizes such value-laden terms as authoritarian, democratic, and laissez faire—it may be useful to seek another system. Many exist. This can be illustrated by looking at three different studies on leadership.

A recent study of educational administrators categorize them as either "gatherers" or "hunters." The gatherers forage passively in a small area, seeking only to be able to meet day-to-day needs. By contrast the hunters (1) emphasize a range of opportunities and create a climate that fosters new ideas, (2) cultivate a distinctive institutional image, (3) display an ability and a willingness to create the inspirational vision that preceded the development of "an insightful, commitment-generating strategic plan," (4) are concerned about both the quality and the outcomes of decision-making processes, and (5) tend to err on the side of over-communication.

In the same essay the author, David Whetten, distinguishes between "charismatic" and "catalytic" leaders. The former seek to persuade people to follow the initiative of the magnetic leader while the latter work within a group to build cohesion, solidarity, and commitment to goals or objectives that emerge from that group. Whetten observes that the effective university administrators usually are viewed by colleagues as either catalytic or charismatic, but rarely as authoritarian.[26]

In discussing leadership in community service organizations, Ray Johns, who reflects the human relations approach of Lippit, Lewis, MacGregor, and others, identified two basic types of leadership in an organization. One type is concerned primarily with institutional maintenance, and the second is concerned with organizational change.[27]

A third set of simple, but very revealing, categories can be found in one of the most influential books on leadership to come out in recent years. James MacGregor Burns divides the world of leaders into two basic types.[28] The more common, the "transactional" leader, is the person who takes the initiative to work out an acceptable exchange of what one can offer and what the other(s) needs.

Most of the work of the typical parish pastor fits into the transactional category. The congregation provides a place to do ministry, an economic stipend, and a group of cooperative members. In exchange the minister completes the transaction by conducting worship, preaching, administering the sacraments, fulfilling the priestly obligations, visiting the sick, burying the dead, and administering the parish. Some people will argue that Burns' category of transactional leadership really is the equivalent of the effective manager.

The second type of leader identified by Burns is the transformational leader. The transforming leader raises the level of both conduct and aspirations, transforms followers into leaders, and helps to change the world. The transforming leader is an intentional agent of planned change. Gandhi, Mao Tse-tung, and Franklin D. Roosevelt were highly visible examples of transforming leaders. In a fascinating book on leadership, Aaron Wildavsky, a political scientist, identifies the accomplishments of Moses in the "transformation of three regimes—from slavery to anarchy to equity to hierarchy."[29] The biblical narrative makes it clear that Moses concluded that an egalitarian system produced uncontrollable enthusiasm and unacceptable carnage among competing leaders. Thus the final step in this sequence was to transform equity into hierarchy with Moses himself at the top of the pecking order, and at the top of the mountain, in receiving God's revelation. The elders were below Moses and above the people in that hierarchy.

The parish version of the transforming leader may be the new minister who helps a congregation move from a plateau—in which the Sunday morning worship attendance averages 160 to 200—to reach more people—with the attendance climbing to 300 or 400 or 500 on the typical Sunday morning. This transformation might include (a) persuading the people to accept a change in the schedule to two worship services on Sunday morning, (b) a redefinition of the organizational structure that strengthens the committee system and allows the governing board to focus on planning, setting direction, and general oversight rather than being concerned with details, (c) expansion of the program, (d) doubling or tripling the paid staff, (e) enlisting and training several dozen additional lay volunteers to staff these new ministries—with many of them subsequently identifying that as a life-changing experience for themselves, (f) enlarging the meeting place, (g) raising the per member level of giving substantially, and (h) launching an aggressive new member enlistment effort. Nine years after the arrival of that minister one of the longtime members said, "This surely is a different church from the one I joined fifteen years ago!" The reason the oldtimer says that is because of the transformation that has occurred in a relatively short time.

Another transformational leader may lead the congregation to relocate and build a new meeting place, or to launch a Christian dayschool as part of a larger effort to reach and serve the parents of younger children—and through that effort transform an Anglo congregation into a racially integrated church—or to lead that congregation out of the denomination (a century ago the equivalent of this contemporary trend was to lead an independent congregation into affiliating with a denomination), or to lead a noncharismatic congregation into becoming a part of the charismatic renewal movement, or to help the small rural congregation of 1960 become a large suburban church in 1990, or to change from a chaplaincy style of congregational life to an aggressive concern with social issues.

The transformational leader not only produces radical changes, substantial discontinuity, and a cadre of new leaders, but also usually has to live with the emergence of a group of longtime members who regret the changes and long for a return to the good old days (see Num. 14:3-5). That cluster of alienated and angry ex-leaders may be the source of that repeated comment, "It surely isn't like it used to be around here!"

It also should be noted that the transforming leader rarely is able to function in a democratic setting with majority support. Most transformations are accomplished by a minority who act contrary to the wishes of the majority.

101

In addition to choosing the set of categories one is comfortable with in describing various approaches to leadership, it is important that the institutional context not be neglected.

What Is the Context?

The context often is at least as influential in defining the role of any one individual in an organization as that person's gifts, talents, skills, and position. This can be illustrated by three different examples which also help to explain the concept of role. The first example contrasts the roles of two different pastors, the second one identifies two sharply different sets of roles for two women who carry the same title, and the third illustrates the change in roles of the pastor who becomes a denominational executive. All these examples illustrate that role is what a person does, and also why it may be difficult to define roles through a job description.

The first example contrasts the roles of two ministers. One is the Reverend Sally Carson, who is in her third year as a pastor of a stable midwestern congregation located in a village of 740 residents, nearly one-fourth of whom are past sixty-five years of age. Sally is the second woman and the nineteenth minister to serve as the full-time resident pastor of this ninety-seven-year-old congregation. Reliable records exist only as far back as 1948, but they indicate the congregation reached its peak in size in 1957, when Sunday morning worship attendance averaged 119 and the Sunday school averaged 77. For the past twenty years worship attendance has ranged from a low of 64 in 1979 to a high of 93 last year.

The Reverend Terry Carter is the founding pastor of a nine-year-old new mission in the Sunbelt that is now planning its second building program. After meeting for three years in a public school the congregation completed its first building, but that has been outgrown. It has been necessary to go to two worship services on Sunday morning in that big, general purpose room that serves as a fellowship hall, doubles as the sanctuary on Sunday morning and also accommodates four classes during the Sunday school hour at 9:30 A.M. Last year Sunday morning worship attendance averaged 180, up from 133 the previous year and from 138 the year before that. The tentative proposal is to construct a one-story wing with eight classrooms.

When asked to identify and rank their roles and responsibilities in order of importance, Sally and Terry came up with substantially different rankings.

Sally	Terry
1. Shepherd	1. Leader
2. Pastor	2. Preacher
3. Friend	3. Administrator
4. Equipper	4. Visionary
5. Counselor	5. Motivator
6. Visitor	6. Evangelist
7. Teacher	7. Fund raiser
8. Nurse	8. Planning consultant
9. Preacher	9. Shaper of traditions
10. Cheerleader	10. Organizer
11. Youth counselor	11. Encourager
12. Theologian	12. Counselor
13. Umpire	13. Initiator
14. Organizer	14. Teacher
15. Community leader	15. Prophet
16. Celebrant	16. Conceptualizer
17. Administrator	17. Builder
18. Prophet	18. Innovator
19. Denominational volunteer	19. Friend
20. Model	20. Theologian

When asked to elaborate on her list, the forty-seven-year-old Sally, the divorced mother of two teenagers, replied, "You asked me to identify twenty different roles I fulfill as the pastor of the congregation. That was hard. I never thought I did that many different things. Obviously there is considerable overlap, but each role has its own distinctive characteristics. For example, while I never thought of myself as a nurse, and I have had no training as a nurse, when I go to visit some of my members who live alone, I find myself filling the role of nurse. Likewise I am the umpire who has to settle minor disputes, the cheerleader who keeps urging the people that we can do what we set out to do if it is consistent with God's will, and the equipper who is always seeking and equipping new volunteers. We have plenty of policy makers, but we're always short of people who will pitch in and do things like teach Sunday school.

"The biggest surprise, I guess, is that I placed 'preacher' ninth on the list. I was thirty-nine years old when I started seminary, and I worked in a big church near the seminary to support myself and my two boys. I just assumed that when I graduated and started to serve a church, my number one responsibility would be preaching. That's not how it is here, however. As I worked on this list, it became clear to me that my primary emphasis here has to be on relationships, on nurture, and simply on being a friend to a lot of people who have seen most of their friends and relatives move away or die."

"What do you mean by that last item on your list?" came the question from the person who had asked Sally to go through this exercise.

"That's the one that has surprised me most, and perhaps it should be much higher on the list," reflected Sally. "I knew when I came here that I was following a woman who had been pastor for three years, so I wouldn't be a pioneer. She came straight from seminary and soon fell in love with a parishioner who had a lot of relatives in this congregation. Within a year after they were married, she decided it would be wise to move on, and she is now the minister of a church about two hundred miles west of here where she doesn't have to deal with the role conflict that goes with trying to be both a pastor and an in-law. For some, I am the model of a woman in the ministry, for others I am the model of a second-career professional, for quite a few I am a model for the fact there is life after divorce, for perhaps a few I am the model of a committed Christian, for several of our older members I am the model of how they wish their kids had turned out, and for at least a couple of women I am a model of a mother who also is employed outside the home."

"You asked me to list twenty roles," explained Terry, the new church developer, "and I did as you wanted, but the top four are clearly the critical ones. Since I was the organizing minister here, I have seniority on everyone else, and they respect that. I am *the* leader here. Second, I see preaching as my most important ministerial duty. Those first-time visitors won't come back unless they are fed spiritually on that first visit. This sounds terribly immodest, but a lot of our members really joined *me* and subsequently transferred their allegiance to this congregation, and a big reason why they came is my preaching. Third, there is a huge administrative burden that goes with creating a new church out of a five-acre parcel of land and no people. Fourth, sometimes I'm the visionary, the motivator, the innovator, the initiator, and the hustler who has to run against the tide. A couple of years after we moved into this building, we leveled off at about 135 in attendance on Sunday morning. That's all the room would hold. I was the one who pushed for going to two services a little over a year ago. Last year our attendance was up by a third as the result of going to two services. There's still quite a bit of opposition to the idea. Some object that we're dividing the congregation into two groups, others point out they preferred the atmosphere when the room was full to today when it's half empty at eight-thirty and a third empty at eleven o'clock, but I point out that the Great Commission requires us to reach everyone we can."

"What else on your list needs a word of explanation?" was the next question.

"This is my third pastorate," replied Terry, "and both of my previous pastorates were with long-established congregations that were filled with tradition. Here less than a fourth of our people came from this denominational heritage. That means we're creating new traditions all the time. Thus the role of helping to create and shape traditions is in the top half of my responsibilities. At times it's kind of scary when I stop to wonder how my successors here will view some of these traditions that we're building, but I expect to stay for a good many more years, so I don't worry about that a lot."

This last comment of Terry's refers to a distinctive role for the minister organizing a new congregation. The new mission has very few traditions. Thus the first leaders, and especially that first mission developer, should recognize the responsibility to build traditions and precedents that reflect the nature of that worshiping community, rather than simply reflecting the personal predilections of that leader. These early decisions do become precedents. They must be consistent with what eventually emerges as a set of rules or a constitution, with the basic statement of purpose, and with the commitments of the first members to that new congregation. The first pastor helps to create the congregational culture.

A comparison of these two lists reveals a substantially different set of roles for Sally than for Terry. In part this reflects the huge differences in the cultures of these two congregations and in part the differences are a reflection of the gifts, talents, experiences, values, and priorities of the two ministers.

A second example of the concept of role can be seen by comparing the roles and responsibilities of Mrs. Rogers, the forty-three-year-old part-time secretary at the 375-member Hilltop Church with the roles and responsibilities of Mrs. Brown, the forty-five-year-old full-time secretary to the pastor at the 930-member First Church.

When asked what she does, Mrs. Rogers replied, "I answer the telephone; type; file; mimeograph the church bulletin; duplicate, address, and mail the monthly newsletter; and do whatever else the pastor asks me to do. I'm paid to work twenty hours a week. Sometimes I have time left over to straighten up the office and catch up on a lot of little things that have been neglected. Other weeks, especially the week we get out the newsletter or some other big mailing, I may stay late on two or three days."

When asked what she does, Mrs. Brown explained, "While I was hired to be the pastor's secretary, I also have to manage the office. We have a full-time receptionist-typist who does most of the routine typing and a part-time financial secretary who takes care of the financial records, but I keep the membership records. I also coordinate the calendar, schedule the use of the building, take about half of the telephone calls that otherwise would go to the pastor, serve as a friend and advisor to a lot of folks who just drop by the church office, schedule all the weddings, serve as secretary to both the trustees and the finance committee, help members who are trying to enlist volunteers, answer questions no one else is prepared to deal with, serve as an intermediary between the pastor and some of the members who are afraid of the minister or reluctant to call someone they believe is too busy to be bothered with their concerns, keep track of who is in or being discharged from the hospital, and work on the annual stewardship program. In general, I am our pastor's girl Friday. I do not make the coffee, and I don't wash windows, but I've cleaned this office more than once. Oh, yes, I also type all the pastor's correspondence and answer some of the letters myself."

Both Mrs. Rogers and Mrs. Brown are referred to by the parishioners as "our church secretary," although the two roles are vastly different. To some extent this is a reflection of the differences in gifts, talents, interests, personalities, skills, and experience. To a substantial degree the differences in role are determined by the differences in the congregational context.

This comparison also illustrates the fact that it is relatively easy to write a job description for someone who has a job such as that filled by Mrs. Rogers, but it is far more difficult to write a job description for someone like Mrs. Brown who fills a distinctive and very complex role at First Church.

The impact of the institutional context also can be illustrated by the experience of the Reverend Harold Hawkins. At age fifty-three Harold was in his eleventh year as the senior minister of a 1,740-member congregation that had been experiencing a net annual increase of nearly one hundred members since Harold's arrival. A skilled, energetic, rational, enthusiastic, and gifted individual, Harold saw his seven basic roles as (1) preacher, (2) chief of staff, (3) cheerleader, (4) worship leader, (5) pastor, (6) administrator, and (7) innovator.

His friends and colleagues in the denomination saw his two principal gifts as preaching and administration. They persuaded Harold to accept the recently vacated position as the executive for the regional judicatory of that denomination in the same state in which he had been serving as a pastor. Harold was not sure that was what the Lord was calling him to do, but the combination of persuasive friends and itchy feet made him accept.

Four years later an unhappy and frustrated Harold Hawkins explained to a friend why he was interested in returning to the pastorate.

"At the end of last year," explained Harold as he pulled a typed sheet of paper out of a manila folder, "I sat down and tried to identify my responsibilities in this job. The people who wrote that job description probably were well intentioned, but they either did not understand or they were unable to communicate the ambiguities and the subtleties of this office and of how much the personality of the person who holds this position influences the expectations people project on the person who sits in this chair!

"This is the list prepared in the order of the amount of time each required, and as you can see, there is not much overlap between this list and my job description. First of all, I'm seen as a problem solver. People bring me their problems and expect me to solve them. That's my most time-consuming role. Second, I'm expected to be a personnel expert since much of my time is spent on ministerial placement.

"Here's the rest of the list," continued Harold. "My third role is as a referee in a variety of conflict situations. Fourth, I'm a diagnostician. I go into a local church and am expected to be able to listen to the symptoms and diagnose what the real problem is. Fifth, I'm sort of a county agent, you know, the person who tries to help those who are out there doing the work in the parish to change and improve their ways of doing what they're called to do. That's what the county agricultural agent used to do with farmers. He was a graduate of a school of agriculture, but he didn't farm; he tried to help those who were doing the farming do a better job. Sixth, I'm a pediatrician and seventh. . ."

"Hold it," interrupted Harold's friend, "what do you mean by pediatrician?"

"Don't you know what a pediatrician is?" asked Harold with a smile. "A pediatrician's number one job is to say to those anxious mothers, 'What you're doing is exactly right, and your baby is behaving in a normal and predictable manner!' That's what I have to do with a lot of anxious young pastors. Seventh, I'm the administrator of an office which includes my assistant, a secretary, and a part-time volunteer. Eighth, I'm expected by many to be the prophetic voice for our denomination in this region. Ninth, I'm a marriage counselor for a surprisingly large number of parsonage families. Tenth, I'm supposed to be the pastor to pastors, but that's incompatible with my role in ministerial placement."

"Wait a minute," commented the friend, "I thought people like you were supposed to make serving as the pastor to pastors one of your two or three top priorities."

"That's true," agreed Harold. "That's what I was told when I took this job, but in point of fact it ranks about in the middle of my list of twenty in terms of the time I can spend on it."

"In addition to those ten roles," continued Harold, "I'm also a fund raiser for the denomination, a teacher, a preacher, a missions interpreter, an innovator, a confidant and a friend to a fair number of folks who appear to need someone they can confide in, the chief representative of our denomination on the ecumenical scene, an entrepreneur as I attempt to launch new programs, an uninvited interventionist as I see the need to intervene in some situations without being asked, and finally, the role I hate the most, hitman."

"What in the world do you mean by that?" inquired the friend.

"Don't you know what a hitman is?" replied Harold. "That's a gunman from Detroit you contract with who, for a fee, will come and rub out someone you don't like. Three or four times a year I'm called in either by some congregational leaders who want me to tell their pastor to resign or by a senior minister who wants me to fire a staff member or by a pastor who wants me to come in and straighten out a member that the pastor can't deal with in a constructive manner."

"That's an impressive list," agreed the friend, "but I'm surprised you didn't mention meeting-goer or board member. I always thought people like you had to spend a lot of time in meetings. That's why I'm glad I don't have a job like yours."

"Oh, I do go to a lot of meetings," replied Harold, "and that was a part of that misleading job description someone prepared for this position. I'm on ten or eleven different permanent committees and boards. That's a different way of dividing up my time. That describes where I go. The roles I've listed are what I do when I get there. For example, on one board, I play the role of interventionist, problem solver, referee, and fund raiser. Before and after the meetings of that board, I spend a lot of time in my roles as pastor to pastor, diagnostician, friend or confidant, county agent, pediatrician, and administrator of this office."

Harold took the next hour to explain to his friend, who also was one of the persons who had persuaded him to accept this position, why he was unhappy. In simple terms it boiled down to the fact that most of the leadership roles he had filled in the pastorate, and filled with a high level of competence, immense personal satisfactions, and a sense of responding to a call, were rarely a part of the day's work as a denominational executive. Most of the roles he was thrust into in his present position were ones with which he was not comfortable or did not feel competent to fill or simply did not produce the personal satisfactions he had enjoyed as a pastor. As a pastor he enjoyed the continuity of relationships with his staff and his members. As a denominational executive Harold found he had far less continuity in his relationships with people, and many he saw only once or twice a year or less. Harold clearly enjoyed the greater depth of more frequent encounters with people.

As they talked, the friend said, "You know, Harold, there are dozens of ministers elsewhere in our denomination who occupy the same office as you do in this region for us, and they are happy in their work."

"I know that's true," agreed Harold, "but I find it difficult to understand how they can be happy in a job like this."

Harold's story illustrates several points about leadership and roles. Obviously it illustrates that the gifted and effective leader with one set of roles in one position may not be either happy or effective in a leadership position that requires a different set of roles and far greater discontinuity in interpersonal relationships. In addition, as the pastor of a rapidly growing congregation, he had many opportunities to express his gifts of creativity. As the regional executive of a long-established denominational agency, he was placed in a position in which he was pressured to react rather than to create.

That same point is illustrated by the radical change in role expectations placed on the member of the state legislature who is elected to the office of mayor in a big city, by the star baseball player who is asked to manage that club immediately after retirement, by the minister who becomes the senior pastor after serving for several years as the associate minister of that same congregation, by the nurse in the physician's office who comes back after a year of advanced training to become the physician's assistant in that same office with the same receptionist and the same patients, and by the graduate student who becomes a member of the faculty after completing the doctorate. As a general rule it usually is easier to change roles when that is accompanied by a change in the institutional context. That is one reason a newly elected bishop in The United Methodist Church cannot serve in the same conference of which he or she was a member immediately prior to election.

Harold's story also illustrates the central point of this section of this book that the institutional setting, as well as the era and the skills, gifts, and talents of the individual, greatly influences the definition of role. This account also illustrates the point that most leaders are called to fill several roles. While this will not surprise some readers, Harold's story illustrates the point that a job description may not convey an adequate description of roles. Finally, these statements on roles may offer a better beginning point for identifying the basic special competencies required than is offered by the traditional job description, but that is part of the final chapter.

What Is Your Leadership Style?

If one accepts the simple concept that the definition of role is determined in part by the leader holding a specific position of leadership and in part by the institutional setting or culture, a simple definition of style is *how* that leader fulfills that role or carries out that leadership role.

Two people may be assigned identical roles, but the way they fill that role or their style of operating may be vastly different. This is illustrated by clerks at the window in the post office, by football coaches, by bus drivers, by tellers at the bank, by flight attendants on an airline, by company commanders in the army, by ministers who are delivering a sermon, by presidents of the United States, and by seminary professors.

There is not necessarily a clear and consistent correlation between role and style. For example, some pastors adopt for themselves a highly nondirective leadership role, but are extremely authoritarian in style when they respond to a plea to be more directive or to accept an initiating role. "Don't ask me what you should do! Go figure it out for yourself!" might be the response by the nondirective leader with an authoritarian style of leadership.

Some leaders prefer a collegial style while others are more unilateral. Many lead with a smile and optimize the values of humor and laughter while others lead with a frown and perceive laughter as a needless and unproductive diversion. Some are always tense while others are relaxed. Some are extremely directive and obviously enjoy issuing commands while others place a much greater emphasis on asking questions. Many of today's leaders are pessimistic about the future while others are overflowing with optimism. A few leaders appear to enjoy polarization and conflict while others are always seeking to build a consensus. Some leaders excel in human skills while others excel in conceptual skills, and many function around a level of technical skills which provides the basis for their leadership role as experts. Some leaders appear to feel a need to be in complete control while others do not display this need.

Countless variations in leadership styles exist because of the many facets of leadership and the huge variation in personalities, skills, gifts, talents, and experience.

Overriding these differences, however, is a leadership style that can be learned, that is compatible with a wide variety of personalities, and that fits most roles. Basically this style of leadership consists of two components.

The first is to affirm and build. In simple terms that means the person following this style of leadership is always seeking to identify and affirm strengths, resources, and assets and to build on these strengths in raising or discussing specific issues. This approach is in sharp contrast to the leader who focuses on faults, problems, shortcomings, limitations, weaknesses, imperfections, and deficiencies. The leader who seeks to affirm and build usually is tremendously impressed and awed by God's goodness, by His creation, by His glory, by His forgiveness of human failings, by His generosity, and by His limitless love. The leader who prefers to focus on shortcomings and problems appears to be more impressed by the sinful nature of human beings, by the terrible things God's creatures have done to His creation, and by the power of demonic forces.

The second component of this leadership style is to place a greater emphasis on statements that end with a question mark rather than with a period or an exclamation mark. The person who practices this style of leadership knows there are no neutral or value-free questions, understands the power of questions, and seeks to load the question in a manner consistent with his or her own values and goals and with an understanding of what God has called that group or congregation or committee or organization to be and to do.

The combination of affirm and build and of asking questions can be a part of the style for the transformational leader who is willing to intervene and to seek to change the agenda. Four different approaches to this interventionist role can be illustrated by these examples.

At Zion Church one of the trustees, who also was a building contractor, was explaining at the monthly meeting of the Board how the wall that separated the nave from the narthex could be moved back to make room for four more pews. That would accommodate most, if not all the people who were now seated in chairs at the eleven o'clock service. Two-thirds of the way through that presentation the newest member of the Board commented, "We've only been here in this congregation for about two years now, but this is the most vital and spiritually alive church we've been a part of in nearly thirty years of moving around the country. We also are impressed with how much this congregation has grown in the short time we've been here. Attendance must be up at least 20 percent in just two years. I wonder whether we should be talking about a modest remodeling job to add four more pews or whether we really should be talking about either going to two services on Sunday morning or perhaps planning to build a new sanctuary. What do you all think?" An hour later nearly everyone agreed that changing to two services made more sense than going to all that work simply to add four pews.

By first affirming the positive aspects of this congregation, that new Board member earned a sympathetic hearing. By asking a question which posed two alternative courses of action, that newcomer changed the agenda from how much it would cost and how long it would take to move that wall to a discussion of other courses of action.

For more than a decade the youth program at Redeemer Church had been allowed to run down until the junior high youth group included only seven or eight youngsters and the attendance at the weekly meetings of the senior high group rarely was even that high. Finally, the husband-wife couple who were counselors for the older group and the pastor, who worked with the junior highs, concluded that the best course of action would be to merge the two groups.

When this proposal came before the church council, the discussion revolved around a series of questions. What could be done to make the parents of the youth who were not participating insist that their children attend? When would the change be made? Now? In June? In September? Would this couple continue to work with the pastor in the youth program after the merger of the two groups? Would it be better to merge each group with the equivalent age group in the youth program carried on by the church across the street and run a joint program rather than try to include thirteen-year-olds and eighteen-year-olds in one group? When would the newly merged group meet?

After half an hour of depressing debate, one member of the council said, "I knew this was going to be on the agenda tonight, so before I left the house I went through our membership directory and, according to my count, we have thirty-one junior highs and thirty-seven senior high age youth in this congregation. That's a lot of kids! Rather than talking about merging these two groups, I believe we need to address a couple of other questions. First, what is the basic organizing principle that is being used in each of these two groups? Are we following a small group approach that naturally creates a small group? With that many kids maybe we need to take a look at what would happen if we changed the organizing principles. Why are 75 to 80 percent of our kids not participating? What are we doing or not doing that causes them to respond by staying away?"

Half of the people in the room could not comprehend what this person was saying, one or two reacted with a hostile silence, but finally someone said, "I don't have any idea what the answers are to those questions, but they sound to me like good questions. I move we appoint a committee to study the youth program and to use these questions as a beginning point."

In both of these examples someone intervened in the flow of the discussion to change the agenda and ultimately produced a different outcome. Leaders do lead, and one aspect of leadership is intervention.

The minister at Pilgrim Church came home after a week at a continuing education event and a few days later came to a special joint meeting of the Christian education committee and the worship committee. The worship committee had proposed adding a third worship service to the schedule on Sunday morning that would be at the same hour as the Sunday school. The members of the Christian education committee had objected strenuously when they heard about it. They feared this would undercut the Sunday school. They were convinced that many parents would place their children in the Sunday school while they were in worship, and this not only would dry up one source of teachers, it also would make it impossible to organize new classes for younger parents. The church council had asked the two committees to meet together and to bring in a recommendation both could support.

The members of the worship committee were adamant. "We have four choices," declared one member of that committee. "Plateau in size, relocate, expand the sanctuary, or go to three services. Three services is the only viable alternative."

At this point the minister intervened. "It seems to me that the debate is over whether we expect our people to come for one hour on Sunday morning or for two hours. Last week I met the pastors of two different churches. One, from San Diego County in southern California, told me they have a four-hour schedule on Sunday morning. The other said they have a three-hour schedule. Both of them said their schedules are designed to offer people a choice of being there for three hours or for two hours on Sunday morning.

"I'm convinced our people are as loyal, as committed, and as interested in a strong educational program as the people in those two churches," continued the minister. "Although we are crowded for space, we do have two excellent rooms for adult classes, we have a dedicated and capable teaching staff, we have a growing congregation, and we have a fair amount of off-street parking. Why don't we take a look at a three-hour schedule in which we would offer adult classes at all three hours. That way someone could be in an adult class, teach, and also be in worship. That would alleviate our space problem, at least for awhile. We could tell people we offer them a choice between coming for three hours or only two hours."

"What about those parents who want to stick their kids in Sunday school while they're in worship and be here for only one hour?" demanded a member of the Christian education committee.

"That would be possible," agreed the minister, "but we wouldn't advertise that option. Some of our members currently choose the option of not coming at all on Sunday morning, but we never advertise that possibility. People do respond to challenges and to high expectations. Let's raise the level of expectations we hold out to our people. Now, what do you see as other facets of a three-hour schedule that we need to explore together?"

In this case the minister intervened and changed the agenda from "Should we add a third worship service?" to "How can we build a schedule that will encourage our people to be here for either three or two hours on Sunday morning?" Frequently transformational leaders find it necessary to rephrase the question.

The twenty-nine-year-old pastor of a ninety-year-old congregation that averaged between one hundred twenty-five and one hundred thirty at worship on Sunday morning was growing increasingly frustrated after two years. Nearly every suggestion he made had been rejected with the comment, "In a small church such as ours, we could never do that. Preacher, you're simply going to have to adjust to the fact that we don't have the resources here that big church had back where you spent your intern year."

Sometimes the rejection was even briefer, "Reverend, we're just a small church. Why don't you leave us be rather than trying to impose a lot of big church programs on us?"

One morning this minister spent two hours working with the statistics in the denominational yearbook. After that he prefaced every suggestion with one of three comments. "Although you may find this hard to believe, our attendance on Sunday morning is larger than two-thirds of the churches in our denomination. Therefore, don't you think we might try . . .?" Or, "In a congregation as big as ours, don't you think we could . . .?" The third prefactory comment he used to introduce his ideas for expanding the program was, "When you stop to think that we rank among the largest third of all the churches in our denomination, don't you think we should be able to . . .?"

After two years of these kinds of affirm and build comments, this minister had (a) raised the level of congregational self-esteem, (b) strengthened the corporate self-image, (c) changed the congregational culture, (d) gained a hearing for several of his earlier proposals which previously had been dismissed as too extravagant for a small church, (e) earned a reputation as an irresponsible and incurable optimist, (f) persuaded the leaders to undertake several new programs, three of which were such success stories they surprised nearly everyone, (g) celebrated each of those three victories and thus reinforced the self-image and raised the congregational morale, and (h) become the pastor of a congregation averaging 160 at worship on Sunday morning without moving.

In summary, a useful style for the leader who is willing to intervene is to affirm resources, to ask questions, to be willing to redefine the issue or to revise the agenda and to give people a chance to talk themselves into a new view of the situation before asking them to make a decision. This requires patience, persistence, and understanding of the difference between articulating the issue and making the decision, a willingness to speak first, and a recognition of the fact that the longer the organization has been in existence, the more likely it will be hostile to new ideas. The response to this last fact of life, however, deserves a separate chapter.

THE FUTURE OF
A NEW IDEA

"Instead of paying that much interest over the life of a ten-year mortgage," questioned Harvey Williams as he was having a cup of coffee with his friend Jim Merton during the fellowship period between Sunday school and worship at First Church, "why don't we simply go out and raise the whole $300,000 on one Sunday? Last winter, when my wife and I spent a week in Florida, I read in the paper about a church that raised $2,000,000 on one Sunday. They have about three times as many members as we do, so if they could raise two million in one day, we should be able to raise a third of a million."

Harvey and Jim were both longtime members at First Church, and while Harvey had never served on any policy-making body, Jim was in his second term on the Board. The trustees had recommended that a major remodeling be undertaken on the sixty-five-year-old building, and the cost was estimated at $300,000. The trustees also were recommending that the congregation borrow the $300,000 on a ten-year mortgage and that the monthly payments be incorporated into the regular budget. Their report had been carried in the church newsletter the previous week. When he read it, Harvey made some quick calculations and concluded that the interest alone would amount to between $175,000 and $200,000 over the life of that ten-year mortgage.

"The Board will be officially receiving the trustees' report at their monthly meeting on Tuesday evening," responded Jim Merton. "Why don't you come down and present your suggestion to the full Board? I believe it has a lot of merit."

The following Tuesday evening Harvey left the weekly meeting of his service club early to be at the church at 7:20 P.M. He approached the person who chaired the Board that year and asked if he could have permission to speak when the trustees' report was being discussed. He was assured this would not be a problem. Every member was welcome to attend Board meetings and could be given the privilege of the floor.

At the appropriate time Harvey presented his suggestion. Before the evening was over, Harvey's proposal to raise $300,000 on one Sunday, along with the trustees' proposal to borrow $300,000, was referred to the finance committee for their consideration.

Ten weeks later, at a congregational meeting which took place on a night when Harvey was out of town on business, the congregation approved both the remodeling plan, with a few modest changes, and the proposal to borrow $300,000 on a ten-year mortgage.

During the discussion period Harvey's good friend and neighbor, Jackie Moore, asked, "Whatever happened to the proposal that we avoid paying all that interest by raising the entire $300,000 in one day?" The chairman of the finance committee replied that careful consideration had been given to that suggestion, but the committee had decided to go along with the recommendation of the trustees to borrow the money. Among the arguments in favor of that course of action were (1) future generations of members who would enjoy the benefits of the remodeling would help pay for it, (2) the prospects for continued inflation made it likely that in a few years the members could use cheap dollars to repay the expensive dollars they would be borrowing, (3) members could use the extra contributions they made to cover the interest payments as deductions on their income taxes so the real cost of that interest was less than it appeared to be, and (4) the members of the finance committee had serious doubts about whether it would be possible to raise that much money in one day, and the committee was not interested in scheduling a psychological defeat which would undermine congregational morale and perhaps even scuttle this overdue remodeling program.

Two days later, after Harvey had returned from his business trip, Jackie Moore went next door to explain to Harvey what had happened. Harvey obviously was both surprised and hurt. "I thought the idea had such obvious merit that it would carry itself. Everyone would be quick to understand the advantages and would be eager to give it a try. Suppose we had only raised $150,000. That wouldn't have been a defeat. We would have had $150,000 more than we now have, and we would have saved half of those huge interest payments."

"You shouldn't feel that you were rejected," counseled Jackie. "This was not a rejection of you personally. You need to understand that in every organization any unsolicited idea that comes in from the outside tends to be rejected. In the research lab where I work we call that NIH—not invented here. Second, in any organization the natural and predictable course of action is to accept and endorse the proposal of a powerful standing committee. Third, while your idea had merit, it didn't have any inside support. Your idea needed to be proposed by an influential insider, and it needed the support of at least a couple of other influential insiders. In addition to merit, your idea needed allies. Finally, you realize First Church is a big organization, and the natural tendency in big organizations is to choose the safest and most risk-free alternative possible."

"You make it sound like a business," protested Harvey. "Our pastor is always telling us that being a Christian means taking risks. Christ took risks. Why couldn't we venture down this road? After all, we really had nothing to lose. Suppose we only raised $100,000, we would still be that much better off than we are now."

"What you forget," admonished Jackie, "is that on issues like this one, our people tend to respond like church members, rather than like Christians."

What Jackie neglected to add was that to be implemented, Harvey's proposal would have had to survive four potential vetoes—the finance committee, the trustees, the Board, and the congregational meeting. That is a lot to ask of a new idea that has the strong support of only two people—when neither of those two supporters is an influential insider.

That is the true story of one idea.

For a different response look at the true story of another new idea.

Twenty-Seven Thousand Cookies

When the time came for the First Baptist Church of Montgomery, Alabama, to celebrate its one-hundred-fifty-fifth anniversary, an unusual format was chosen for that occasion. Instead of using that anniversary celebration, as thousands of congregations have done, to raise extra funds for missions or to publish a comprehensive church history or to remodel the building or to retire a debt, a different focus was chosen at First Baptist Church. It was decided to thank the people of Montgomery for their support, for the privilege of being a downtown church, and for the joy of being a part of that community. That was the heart of the month-long anniversary celebration called "To Montgomery with Love."

A many-faceted approach was used to express the gratitude of this historic congregation to the people of Montgomery. Elderly residents living alone were told they could call First Baptist Church and volunteers would come out and repair the front steps or wash the windows or paint the house or cut the grass or fix the plumbing or other minor home repairs. Several billboards around the city carried the message, "First Baptist Loves Montgomery." A big red heart replaced the letter *O* in the second syllable of the word Montgomery in the signs and the calling cards, and the members were given and wore three-and-one-half-inch plastic buttons that carried the message, "First Baptist Church Loves Montgomery." That slogan was based on I John 4:7, "Beloved, let us love one another . . . ." Radio and television stations carried the offers of help to those in need, and a mailing was sent out to every home in five zip codes.

In preparation for this month-long celebration of that anniversary the bulletin one Sunday morning carried, under banner headlines, "First Baptist Loves Montgomery," a plea to the members to volunteer their time, talents, energy, and skills.

The first Sunday of this month-long celebration was designated as a special day of recognition for officials of the criminal justice system. Nearly a thousand people were in attendance on that third Sunday in August, and a luncheon was held immediately following the eleven o'clock worship service for these officials and leaders and their families. During the next month the events offered by First Baptist Church included a day of prayer for government officials, free baby-sitting for single parents, the landscaping of the grounds at a local correctional center, free workshops for anyone from Montgomery who wanted to attend on nutrition, cardiopulmonary resusitation (C.P.R.), physical fitness, dating and sexuality, how to stop smoking, money management, living with stress, helping teenagers raise their parents, and other current concerns.

The fourth Sunday of August was set aside by the Baptist Young Women for members to bring chess sets, basketballs, toothbrushes, white socks, and other personal and recreational items that could be included in boxes being prepared as Christmas presents. The goal was that every prisoner in the state of Alabama would receive a Christmas present from this congregation. The theme for that Sunday was "Christmas in August Is Love."

The first Sunday after Labor Day was designated "Marriage Enrichment Sunday," and an eleven-hour day was planned on that theme, including a free lunch, lectures, worship, and a variety of workshops. This was

open to anyone who wanted to come at no cost to the registrant. The last Wednesday of August was set aside for a reception to honor all the public school teachers in Montgomery.

The morning of the fifth Sunday of this month-long celebration was Maxwell-Gunter recognition day for persons stationed at either of those two air bases. The capstone of the anniversary celebration was a free concert open to the general public at the Montgomery Civic Center starring Tom Netherton and attended by nearly five thousand persons.

Perhaps the most novel feature of "To Montgomery with Love" was the goal to personally deliver to every firefighter, police officer, teacher, nurse, and public servant in Mongtomery a bag of homemade cookies with a word of gratitude for their work. At 3:00 A.M. one morning, for example, volunteers from First Baptist Church took cookies, tea, and coffee to nurses on duty in a local hospital. Other volunteers took cookies to the engineers and program people working the midnight-to-eight shift at the local radio and television stations. Every shopping mall had a stand supplying free coffee, tea, and cookies to those who worked there. A total of 27,000 cookies were baked and personally delivered, each with the message, "To Montgomery with Love."

Not only is this a remarkable example of a unique approach to celebrating a church's anniversary, it also is an excellent illustration of fostering creativity. The process of implementing this idea is as interesting as the content. Seven components merit attention. First, someone had a brilliant idea, but instead of simply thinking about it and dismissing it with the usual, "Someday when we have more time, we ought to give it a try," that idea was turned into a plan of action.

Second, the decision-making process at First Baptist Church did not require this new idea to survive a series of potential vetoes as it passed through various committees and boards, each with the power to reject it. From the time the idea was first hatched until it was implemented, the key test was not, "Do you approve it?" but rather, "Will you help implement it?" This plan needed hundreds of *yes* votes. The *no* votes were not sought, since they would not be useful in implementing it.

Third, the criteria used in evaluating and refining the original idea were not the usual, "Do I like it?" or "Do I like the person who originated it?" Instead, three carefully thought-out criteria were used for evaluation. Every activity had to meet at least two of these three criteria:

1. Will it involve our people in reaching out?
2. Will it make a significant impact on our community?
3. Does it offer the possibility of becoming a continuing ministry within our program here at First Baptist Church?

Fourth, instead of assigning the implementation responsibility to a standing committee or board, where there might be differences of opinion on the merits of the plan, a special ad hoc or steering committee was created. By definition only those who were enthusiastic about the idea were asked to help implement it. All too often the stance of the members of a standing committee or official governing board is "We can do only that which is clearly permitted." By contrast the members of the typical ad hoc or temporary committee usually are willing to undertake any responsibility except that which is clearly and specifically prohibited.

Fifth, and some will argue this is the most critical point in encouraging innovation and converting creative ideas into action plans, an exceptionally gifted, busy, strong, and entrepreneurial individual was asked to be the volunteer director of "To Montgomery with Love." The job description for this director consisted of seven brief statements.

1. Pray for God's guidance in our ministry.
2. Select a proposed activity and present it to the steering committee for approval.
3. Upon approval, enlist necessary persons and secure resources necessary to accomplish that activity.
4. Make timely progress reports to the steering committee.
5. Attend scheduled committee meetings.
6. Complete the activity.
7. Understand there is no budget for this program.

As soon as it was agreed that a specific action proposal met the criteria for evaluation, the clear message was, "Let's go!"

Sixth, "To Montgomery with Love" gave hundreds of volunteers a chance to vote their approval of the concept by expressing their creativity through their hands by the giving of their time and energy, by the exercise of their talents, and by helping others.

Finally, the entire program was based on the assumption that the members would respond when challenged. Too often creative ideas are not implemented because those creating the new idea do not have that degree of confidence in people. That was one of the reasons Harvey Williams' proposal to raise $300,000 in one day was never implemented. Too often people are viewed as liabilities rather than as assets.

A persuasive argument could have been made, for example, that mid-August to mid-September in Alabama is a time for vacations or for staying in air-conditioned buildings, not for going out to say "Thank you!" to strangers. The leaders at First Baptist Church, however, had confidence the members would respond to a creative challenge. After all, 27,000 homemade cookies is only two thousand two hundred and fifty dozen!

Another way of looking at what happened to that novel approach to celebrating an anniversary at First Baptist Church is to use the three-phase theory of innovation described by Rosabeth Moss Kanter.[1] She states the prototypical innovation goes through three phases. First, the project has to be defined. At First Baptist Church the project was defined in general terms as the celebration of an anniversary. In more specific terms it was defined as (a) reaching out beyond the membership to the entire community, (b) maximizing the involvement of a huge number of members, and (c) making an impact on the entire community.

Kanter identifies the second state of innovation as building a coalition. Too often that second step consists of going around and seeking the approval of every potential veto group. This creates a situation that invites opponents to register their negative votes. At First Baptist Church the process of building a coalition focused on participation, rather than overcoming potential vetoes.

The third stage is the action phase or implementation. In this large, diverse downtown congregation members were offered literally scores of opportunities for helping to implement the plan. The need for 27,000 cookies gave many people, who otherwise might have felt they had nothing to offer, a chance to contribute and to register their support by their actions.

Another way to describe this response to a new idea is that it represents an exercise of entrepreneurial leadership. The entrepreneurial leader in any organization usually needs more power than normally goes with that particular office or position. In this same essay Kanter makes the point that in large organizations powerlessness tends to corrupt. The lack of power tends to attract persons who are more comfortable guarding their own turf rather than encouraging creativity. The entrepreneurial personality frequently oversteps the boundaries of that office and gathers the power that makes possible the mobilization of the resources necessary to implement that new idea. It may be, as Kanter suggests, that the critical characteristic in the leader who will produce innovative achievements is the capability to see a vision that goes beyond the scope of that leader's legitimate authority and a willingness to mobilize those additional resources necessary to turn that vision into reality.

One approach to nurturing a fertile organizational climate for such an entrepreneurial personality is to create a new position and make the holder of that new office accountable to a new ad hoc committee. In that arrangement there are no precedents that limit the power of either the individual or that special committee. That was the approach followed at First Baptist Church.

The same point can be illustrated by the story of Harvey Williams and his idea of raising $300,000 in one day. If there had been any real interest in Harvey's proposal, the most productive response would *not* have been to refer it, along with the trustees' report, to the finance committee. A far more positive approach would have been to create a special committee to examine Harvey's proposal and to give that committee the authority to plan the effort to raise that much money in one day, to formulate guidelines, and to identify the person who would direct that program. That procedure would have placed the focus on action rather than on overcoming potential vetoes.

The effective leader who seeks to encourage creativity and innovation can recognize those occasions when it will be necessary to create a special ad hoc committee rather than "work within the channels." Those leaders also understand the distinctive contributions that can be made by entrepreneurial individuals if they have the organizational freedom to act.

ALLIES, COALITIONS, AND MEETINGS

The Parkview Community Church was founded on the growing edge of a sunbelt city in the late 1960s. Approximately a dozen years later it was averaging nearly two hundred at worship on Sunday morning when the mission-developer pastor resigned to accept a call to a church in Iowa. The next several years brought (a) a prolonged, disastrous, and divisive pastorate, (b) a decline in worship attendance to fewer than one hundred on the typical Sunday morning, (c) a cutback in programming to only worship services, Sunday school, and a weakened women's organization, (d) a financial crisis as the congregation became unable to meet the $5,000 monthly payments on the mortgage on that beautiful new building that had been completed in 1975 and had to seek an annual subsidy from the denomination, (e) a serious morale problem, and (f) an intentional interim pastorate by a sixty-nine-year-old retired minister who loved the people, halted the decline, restored a reasonably strong self-image, and encouraged the members to seek a new permanent pastor.

Three years ago the new pastor arrived. This new minister is a gifted preacher, a hard worker, an excellent teacher, and convinced the best days of this congregation lie in the future. This optimistic attitude has given new hope to several of the leaders, most of whom have been in office for at least a decade. The new pastor also is basically a task-oriented individual who is moderately introverted and somewhat quick to make decisions and to judge the actions of others.

Recently the denominational executive for that region came by to spend an afternoon and evening at Parkview. He is concerned that the denomination is still providing one-half of the money for those $5,000 monthly payments on the mortgage, but is delighted to learn the Sunday morning worship attendance is now averaging close to 140.

After listening for an hour to the pastor describe a detailed and impressive strategy for program expansion, new member enlistment, and leadership development, the denominational executive asked, "Your three-part plan makes a lot of sense to me, and I gather you are ready to begin implementing it. Your plan certainly appears to fit the circumstances, but you haven't mentioned allies. Who are the folks here who will help you turn your plans into reality?"

"I'm not sure what you mean by your question," responded the pastor. "If I understand your question correctly, the answer is the officers. They approved every phase of it at last month's Board meeting. My plan was approved, not only without any dissenting votes, but without even any negative comments."

"That raises another question, but let's hold that for a minute," continued the denominational executive. "I don't doubt for a minute that you have everyone's approval. The folks here have been waiting for nearly a decade for a pastor to lead them, but that's not my question. By allies I mean people with clout in this congregation who not only will influence others to help, but will themselves pitch in and work to turn your dream into tomorrow's church. Who are they?"

After a minute or so of silent reflection, the pastor replied, "I guess my three best allies are Harold Wilson, Ian MacGregor, and Jack DeYoung."

Later that afternoon this denominational official was talking with Harold Wilson and asked, "What do you think of your pastor's plans to rebuild this congregation?"

"I have nothing but favorable comments," came the quick response. "Our new minister is a very gifted individual, and I think it's a great program. No one is a stronger supporter of our new minister than my family and I are."

"I agree it's a great plan," concurred the denominational executive, "but I believe that plan will require the assistance of some influential leaders here who also will pitch in and give the time and energy necessary to turn that vision into reality. Could you predict who will be this minister's most influential and effective allies?"

"That's a good question!" reflected Harold. "I agree that our minister can't pull that off alone. Let's see now, who will be the best allies? Right offhand, I can't answer that. About all I can tell you for sure is I don't meet your definition. Since I am one of the few charter members still around, I guess I do have some influence with

"Ideas need allies!"

—FRIAR TUCK

a few of the old timers, but we now have two kids in college and two in high school, so about a year ago I took a second job in order to pay the bills. In addition to my regular work, I have a sales job that takes three evenings a week plus all day Saturday. I'm afraid I simply can't be one of those allies."

A similar interview with Ian MacGregor produced this response, "You're right, the minister is going to need allies, but I guess I won't be one of them. A week ago I was told I have to start chemotherapy treatments and that if I'm lucky I'll probably need at least six months of them to get this problem licked. I guess you know what those treatments do to a person, so I'm afraid I won't be of any help, but please understand, I strongly support what our minister has proposed."

Jack DeYoung's response, when asked if he could be counted on as an influential and active ally, was one of surprise, "You gotta be kidding! In the first place I don't have a nickel's worth of influence around here. Sarah and I joined Parkview shortly after our new minister arrived and about a year ago, when Kelly Smithson moved away, I was asked to fill that vacancy on the Board. Why they asked me I don't know, since I really haven't been that active here. Now my wife, Sarah, she may be the one you want to talk to about being an ally since she's been much more active here than I have."

Later Sarah explained her role, "I think we have a wonderful minister, and I wish I could do more to help because I believe that's a great program, but we've got a five-year-old and a pair of twins who just turned two. Besides that I keep the books for a man who builds houses and he comes over about two evenings a week for an hour or two to go over the accounts, so I'm really tied down to my home."

What do you estimate are the chances this minister's carefully worked out action plan will become reality?

Supporters or Allies?

This brief case study illustrates four issues that repeatedly confront leaders, both inside and outside the church.

The first is the distinction between the official support or approval for a course of action and the help necessary to implement the plan. This minister appears to have widespread approval for the proposed program, or, to be more precise, there appears to be a complete lack of opposition. That is a significant component of the climate for action, but it is not the same as getting the job done. It appears this pastor misread the lack of opposition and the passive approval as representing active support.

The process or sequence for planned change provides a conceptual framework for examining this. The first step in initiating change from within a voluntary organization is dissatisfaction with the status quo. There was dissatisfaction with the status quo at Parkview. The longtime members long for a return to the day when the sanctuary was filled nearly every Sunday. They are not happy with the present situation.

The second step in planned change is the creation of an initiating group that will respond to that discontent with a proposed course of action. At Parkview the minister constituted a one-person initiating group to respond to the discontent and unilaterally had developed an impressive plan of action. The third step, the organization of a support group, apparently has been overlooked as the pastor is ready to begin to implement that three-part action plan without the commitment of allies. One of the most well traveled roads to frustration in planned change is to ignore this step.

The effective leader recognizes the value of allies and does not act alone when allies are essential to the implementation of a program. That third step of building a support group should precede any effort to implement what appears to be a highly meritorious plan. The fourth step is to implement the plan.

This minister is confronted with what boils down to four tactical choices in enlisting allies. One choice is to seek out individuals who not only will endorse his strategy, but also actively work to help turn that dream into reality.

A second choice is to enlist committees as the primary allies and work with and through committees. A third choice is available to those charismatic personalities who can attract loyal followers who will obey the leader's wishes and orders. A fourth alternative is to plug along single-handedly and become increasingly frustrated because the size and the nature of the task exceeds the resources one individual can bring to that assignment. This fourth alternative tends to produce both a high level of frustration and short pastorates.

The leadership role chosen by a minister will have a profound impact on the appropriate procedure for enlisting allies. The minister who chooses to function as one leader among a group of leaders will need individual fellow leaders as allies. The minister who decides to be a catalytic leader probably will be more

effective by placing a major emphasis on working with committees, choirs, classes, and other groups as the principal allies. The pastor who is a charismatic or magnetic personality may choose to depend on loyal followers who are attracted by his or her personality rather than the merits of a specific proposal, or rather than attempting to enlist committees or groups as allies.

One of the reasons this is both a significant and difficult issue is that many seminaries still teach the concept that a pastor should function in a shared leadership role as one among a team of leaders, but most systems of congregational self-government called for by the denominational polity are designed on the assumption the pastor will be *the* leader in that congregation. This expectation often is reinforced by the congregation's culture, traditions, and choice of lay leaders. Too often this produces what was mentioned in the previous chapter as the corruption of powerlessness.

The Value of Coalitions

A second point illustrated by this episode at Parkview Church can be summarized by five words: size, self-image, inertia, powerlessness, and coalitions. This is not a small congregation. The average attendance of 140 at worship on Sunday morning means it is larger than three out of four Protestant congregations on the North American continent. It is too large for the minister to function effectively without active allies. This introduces a second factor. The congregational self-image is that of a small church. The people perceive a limited future ahead. This means the self-image must be enhanced as a part of that overall strategy.

Third, Isaac Newton's first law of motion also applies to religious organizations. A body at rest tends to remain at rest, and a body in motion tends to remain in motion. The pastor at Parkview Church needs the help of others in overcoming this inertia or passivity in a congregation that has been at rest for several years. The momentum that had been created during the early years of that first pastorate has been lost.

The fourth word to help explain this case study is powerlessness. Whenever one individual functions alone in a large and complex organization, and Parkview is both large and complex, that individual often feels isolated—and isolation often produces the feeling of powerlessness.

One response to that feeling of powerlessness is to spend most or all of the time on routine duties and to respond when someone raises questions or seeks help. It is easy to justify this reactive stance with the explanation, "All the people here really want is a chaplain, they don't want a minister who will challenge them with a call to mission and ministry." That may be an accurate portrayal of what the people appear to want, but not of what that parish needs if it is to be faithful to the call of the Lord. That response usually represents an abdication of a leadership role.

A second response is to turn to the Gospel According to Luke for justification (Luke 10:10-11), make it known to the denominational leaders that the time has come to move on, and prepare to shake the dust of that community from your feet. This is both a common cause of short pastorates and a means of postponing the decision about accepting the role of an initiating leader.

A third, and far more productive response, to that feeling of powerlessness, is to build a coalition. Coalitions or alliances usually display four or five common characteristics.[1] First, as was pointed out earlier, this process requires that at least one individual or group be sufficiently discontent with the status quo to be motivated to alter the present state of affairs. Second is the need to articulate that source of discontent in terms that will attract allies. This is the common denominator of the coalition. All participants share a common pain or point of discontent. Third, a course of action can be identified and accepted by all members of that potential coalition as a promising way of relieving their discontent. It is not uncommon for some discontented people to stay out of that coalition because they are not convinced that course of action is the appropriate response to the problem.

Fourth, a plan to implement that course of action is developed and carried out. Frequently this requires the support of those who are not members of that original initiating group, but who can provide support or resources (votes, money, time, energy, skills) that are essential to implement the plan.

Fifth, while it is not essential, a valuable component for any coalition that expects to remain together to implement new goals is to celebrate every victory and institutionalize the coalition as an ongoing group.

A simple example of this process can be seen in what happened at the Hilltop Church when Alice Jones was asked to replace Ethel Baxter as the teacher of the third- and fourth-grade Sunday school class in that room at the end of the hall. Ethel had taught that class for nine years but finally decided she would not teach another year. After her third Sunday on the job, Alice said to Ethel one day, "How in the world did you teach that many kids in that tiny room for nine years? Why didn't you demand that the trustees do something to improve that room? The acoustics are terrible, the door won't close, and there simply are too many kids for that size room."

Ethel replied, "I know exactly what you mean, and it'll be worse in the winter when you discover how cold it can get in there. I tried for eight years to get someone to do something about it, but no one would pay any attention to me, so I told the committee that this past year would be my last. I felt I had done my share."

That is a classic statement of powerlessness, and of one response to it. Alice soon discovered the trustees had a high level of competence and long experience in ignoring the pleas of Sunday school teachers. "After all, it's only for one hour a week. If Ethel could do it for nine years, you should be able to survive for another year or two until we can find the money to fix it up."

Alice persisted, a key factor in coalition building. Eventually she enlisted the interest of two mothers of fourth-grade children, the father of a third-grader who had just moved to this community from a congregation that had far better facilities for Sunday school, the minister, and one sympathetic trustee. Alice had completed the second step. She had her allies. What Alice really wanted was the construction of a new church school wing to this eighty-three-year-old structure, but when she found zero support for this among her allies, she settled for the short-term and attainable goal of remodeling her present room. Coalition builders frequently have to accept compromise.

After studying the situation for a couple of hours one Sunday afternoon, this initiating group came up with a list of changes and repairs that included knocking out the wall next to the corridor and extending that room into the hall, building a new entrance for the room across the hall as well as a new entrance into this enlarged room, the installation of acoustical tile on the ceiling, storm sashes for all four of the windows, two large bulletin boards, drapes on the windows, carpet for the floor and, of course, repainting all the walls. They made two dozen copies of this list, placed one in a small box neatly wrapped in Christmas wrapping paper, called on all the parents of the children in that class plus some other members who were presumed to be sympathetic to the change and asked, "Would you like to contribute some money and/or work for a Christmas present for the

WHEN THINGS ARE GOING RIGHT ONE CAN DEFY GRAVITY!

WHEE!

YIPPEE!

BANDWAGON

HURRAY!

Momentum comes with celebrations!

—FRIAR TUCK

third- and fourth-grade Sunday school class here at Hilltop Church?" They received $961, two good used rugs, and nearly 200 hours of volunteer labor. On the third Sunday of Advent most of the children and well over one-half of the adults gathered at the door of the remodeled room before the Sunday school hour for a brief open house. A fourth-grade boy and a third-grade girl untied a huge red bow that Alice had tied across the doorway earlier that morning and invited everyone in to see the attractive "new" room. When Arthur Moore, a trustee, questioned, "Who gave permission for this remodeling?" his wife, who taught the first- and second-grade class at the other end of the hall, replied, "Art, shut up! Be glad Alice didn't wait for you and the trustees to get around to doing something."

Ethel Baxter felt powerless and resigned. Alice Jones was discontended, articulated her discontent, and enlisted allies, all of whom saw a payoff in a more attractive room for the children. That initiating group devised a plan of action, expanded the coalition to gather the necessary resources, and implemented the plan. Alice also made sure that many adults were present for the highly visible celebration of the victory. When that story was fed into the grapevine, the word was out, "That Alice Jones sure knows how to get things done when she sets her mind to it." That made it easier for Alice to enlist allies for her next project. People tend to be attracted to a winner.

The new minister at Parkview Church needs someone like Alice Jones not only to help him see the value of allies, but also to assist in building a coalition that could help the pastor implement that impressive strategy.

Disagreement or Apathy?

A third point that is illustrated by the story of Parkview Community Church surfaced when the pastor pointed out that not only had there been unanimous approval at the Board meeting, but also no negative comments were heard.

While there are many exceptions to this generalization, that lack of any negative comments should have been read as at least an amber flag, not a green light.

This lack of articulated disagreement on an important issue often suggests (a) passivity or (b) a climate or atmosphere that inhibits the freedom to voice one's real feelings or (c) a lack of involvement or interest by any of the participants in what is being discussed or (d) a feeling that what is being proposed is so far removed from reality that it does not deserve serious criticism.

The sensitive leader listens for what is not being said, as well as for agreement or disagreement.

Dual Leadership

A fourth issue illustrated by the situation at Parkview Church is the concept of dual leadership. The basic generalization is that every organization needs both a task-oriented leader and also a person-centered or social leader.[2]

The pastor appears to be a creative and determined individual who also has a strong task orientation. The focus tends to be on the problem and working out a solution, rather than on enlisting allies. This in itself is not bad. Most adults are either strongly task-oriented or primarily person-centered. Few are able to fulfill both roles, but both roles are needed. The first keeps the world moving. The second keeps it from flying apart.

This strongly task-oriented pastor, who also appears to be somewhat introverted, not only needs allies and a greater sensitivity to the distinction between lack of disagreement and apathy, but also would benefit from understanding the role of dual leadership.

The effectiveness of this minister probably would be greatly enhanced by enlisting as an ally a close personal friend from among the membership who is extroverted, basically person-centered, respected, likes people, and also is strongly supportive of that three-part action plan devised by the minister. It obviously would help if this close friend, co-leader, and ally had been involved in the development of this plan of action, or at least in the revision of the basic design.

This concept of dual leadership, which can be traced back to the Laboratory of Social Relations that was organized at Harvard University in 1947,[3] has widespread application. One version is the person-centered and extroverted college president who works very closely with a task-oriented dean or vice-president of academic affairs.

Another is the competent, serious, hard-working, and task-oriented senior pastor who encourages the congregation to find a warm-hearted, person-centered, loving, and extroverted person to serve as the associate minister, to staff the Christian education committee, call on prospective new members and shut-ins, work with the youth, and preach a dozen Sundays a year. The members brag about their wonderful ministerial team, are delighted at how everything in the parish appears to run so smoothly, and are disappointed four years later when the widely loved associate minister moves on to become the pastor of a smaller congregation. The leaders are surprised, but pleased, when the freewill offering for the departing minister adds up to an impressive $3,285. Several years later, after a total of eleven years with that congregation, the senior resigns to accept a position as a denominational official. The members get together and contribute a total of $2,500 as a farewell gift to their senior minister. The reason the gift is that large is that the two leaders who spear-headed this effort each contributed $300.

Both leadership roles are needed. The task-oriented leader challenges people to exceed their own self-imposed limitations, contributes what everyone agrees are excellent ideas, rarely is late for a meeting or fails to keep an appointment, keeps things moving, reminds everyone of what their assignment is, shakes a lot of hands, intimidates at least a third of the members but is never aware of that fact, earns the respect of many, wins few close friends, and frequently, but almost always, undercuts the unity of the organization or committee.

The person-centered leader helps keep each member aware of his or her individual importance—both as a child of God and as a member of the group—restores a sense of unity, frequently is late for meetings or appointments, spends a fair amount of time every week hugging people, draws out the shy or bashful and the inarticulate, wins a host of friends, contributes few original ideas but creates lots of laughter, does not intimidate anyone, and is greatly missed following his or her departure.

The most effective leaders understand and appreciate, but are not seriously threatened by, this concept of dual leadership.

Institutionally, most of our society is still organized on the principle of single leaders. Whether one looks at government, business, the church, educational institutions, health delivery organizations, or the military, the dominant pattern is still of one-person leadership positions, sometimes with an assistant, but rarely with an institutionalized version of dual leadership.

Recent years have brought literally hundreds of efforts to create "co-pastorates" or "joint pastorates" or "team ministries" or "dual pastorates." (The survivor of one dual pastorate commented, "The error was that this arrangement was explained to me orally, never in writing. The correct spelling was duel, not dual.") An increasing proportion of these co-pastorates have been designed to accommodate the career ambitions of clergy couples, but that is another story. For those composed of two unrelated individuals, however, the emphasis frequently has been on collegiability, personal compatibility, and professional responsibilities. Rarely has this concept of dual leadership been a central criterion in creating a co-pastorate.

The importance of this concept of dual leadership originally surfaced in the studies and experiments first conducted forty years ago to identify the characteristics of an effective committee—and that raises a related subject that is of central importance to the wise leader.

Committees and Meetings

"We must include a couple of people from the Fellowship Class," declared a well-informed member of Bethany Church. "Everyone knows that class includes at least half of the most influential members in this church. If we want this project to go, we'll need the support of the people in the Fellowship Class."

"We should have at least one of the new younger members," added a sixty-three-year-old. "The young people of today are the church of tomorrow."

"Don't forget we need to put a teenager on every committee."

"Yes, and we also need to include someone from the choir and the women's fellowship," suggested someone else.

Fifteen minutes later the person who had called this ad hoc group together in his home interrupted by announcing, "When we began, we agreed we wanted no more than ten or twelve people on this committee and so far we have suggestions that total sixteen. Where do you want to cut?"

"Before we forget, we must be sure to include someone who lives on the east side of town," declared someone else. "Although most of our members live north and west, we do have quite a few east siders, and we don't want them to feel they aren't represented."

This conversation illustrates one of the organizing principles for constituting a committee. This is to make sure every faction, interest group, class, organization, and segment of the constituency is represented. Frequently this results in a committee of from a dozen to several dozen members.

A better approach would be to begin with two questions. First, what do we want to happen? Second, what has been learned by the people who have researched this subject that can be useful to us in creating a new committee?

Experience suggests at least a half dozen reasons why some people favor large committees that may include as many as seventy people. (1) This is a means of assuring that every point of view, faction, potential opponent, and interest group is represented. (2) A very large committee creates the possibility of many different lines of communication directly from the committee to the constituency. (3) The larger the committee, the greater the probability that either the staff and/or a small number of hard-working, knowledgeable, and dedicated volunteers who do their homework can determine direction, priorities, and recommendations. (4) Those opposed to radical change are comforted by the knowledge that large committees are more likely to seek the lowest common denominator of agreement and protect the status quo rather than to come forth with revolutionary ideas. (The Federal Convention of 1787 was an outstanding exception to this generalization. It was composed of fifty-five delegates, and they came up with a revolutionary document called the Constitution of the United States of America. It should be noted, however, that only thirty-nine delegates signed it and several left early in protest over the direction the Constitution took. The Commission for a New Lutheran Church may turn out to be another exception to that generalization.) (5) A very large committee enables many different individuals to share in the deliberations and thus should broaden the base of ownership of the recommendations. (6) The very size of the committee stands as evidence against charges of elitism because it allows for inclusion of representatives from a variety of minority groups.

Critics of large committees add that the large committees (a) encourage absenteeism, "No one will miss me if I don't go," (b) too often become polarized and produce majority recommendations and minority dissents which then polarize the congregation, (c) avoid conflict by producing watered-down compromises, (d) require too much time to rebuild a sense of community at the beginning of each meeting, and (e) spend too much time "playing catch up" at the beginning of each meeting.

Others will not be impressed by these arguments and will urge, "We should utilize all this accumulated wisdom and research to create what is most likely to be an effective committee of people who will be compatible, creative, and productive, and who will come up with the best possible set of recommendations." How do we create such a committee?

While there are few guarantees in life, a dozen generalizations can be offered that will increase the probability of securing that result.

How Large?

First, and perhaps most important, the most effective committees are composed of five or seven persons. Not three, not nine, not twelve. (The biblical evidence suggests that with a committee of twelve, it will not a long before one will deny he ever knew you and another will betray you.) If it appears that a problem of power may arise, a committee of three should be avoided. It is difficult for three people to meet and survive what in a group of seven would be termed "healthy disagreement." In a committee of three the one who disagrees often ends up a solitary loser. In a committee of five or seven that same person with the same point of view also may end up on the losing side, but at least has the possibility of the solace of one or two others who share the same strongly held minority conviction.

If at all possible, choose a range of types of personalities for the committee. If they are all hyperactive, high participant types, this probably will result in excessive competition. If most are shy or introverted, the meeting may drag, bore the one or two high participant types, and be short on creative ideas and stimulating exchanges. Include both articulate leaders and persons who are active and reflective listeners.

When the committee exceeds seven, it is easy for one or two to stop talking to all the others at the table and to focus their attention solely on one or two of the leaders or to "drop out" completely and simply become passive observers.

The temptation to include representatives from a variety of points of view, organizations, groups, and other segments of the population frequently produces excessively large committees. Unless the agenda includes a major emphasis on information giving and receiving, it usually is appropriate to limit the number of persons attending a meeting to no more than five to ten.

The larger the number of persons invited to a meeting (a) the lower the proportion who will attend, (b) the larger the proportion who either will arrive late and/or leave early, (c) the greater the skill required of the presiding officer, (d) the greater the temptation for most persons to assume a passive role, (e) the easier it is for a few individuals to dominate the meeting, (f) the shorter the period of time between necessary breaks, (g) the greater the need for clearly defined and widely accepted rules of procedures (such as *Robert's Rules of Order*), (h) the sooner that meeting will reach the point of diminishing returns, (i) the more difficult it will be to resolve a complex or controversial issue, (j) the more likely some participants will leave convinced that their point of view was not heard, (k) the greater the need to minimize the emphasis on abstract verbal communication and to maximize visual imagery, (l) the greater the need for deliberate and skilled efforts to build and maintain a group identity, (m) the weaker the motivation of the particpants to focus on group goals and the greater the chances that individual goals will override the goals of the group, and (n) the more important are such physical factors as comfortable chairs, excellent acoustics, an attractive physical focal point, good sight lines for each participant, a comfortable room temperature, and an agenda for each session that has been given to everyone well in advance of the meeting.

In other words, a great deal more effort is required to plan and conduct a productive meeting of a large number of persons than is necessary for a smaller number.

Who Is in Charge?

A second characteristic of the effective committee is very simple to describe, but often ignored. Someone is in charge of preparing the agenda, planning the sequence of the discussion, reminding each participant at least once of the time and place, calling the meeting to order at the appointed hour, declaring the time has come for a break if that becomes appropriate, and terminating the meeting when it is over, rather than allowing it to die by apathy.

What Is the Purpose?

A third factor that applies to all types of meetings in general and to committee meetings in particular is to be clear in conceptualizing the type of meeting that is being scheduled. Most meetings fit into one of seven categories.

1. Information giving
2. Information giving and receiving
3. Planning
4. Problem solving
5. Decision making
6. Social or inspirational
7. Therapeutic

Participants will find meetings more satisfying if care is exercised to run various types of meetings sequentially, not concurrently. For example, a therapeutic meeting to respond to someone's wounded feelings should not be carried on concurrently with a decision-making meeting. A common practice is to encourage the "social meetings," the "information sharing meetings," and the "therapy meetings" to be held during the coffee break and/or after the decision-making meeting has been concluded.

Another value in looking at meetings by type is that this should influence both the size and the composition of the group. For example, planning meetings and problem-solving meetings should include no more than five to seven persons while an information-giving meeting may include hundreds of people, and the large size provides for a more productive meeting of that type.

Every participant should know why this committee is meeting at this time. The assignment or task or charge should be clear, and it is best if the participants can be advised of this at least a day or two before the committee is to meet.

Dual Leadership

Fourth, as was pointed out earlier, most committees will function more effectively if the group includes one person who fills the need for a task-oriented leader and another person who fills the role of the person-centered social leader and also has a good sense of humor.

The Setting

Fifth, the longer the committee is expected to meet, the more important the physical setting.[4] An open circle is useful if the focus is to be on interpersonal relationships. If the focus is on "business or a "task," it usually is better for all the participants to sit around a table. A round table is ideal for five, a square table can work for seven, but a round table is better.

If it is necessary to have a session or council or consistory or board involving no more than fourteen or fifteen participants, it may be possible to meet seated around a large table. When the size of the group reaches eighteen to twenty or more, it almost certainly will be better to have the two or three leaders seated at a table facing the rest of the participants who also are seated at tables facing the leaders.

The longer the meeting is to last and/or the larger the group, the more important are comfortable chairs, tables, good lighting without glare, an absence of distracting noise, recesses or "breaks" every fifty to ninety minutes, and, perhaps most important of all, laughter. Laughter is the lubricant that keeps large and extended meetings from becoming abrasive experiences.

Refreshments

Sixth, occasionally it is necessary to bring a large group of people together for some type of meeting, and the meeting may run for two hours or more. This raises the issue of refreshments. As a general rule, the larger the group, the more important are refreshments.

In more specific terms, a useful guideline follows this general pattern:

3-7 persons:	a choice of beverages
7-10 persons:	a wider choice of beverages
10-20 persons:	a choice of beverages and a snack
20-35 persons:	a choice of beverages and a choice of snacks
35-50 persons:	a wider choice of beverages and a wider choice of snacks, or, if it is evening, begin with a beverage and a dessert
50-plus persons:	schedule the meeting around or after a meal

(In selecting beverages it should be noted that 70 percent of all coffee is consumed before 10:00 A.M.)

A related generalization is that if it is essential that everyone be present at the beginning of the meeting, and if more than thirty-five persons are invited, refreshments should be served at the beginning. If having everyone present at the beginning is not a high priority, it may be better to serve the refreshments later and thus encourage the expression of "second thoughts" before the participants leave.

If the business part of the meeting is to extend for more than thirty-five minutes, and more than two dozen persons are present, it may be wise to serve refreshments during the mid-meeting "break-to-stretch" interruption. If the meeting is to extend for less than 105 minutes, it may be better to combine refreshments with the various therapeutic meetings, social meetings, and information-sharing meetings that have been postponed for nearly two hours and that often follow such a business meeting.

It also is useful to remember that the smaller the number of participants, the easier it is to combine refreshments with the meeting without that being disruptive.

Overcoming Negativism

Seventh, some committee meetings begin on a negative note and continue in that vein until adjournment. Not only are such meetings rarely productive, they also often "ruin the rest of the day" for many of the participants.

One widely used method for increasing the level of disagreement from the very beginning is to choose only highly articulate individuals who possess firmly held opinions on nearly every subject that may come up during the course of this meeting. The resulting competition is likely to produce quick disagreement on a variety of subjects.

At least four approaches exist that can be used to minimize the tendency to begin with disagreement. The first was mentioned earlier. One criterion in selecting the members of a committee could be to choose a couple of highly articulate individuals, at least one or two reflective types who usually think and listen before speaking, perhaps one or two widely respected persons who identify themselves as "listeners, not talkers," and a maximum of one person who is long on opinions, short on problem-solving skills, and tends to arouse hostility.

A second approach is sometimes referred to as the "itemized response." Before anyone can offer a negative opinion, that person must state three positive aspects of the proposal before the group and ask at least one information-seeking question. Only after that sequence has been completed is the person free to voice a negative opinion.

If it is a problem-solving meeting or a decision-making meeting, perhaps the best approach is to begin with a review of the facts. Delay any opportunity for participants to inject opinions or to discuss specific courses of action. Begin by going over the facts. Lay a factual foundation for the discussion that will follow. Next, ask for reactions to the facts. How do people feel about them? After those two preliminary steps have been taken, it is appropriate to elicit opinions on what should be done to solve the problem or on the course of action to be chosen.

In some settings an effective means of minimizing that initial outburst of disagreement is to be careful in stating the question. Most planning committees are created, for example, because the people have decided the status quo is no longer a viable alternative. Therefore do not begin with a statement that suggests, "We have two alternatives. One is to seek to perpetuate yesterday into tomorrow. The other is to change." A better beginning point would be to suggest, "The reason we are meeting is that it appears we no longer can continue as we have been in the past. One alternative is to make this set of changes. Another is to choose a different course of action and makes these changes. Does anyone have any facts to introduce into our discussion about either alternative?"

If strong disagreement surfaces early in the meeting and threatens to become disruptive, a useful tactic is to shift the discussion back to the facts.

It also must be recognized that frequently what appears to be disagreement is actually a breakdown in communication. The two who impress one another as disagreeing with each other may in fact be talking about different subjects or experiences. The words may not represent the thoughts of either participant.

When this happens, it may be useful for the person chairing the committee to rephrase and "play back" first what one person appears to be seeking to communicate and subsequently do the same with the other person. "Kim, if I hear you correctly, this is the point you are making. Is this a fair statement of your position?" This interruption not only may improve the communication process and help each person state his or her position more clearly, the time used for this also may give all the participants a chance to catch up in their own thinking and also allow the temperature of the discussion to drop by several degrees. It may be wise for the social leader in the group to do this while the task leader concentrates on the facts and the assignment.

Is Anyone Listening?

An eighth component in creating an effective committee is to be sure to include at least one person who is a skilled and active listener. Most adults have had far more formal training in communication by speaking and by writing than by listening. Listening is a skill that can be learned, and it may be contagious. (Those last five words express a hope, not a carefully researched and demonstrated fact!) A skilled and active listener can silently communicate to each speaker, "I am listening, I hear what you are saying, and I am offering you nonverbal feedback that not only proves you are being heard, but also can be used by you to determine what you say next." The silent recognition and affirmation communicated by even one good listener in a committee of seven people can reduce tension, decrease the latent hostility, accelerate the pace of the meeting, and share the disappointment of the one whose suggestion is not adopted. Most people can adjust to the fact that their suggestion has come in second to an even better idea if their proposal has received a fair hearing. It is harder to accept the fact that the group really did not reject your suggestion, they simply ignored it. The most influential and respected leaders usually are skilled listeners.

Pace and Style

A ninth characteristic of a good meeting is one that some leaders appear to practice intuitively while others learn it by observation and experience. This is pace and style.

On some occasions people begin to look at their watches within half an hour after the meeting has begun and begin to calculate how much longer it will be before the break or adjournment. Boredom becomes widespread, and it is contagious.

A day or two later some of these same people may attend a meeting and, ninety minutes after it began, happen to glance at their watches and exclaim, "Gracious! I didn't realize we had been here this long already. This is very interesting!"

Sometimes it is the subject, but more often it is the style and pace of the meeting that maintain interest and evoke enthusiasm. The leader(s) changes the pace; breaks the tension with anecdotes with which the participants can identify; listens carefully to comments, rebuttals, and questions; does not allow a "scene stealer" to usurp the meeting; and recognizes the egocentric nature of human beings.

This last concept, which Anthony Greenwald, a psychologist at Ohio State University, has labeled the "egocentricity bias," reflects the fact that we all tend to see ourselves at the center of the universe. This egocentricity bias has been identified by some clinical psychologists as a sign of mental health as long as it is not exaggerated. A simple illustration of this concept is that most people can recall more clearly what happened to them on a particular date five or ten years ago than they can recall what happened with other people on that date.

Likewise the man born in 1937 may watch intently a television documentary recounting the highlights of growing into adulthood during the 1950s yet be bored by a skillfully prepared documentary about the stock market crash of 1929 and the Great Depression. His uncle, who was born in 1919, watches this second program with great interest. The younger person identifies with the first program and regards the second as ancient history.

So it is with a meeting; time passes quickly and boredom is a minor consideration in those meetings when each participant feels he or she is at or near the center of the agenda. The larger the group, the more difficult it is for this to happen. This is one of the reasons for keeping committees to seven or fewer members.

The perceptive leader understands the value of the egocentricity bias in reducing boredom and helping everyone gain a sense of involvement in the meeting. This is especially important when the group numbers more than ten or twelve.

The most effective technique is for the leader of the meeting to call every person by name at least once during the course of the meeting. A second is to ask, "Florence, what do you think?" or "Harold, you've been involved in similar situations before. What's your opinion?" A third is to encourage everyone who wants to speak to have the floor at least once before anyone speaks a second time. A fourth is to affirm the specific gifts and experiences of those who appear to be drifting toward the edge of boredom. A fifth, as was pointed out earlier, is to relate experiences and use illustrations with which most of the people in the room can identify very easily. A sixth is, whenever it can be done authentically, for the leader to identify himself or herself with the experiences of many of the people in the group. Effective teachers, successful politicians, and popular public speakers repeatedly illustrate the concept of the egocentricity bias.

Time for Second Thoughts

A tenth, and perhaps the most widely misunderstood characteristic of effective committees is illustrated by comments such as, "We need to have someone study that in more detail and come back with the facts," or "I cannot respond to that until I have more facts on which to base an opinion."

On the surface these appear to be pleas for more factual data. Sometimes they are that. Frequently, however, they can be translated into statements such as these. "I need more time to think about that; perhaps a search for more facts will give me the time I need." "We are moving too fast for some members of this group; we need a recess to allow everyone to catch up." "Our differences have become so pronounced that it is doubtful if we ever will come to an agreement. Perhaps if we go back and seek a common beginning point around the facts, we can restore a sense of unity and overcome the gap that separates us." "This argument has moved from disagreement to becoming disruptive. We need to find a new point of agreement, or this committee will fly apart. Emotions have replaced reason, and we need time for people to cool down."

Effective leaders understand that a demand for "more study" may be of far greater significance than simply a request for more facts.

The Value of Shared Experiences

Some would place this first, rather than eleventh, on a list of factors that produce effective committees while others would place it under the category of planned change. Very simply it is the value of shared experiences. The committee created to plan a new building will find it useful to visit a congregation that has just completed a building program. The planning committee that has been asked to bring in recommendations on the future of what is now clearly an ex-neighborhood church will find it helpful to go visit a congregation that has redefined its role.

One value of such trips is to learn from others. An equally important value is the shared experience and the common reference point.

The officers' retreat that begins with the evening meal on Friday at a camp or retreat center, has a two-hour meeting that evening and a three-hour session on Saturday morning before leaving immediately after lunch probably will be more productive than the 8:00 A.M. to 4:00 P.M. Saturday session held in the church building. Shared experiences away from home encourage both creativity and cohesion. This is especially important if the focus of that retreat is to define a new role or to outline a new chapter in that congregation's ministry. It is easier to retrain people, and especially mature adults, in a group setting which provides mutual support for the participants.

Do We Trust Subcommittees?

Finally, the effective committee treats its subcommittees and study groups with respect. The worship committee at First Church has been asked to review and report on a study conducted by a special subcommittee. The subcommittee has suggested a change in the Sunday morning schedule from one worship service to a new schedule that calls for an early worship service followed by Sunday school and a second service at eleven o'clock. The first person to speak is an influential member of long standing who challenges the proposal. "This is the dumbest idea I've ever heard! This would split the church into two congregations. We would have an early service crowd and a late service congregation. People wouldn't see each other. It would destroy the friendliness and the caring for one another that we all value so highly. Who would sing at the early service? You can't expect the choir to sing at both services, can you? I'll bet the building will be three-quarters empty at the early service. How can you get a feeling of worship when you're seated among a bunch of empty pews? I move we reject this proposal and continue our present schedule."

A few minutes later the worship committee voted to reject the proposal the subcommittee had labored over for five months. The following week three of the five members of that subcommittee resigned from the worship committee.

Could this have been avoided?

The worship committee chairperson might have considered four other possible courses of action that could have produced a different outcome.

First, common courtesy dictates that when a subcommittee invests a large amount of time and energy in studying an issue, the only motion the chair should entertain is a motion to approve the committee's recommendation. The debate should begin with a presumption in support of the committee's work, not a motion against it.

Second, a common practice is to ask those who support the motion to speak first. Those opposing the motion speak second, and those favoring the motion have the final turn in the debate.

Both of these procedures are based on the premise that the first person to speak on an issue has an advantage over subsequent speakers and that most motions are adopted rather than defeated. Perceptive leaders recognize there is no such thing as a neutral or unbiased procedure; therefore, the bias should be in support of those who contributed considerable time and effort to study an issue, rather than to bias the procedure against them.

Third, as was pointed out earlier, it may be wise to use the "itemized response" procedure. This requires anyone speaking on a motion, first, to identify three positive aspects of the proposal; second, to ask questions for clarification or for additional information; and third, to voice any reservations or objections that person may hold about the proposal.

Thus the person opposing the proposal for two worship experiences on Sunday morning might say, "The only advantages I can see are that we would get more work out of our preacher, perhaps the folks who can't carry a tune will all attend the early service, and, third, this may reduce the chances of someone's sitting in my pew at eleven o'clock if I get there a little late. Now, my question is, who will provide the special music for the early service? Finally, here are the reasons I oppose this . . ."

Obviously some opponents of innovation may be immobilized since they will find it impossible to identify three positive characteristics of anyone else's idea.

Fourth, the worship committee might have followed the common procedure that no action proposal can be voted on at the same meeting at which it is first introduced. This is based on the assumption that normal people do their best thinking on the way home from the meeting. Therefore, no action proposal can be adopted or rejected until the committee has had the benefit of everyone's second thoughts.

What is the bias on the procedures followed by the committees in your church? For or against change and new ideas? How much respect is accorded special study groups and subcommittees? Who do you allow to have the advantage of speaking first? Why? Which procedure will increase the effectiveness of your committees?

Effective leaders understand the importance of these and similar organizing principles in planning meetings and in working with committees.

WHAT DO WE SEEK IN OUR NEXT MINISTER?

"We all agree that the number one characteristic we are looking for in our next minister is someone who is a good preacher," summarizes Kris Hudson after an hour's deliberations of the pulpit search committee's third meeting. "But there are two other things I would like to suggest should be high on the priority list as we build a profile of the person we're seeking. The first is I hope we can find someone who not only is a good preacher, but who also can inspire and motivate the folks here. This really is an apathetic congregation. The second is an ability and willingness to lead, to give direction, to suggest where we go next. Two years ago we finished paying off our mortgage. About a year after that, our minister announced the date of his retirement. We've been drifting for at least two years like a ship without a rudder."

"I couldn't agree with you more," added Sandy Jones, "and I would like to add two other characteristics to this profile we're building. One is I would greatly prefer someone born after the end of World War II. Both of our last two pastors were past fifty-five when they came. I think we should be looking for a younger minister. Second, somewhere I recently read that about half of all seminarians come out as introverted on some kind of psychological test. I think we should look for an extroverted and younger minister who is excellent in the pulpit, can help us find a new sense of purpose and direction, and also can inspire us to grab that challenge."

"Do you two really believe we can find someone out there with all those characteristics?" asked the person chairing the search committee.

"Yes, and if we do, would that person be willing to come here for the salary we're willing to pay?" interjected Terry Holton. "I think we need to get busy and finish writing a job description. We really don't have a right to even talk about the characteristics until we agree on a job description. So far we've agreed the job requires someone who is a good preacher and who can motivate people. A couple of us also want to include youth work as a major part of that, and Bertha insists the job description should require regular calling on the shut-ins and on our older members as well as hospital visitation. What else should we include in this job description? Here we are, at our third meeting, and we still haven't even finished writing a job description!"

"I would rather talk about what our new minister should look like," urged Bobby Becker. "I sure hope we can find someone who is tall. I think we need a pastor our kids can really look up to. Our last two pastors both have been shorter than I am, and I'm only five foot nine. When a tall person walks into a room, everyone looks up."

"Wait a minute," cautioned Kim Nichols. "We agreed at our first meeting that we want to consider both men and women. Are you trying to bias our selection process against women?"

* * * *

During this conversation three different approaches to choosing a new minister were identified. Kris Hudson and Terry Holton wanted to begin by writing a job description. Sandy Jones tried to emphasize the characteristics of youthfulness and extroversion. Bobby Becker wanted a tall minister, which also represents an emphasis on traits. Terry Holton also raised the question of compensation, thus lifting up institutional limitations.

The research on traits (height, weight, age, gender, introversion-extroversion, scholarship, intelligence, appearance, and athletic ability) fails to point to a clearcut correlation between any one of these traits and effective leadership.[1] In general, the more objective and easy to measure the trait, such as age, height, or athletic ability, the more likely that trait is irrelevant in identifying the most effective leaders. Some evidence does exist to suggest that effective leaders tend to have an above average sense of humor, but that is such an elusive trait that it is difficult to measure.

Before becoming too entangled in attempting to write a job description that will satisfy the desires of everyone on the search committee, and perhaps exclude many of the potential candidates since none would fulfill all the requirements, it might be more productive for this pulpit search committee to devote some time to discussing which approach they want to follow in their search for ministerial leadership. They might conclude that preparing a job description is not the most productive beginning point. A range of other organizing principles for developing the criteria to be used in the selection of a new minister does exist.

Some churches place a great weight on the seminary the prospective minister attended. A persuasive body of research exists, for example, that both medical schools and law schools not only teach technical skills, they also provide the professional socialization for future entrants into that profession.

Building on this model, Jackson Carroll studied 1,451 ministers who were recent graduates of twenty-one different Protestant seminaries. He concluded that the graduates of seminaries that could be identified as religious communities displayed the most conservative theological orientation. The ministers who had attended what clearly were graduate schools of theology, with a strong emphasis on securing faculty members who had been trained in research-oriented ministries with a heavy emphasis on scholarship, tended to cluster at the liberal end of the theological spectrum. Those who had graduated from what Carroll labeled the vocational school tended to be closer to the middle of the theological spectrum.[2] Most of the denominationally related seminaries that are not related to a university and that place a greater emphasis on practical skills and on preparation for the parish ministry, rather than on scholarship, could be placed in the vocational school category. Sometimes they are labeled as trade schools or professional schools rather than graduate schools. While it has not received the attention it deserves, an important issue in contemporary American Protestantism is whether theological seminaries should see themselves as religious communities or as professional schools or as graduate schools. It appears this is of greater concern among parish leaders than among denominational executives.[3]

More recently Dallas Blanchard published an article reporting on his research which parallels that of Jackson. Blanchard identified four categories of seminary preparation for the parish ministry. He concluded that ministers who graduated from the graduate school type of seminary tended to place a greater value on their role as teacher, change agent, and volunteer in denominational organizations with less concern for traditional local church roles or working with individuals. The graduates of the religious community type of seminary and the ministers who did not graduate from seminary tended to place a greater emphasis on their congregation-oriented role in preaching, helping individuals, and calling in homes.

Blanchard also found that the ministers who had gone to the graduate school type of seminary tended to be at the liberal end of the theological spectrum with the vocational school graduates and the nongraduates closer to the middle of that spectrum and the religious community graduates the most conservative of the four groups.[4] In another study Blanchard reported that next to the wife's attitude toward the pastorate, the type of seminary attended is the best predictor of whether or not a minister will leave the pastoral ministry. Several observers of the scene also contend that the type of seminary the pastor attended also is a good predictor on whether or not a congregation will be experiencing numerical growth, but the research on this has yet to be published.

The importance of the theological seminary as a socialization force has long been recognized by many denominational families including The Lutheran Church—Missouri Synod, the Southern Baptist Convention, the Seventh-day Adventist, the Roman Catholic Church of the 1980s, the Wisconsin Evangelical Lutheran Synod, the former Presbyterian Church in the United States as well as several dozen smaller denominations. A century or two ago this also was an important topic among Methodists, Presbyterians, and Congregationalists in the North.

During the mid-1970s the Association of Theological Schools in the United States and Canada completed a half-million-dollar research project that covered forty-seven denominations. Church members lifted up as the most desirable trait in a minister a "willingness to serve without regard for acclaim" and were most critical of the pastor who "avoids intimacy and repels people with a critical, demeaning, and insensitive attitude."[5] While this research has been used by theological seminaries in revising their course of study and in developing programs of continuing education, it does not appear to have had much of an impact on how congregations go about the process of choosing a new minister. In real life at least ten different approaches can be identified as in contemporary use by congregations looking for new ministerial leadership.

Job Descriptions, Tests, or Competencies?

The committee faced with choosing a new leader, whether it be a congregation seeking a new pastor or a denominational agency looking for a new executive, has many choices. One may be to promote someone already on the staff. Another is to prepare a job description and seek someone to fill that job. A third is to accept the judgment of a denominational executive, who, it is believed, is personally well acquainted with both that congregation or agency and also with all potential candidates. A fourth and not uncommon approach is for an influential member to recommend someone he or she has met, or perhaps knows only in a remote manner, and for that recommendation to prevail because of the influence of that member. A fifth is when the retiring minister designates the heir apparent, but this is more common in independent or semi-autonomous churches than in congregations with a very close tie to a connectional denomination.

A sixth is the group interview in which all candidates are invited to come to the same room at the same time and are interviewed, as a group, by a skilled and knowledgeable interviewer. The members of the search committee, or the pastoral relations committee, are seated around the periphery of the room. They silently observe and take notes. After the group interview has been completed, the members of the committee gather to share their reactions and to decide on next steps. It is not uncommon for all the members of the committee, acting individually during that meeting, to have identified the same person as the number one candidate and for most or all to have placed another individual as the number two candidate. The more skillful the interviewer, the greater the emphasis on competencies (see below) rather than on credentials, and the more knowledgeable the interviewer is with that particular congregation or agency, the higher the probability that all members of the committee will have ranked the top two or three candidates in the same order. This is an especially useful methodology for selecting pastors who will be developers of new missions, for picking an associate minister, and for choosing the new executive for a regional judicatory. Sometimes the committee will follow the group interview with individual interviews with each of the top two or three candidates before making a recommendation.

A seventh approach, that still is used in several religious bodies, is to write the names of all candidates on separate slips of paper, place these several pages apart in a Bible in a random order with the end of each slip of paper protruding for perhaps an inch, pause while someone leads the group in prayer, and then someone, often a child, comes up and pulls one piece of paper out of the Bible. The name on that piece of paper is the person believed to have been chosen by God for that purpose.

An eighth approach, and one that is widely used, is to advertise and ask all candidates to submit a dossier and be interviewed individually by the selection committee. This system, which sometimes is referred to as the "beauty contest approach," usually places a premium on credentials and personality rather than on the special competencies required for that particular position.[6] From this observer's perspective it ranks, along with the first four approaches identified earlier in this section, as among the least effective means of choosing new leaders. One of the most significant shortcomings of this approach is that it is difficult to distinguish between the candidate whose prime motivation is to leave where she or he is now serving and the candidate who feels a genuine call from the Lord to respond to a new challenge. A not uncommon practice among congregations seeking a new associate minister is to avoid seeking applications and to go out and recruit candidates from among those ministers who appear to possess the necessary special competencies and experience. If, when first approached, a potential candidate replies, "Thanks, but I'm not interested in leaving here at this time," that can be interpreted as a positive signal. The committee now knows that the prime motivating factor is *not* a desire to leave that pastorate. Sometimes, after two or three subsequent invitations, that noncandidate becomes the new associate minister.

A ninth and still controversial approach is to place considerable credence on the combination of the results from a variety of tests plus face-to-face interviews. Obviously the choice of tests will vary with the nature of the position to be filled. Perhaps the test that has been most widely used in ecclesiastical circles in recent years is the Myers-Briggs Type Indicator.[7] The Atkins-Katcher-Porter Life Orientation Survey is useful in helping individuals identify their strengths and how these can be used in a productive manner.

A useful test for selecting new church developers or pastors for churches that appear to have the potential for substantial numerical growth, but that potential is yet to be realized, is one devised by William A. Delaney that attempts to measure entrepreneurial instincts.[8] The Bell System has used Edwards Personal Preference Schedule.[9] The Dominance Scale and the Deference Scale from this test might be useful in selecting both senior pastor and associate ministers who are expected to have long tenure. While the traditional I.Q. test does not appear to have great value in selecting leaders, the Rokeach Survey appears to be a useful tool in the selection of leaders for positions in which a strong goal-orientation is considered to be a positive factor.

Those who have been attracted to the discipline often called "neurolinguistics" may want to include one or more tests that identify communication modes and skills.

Professor Jane Loevinger, a psychologist from Washington University, spent a dozen years devising a test to measure ego development that has been used by Alon Gratch and others to identify potential leaders in a corporate setting. The results suggest the best leaders are between the third ("conformist") and fifth ("autonomous") stages of ego development. They have moved beyond the conformist stage; they may be in the fourth stage of ego development ("conscientous") but have not yet reached that fifth stage ("autonomous"). There also appears to be some evidence to support the contention that persons at the sixth stage of ego development ("integrated") do not make effective leaders. The characteristics of the 2 to 5 percent of the adult population who reach this sixth stage of ego development may be incompatible with the effective leadership of an organization when the role (a) demands loyalty from others, (b) cannot tolerate the complete autonomy of every individual, (c) does not provide the environment that enables everyone to be completely independent in goals and procedures, and (d) provides no rewards for ambition. Ministers who are at this sixth stage of ego development probably will be unhappy serving as senior ministers of large congregations or as the mission developer of a new congregation. Likewise they often fail to meet the expectations placed on them by others when serving as associate ministers in large churches. They probably will feel far more comfortable as chaplains, teachers, counselors, or as part-time pastors of small and very stable congregations. The effective initiating leader is most likely to come from among persons who are in or near the fourth ("conscientious") stage of ego developmet. These "tamed rebels" also frequently are the source for excellent senior ministers.

A remarkable degree of overlap appears to exist between the characteristics of individuals in a particular stage of ego development and those in a parallel stage of faith development.[10] This is a subject that deserves more research. It might produce some useful insights that could be utilized in preparing the criteria for selecting a new minister or in developing the profiles of potential candidates.

It also should be noted that the typical long-range planning committee—that includes members who are at three or more different stages of ego development and/or faith development—often have difficulty agreeing on goals and priorities. By contrast, the planning committees drawn largely or entirely from persons at the same stage of faith and/or ego development appear to find it easier to agree on recommendations that may greatly change the status quo.

Dozens of other tests are being utilized by theological seminaries and career development centers in helping ministers gain a better sense of self-understanding. Unfortunately, however, relatively few congregations make use of these instruments in their search for their next pastor. This probably will not happen until denominational leaders offer to make these resources available to congregations—and that probably will not happen until after a larger proportion of these denominational leaders become convinced of the usefulness of these tests.[11]

From this observer's perspective the most promising approach to matching ministers and congregations would be to place far less emphasis on job descriptions, the recommendations of any one individual, traits, the wants or wishes of the members, promotions from within (the attractiveness of the known versus the fear of the unknown), and the solicitation of dossiers in favor of a greater emphasis on the special competencies required by the position in question. Occasionally a congregation's pulpit nominating committee will at least begin to go down this road by developing what is commonly called a "profile" of what they will be seeking in the next minister.

This tenth approach is sometimes referred to very simply as "practical intelligence," but in professional circles it usually is described as "special competencies."[12] While it is widely used in ecclesiastical circles in an informal and unsystematic manner, this concept of special competencies has yet to benefit from the research necessary to identify the distinctive competencies needed for specific positions such as senior minister, bishop, program director, or conference minister.

David C. McClelland, a professor at Harvard University who has specialized in testing for competence, contends that the best approach is to focus, not on the aspects of the job, but rather on the characteristics of those who are the best performers in that job.[13] This is a radically different approach than that followed by most congregations and denominational agencies that begin by preparing a description of the job to be done. In simple terms it means that a search committee would be well advised to spend less time on writing a job description and much more time going out and identifying the common characteristics of the persons who are doing an excellent job as pastors in churches of that size and type or in similar positions in a denominational agency or as members of a multiple-staff church.

To place the primary emphasis on competencies, however, is neither easy nor universally acceptable. It is more difficult and much more time consuming to identify the common characteristics of the best pastors of middle-sized congregations in county seat communities than it is for a search committee or a denominational official to sit down and write a job description for the next minister of that congregation and to use that job description as the primary tool in interviews with candidates.

Perhaps the most threatening dimension of this emphasis on competencies is that it rarely correlates with the number of academic degrees possessed by a candidate or years on the job. The current ecclesiastical illustration of this is the growing number of ministers who have discovered that the doctor of ministry degree may produce ego satisfactions, but is not necessarily a useful credential in seeking a call to a larger congregation. In those denominations in which the ministerial placement process places great weight on credentials (academic degrees, awards, volunteer leadership roles on denominational committees, membership in professional organizations, foreign travel, pastoral experience, and seniority), a greater emphasis on competencies will be extremely threatening to many, and especially to mature males and to those who control the ministerial placement process.

A greater emphasis on competence assessment also would threaten those individuals who are convinced they can identify the best candidates for a vacancy through an examination of a dossier and face-to-face interviews.

If the data base for key competencies were available for a range of specialized ministerial roles (pastor of a three-church parish, campus minister, district superintendent, senior minister, program director, minister of music, counselor, new church developer, presbytery executive, preacher, bishop, seminary professor, associate pastor, youth director, administrator, pastor of a racially integrated church, conference minister, evangelist, camp director), it not only would simplify the task of the search committee, it also would greatly increase the chances of a wise selection being made.[14] A greater emphasis on "practical intelligence" also would make it easier to identify those seminaries that are most likely to produce graduates who become effective campus ministers or parish pastors or scholars or senior ministers of large congregations or change agents or denominational staff members. Would that knowledge also be extremely threatening?

The Question of Structure

In addition to the factors discussed thus far, two other concerns merit the attention of those involved in ministerial placement. From the local church perspective the most widely neglected is the lack of structure. With the exception of scheduled meetings and the regular worship services, the typical congregation offers very little structure for a minister. The daily schedule is largely discretionary. Should I go out calling this afternoon, or should I first go to the hospital and then, if time permits, perhaps I can make a few calls? Should I spend this morning working on my sermon for next Sunday morning or should I take four hours and lay out my preaching schedule for the next three or four months? Or would it be wiser to spend the morning preparing for two very important meetings I have coming up later in the week? Six mornings a week the typical pastor has to decide, "What should I do today, and what should I postpone until tomorrow or later?"

These time management questions are further complicated by unexpected telephone calls, people dropping by the church office "to see the minister for just a few minutes," the unanticipated accident that summons the pastor to the hospital, or the death of a member that dominates the schedule for the next two or three days.

The nature of the work environment for most pastors makes it extremely tempting to wait until noon to plan the use of that day. Rarely does the governing board or a pastoral relations committee feel competent to offer to structure their minister's day, and even more rarely is a minister open to that possibility.

From this outsider's perspective the evidence is overwhelmingly on the side of the argument that contends most people do need a structured and stimulating work environment and that structure usually is necessary for peak performance, for productivity, for growth, for personal satisfactions, and for fostering creativity.

One expression of this is the Tuesday morning meeting as five pastors gather to use the lectionary in sermon preparation. That setting, plus the use of the lectionary, provides structure for the process of sermon preparation. A second example of structure is the minister who adheres to a carefully designed schedule that provides time each week for study and meditation as well as for hospital visitation, for calling on prospective new members, and for time with the family. A third example of how ministers function in structured settings would be the pastor who conducts worship for three different congregations every Sunday morning. A fourth are those theological seminaries which place high academic demands on the students.

By and large, however, when the seminary student leaves school to become the pastor of a small rural parish or to join the staff of a large congregation as an associate minister, that is a move from a highly structured setting into a far less structured environment.

One response to this by a few denominations is that in sending a minister out to organize a new congregation the selection process and orientation phase include clarity and agreement on structure. This normally includes specific, attainable, measurable, and clearly agreed upon expectations on calling and on finding a temporary meeting place. The regional judicatory or a staff person from national headquarters provides a regular and detailed system of accountability on performance.

At the other end of this spectrum is the first person to hold the newly created position of associate minister in a congregation served by a hard-working, inner-directed, ambitious, overburdened, introverted, self-confident, and highly competent senior minister who is just past the conformist stage in ego development. This "tamed rebel" declares, "I'll do the preaching, I'll oversee the general area of program, and I'll take care of the administration here. I want to turn you loose to develop a good youth ministry, cultivate prospective new members, and build up the Sunday school. If you decide that will help you accomplish what you need to do, it's not even necessary for you to be in the chancel on Sunday morning, except for the five or six Sundays when you'll do the preaching. I'll take care of that. I don't think you need a lot of supervision, and I don't have the time to provide it, so you're on your own!"

The lay leaders who approved creation of this new position had a half dozen reasons for doing so. These included asking the new minister to do what was not getting done, to do that which no one else knew how to do, to relieve the burden on the overworked pastor, to do those things no one else wanted to do, and to expand the ministry with teenagers.

Two years later the "new" associate minister is deeply immersed in beginning a doctor of ministry program at a nearby seminary and spending one day a week serving on denominational committees. The senior minister is convinced this very talented and promising associate minister either (a) never learned to work and/or (b) is not a self-starter. The lay leadership have no clearly defined advance criteria for evaluation and respond primarily to (a) whether the new associate minister has a likable personality or is aloof and introverted and (b) whether or not the size of the youth program has grown.

OOPS! WE LET HIM DO HIS OWN THING BUT WE FORGOT TO TELL HIM ABOUT PARACHUTES!

Structure doesn't occur in a vacuum!
—FRIAR TUCK

From a diagnostic perspective a central issue is structure. The new associate minister wanted and needed a more highly structured work environment than this congregation offered. One alternative was the structured program required for the doctor of ministry degree. A second was volunteer service on denominational committees that provided structure, recognition, satisfactions, an opportunity for expressing one's creativity, and a feeling of being needed.

Instead of discussing whether the new associate was not motivated or was lazy or simply incompetent, a more productive debate would have centered on the issue of structure. The senior minister benefited from a relatively structured set of expectations while the new associate minister was lost in an unstructured work environment that did not offer the precedents of what the predecessor did in that role.

Who Will Be the Leaders in 2015?

The second widely neglected issue is leadership development. This is a never-ending contemporary issue in thousands of congregations. Everyone is convinced of the perpetual shortage of competent, willing, and dedicated volunteer leaders and workers.[15] On a long-term basis, however, another facet of this issue is identifying, enlisting, educating, socializing, nurturing, and training those persons who will be the leaders of the churches in the year 2015. The present generation will have disappeared from the scene, and been largely forgotten, by that time. Who will be the new leaders for a new generation?

It is possible today to identify some of the qualities and competencies that are common among the best and most effective initiating leaders. They tend to display a high level of self-confidence, they are not conformists, and they are willing to take risks. In addition, these self-confident, tamed, and venturesome rebels tend to be hardworkers, curious, impatient, assertive, survivalists, energetic, hardy, flexible, self-starters, tough, persistent, decisive, persuasive, ambitious, and optimistic about the future. They have learned how to manage their time in a productive manner, they are reflective, and when criticized they do not respond in anger but look beyond that anger in an effort to analyze both the content of the criticism and the motivation of the critic.

The leaders of tomorrow
can look beyond anger
and criticism
to truth and love!
—FRIAR TUCK.

The best leaders function in a long time frame and are comfortable conceptualizing abstract ideas in a five- to twenty-year time span. They also display a characteristic of football coaches sometimes called "mental rehearsal." When the team has the football on first down with ten yards to go, the good football coach is mentally rehearsing the choices if two plays later it is third down and six yards to go. When a good baseball manager sends a pinch hitter in to bat in a fourth inning rally, that manager already has mentally rehearsed the choices that will be left if a pinch hitter is needed in the ninth inning. The effective parish pastor who is bringing a controversial proposal to the governing Board on a Tuesday evening will have mentally rehearsed the arguments of the opposition and reflected on alternative courses of action if the pastor's preference does not win the necessary support that evening.

Effective leaders rarely allow themselves to become captives of what others claim is the most urgent immediate issue.[16] Many will argue that the two crucial qualities in a leader are vision and the ability to inspire others to want to turn that vision into reality. A third is a willingness to intervene.

It should be possible for several of those denominational families concerned about the future to begin the process of identifying, enlisting, and training the leaders of tomorrow. This does not require inventing the wheel. Huge sums of money already have been invested in these efforts outside the churches.[17] Models are available to be examined and to be adapted to a particular denomination. All that remains is a willingness to take the initiative and to begin the process. That is called leadership!

2. Tribes, Movements, and Organizations

1. For an elaboration of this point see Lyle E. Schaller, *Understanding Tomorrow* (Nashville: Abingdon Press, 1976), pp. 23-31.

2. Philip Selznick, *Leadership in Administration* (Berkeley: University of California Press, 1963), pp. 40, 108.

3. Robert Redfield, *Folk Culture of the Yucatan* (Chicago: University of Chicago Press, 1941).

4. A brief introduction to several of the sets of categories used to describe movements is Gary T. Marx and James L. Wood, "Strands of Theory and Research in Collective Behavior," *American Review of Sociology*, 1975. A useful textbook presentation is Ralph H. Turner and Lewis M. Killian, *Collective Behavior* (Englewood Cliffs, N.J.: Prentice-Hall, 1972).

5. The pioneering work on the value-oriented movement is Neil Smelser, *The Theory of Collective Behavior* (Glencoe, Ill.: The Free Press, 1962), chapter 10.

6. David Sills, *The Volunteers: Means and Ends in a National Organization* (Glencoe, Ill.: The Free Press, 1957).

7. Lon L. Fuller, "Two Principles of Human Association" in J. Roland Pennock and John W. Chapman, *Voluntary Associations* (New York: Atherton Press, 1969), pp. 3-11. Fuller is widely regarded as one of the intellectual giants in the field of legal philosophy and spent his last years working on a book which he never completed, with the tentative title, "Means and Ends." This essay was to be the introductory chapter in that book. It also can be found in *The Principles of Social Order: Selected Essays of Lon L. Fuller*, Kenneth I. Winston, ed., (Durham, N.C.: Duke University Press, 1981). A sharply different, but very useful, introduction to the nature of public organizations is Charles Perrow, *Complex Organizations* (Glenview, Ill.: Scott, Foresman & Co., 1979). A useful systems approach to the subject is Bertram M. Gross, *Organizations and Their Managing* (New York: The Free Press, 1968). An interesting and critical view of organizational life is Charles Handy, *Gods of Management* (London: Pan Books, 1978). Two books that examine decision making in American Protestantism are Paul M. Harrison, *Authority and Power in the Free Church Tradition* (Carbondale: Southern Illinois University Press, 1971) and Lyle E. Schaller, *The Decision-Makers* (Nashville: Abingdon Press, 1974).

8. Fuller, "Two Principles," pp. 11-21.

9. William A. Westley, "The Informal Organization of the Army: A Sociological Memoir," Howard S. Becker et al., *Institutions and the Person* (Chicago: Aldine Publishing Company, 1968), pp. 200-207.

10. An argument that the religious community type of theological seminary is more likely than the graduate school type to produce parish-oriented ministers can be found in Dallas A. Blanchard, "Seminary Effects of Professional Role Orientations," *Review of Religious Research*, 22, (June 1981): 346-61.

3. Leaders Know How to Organize

1. Among the best congregational histories published in recent years are Coleman A. Harwell, *The Centennial History of Westminster Presbyterian Church* (Nashville: Westminster Presbyterian Church, 1979); James O. Lehman, *Creative Congregationalism* (Smithville, Ohio: Oak Grove Mennonite Church, 1978); John Robert Smith, *The Church That Stayed* (Atlanta: Atlanta Historical Society, 1979); Cheri Register, ed., *A Telling Presence* (Minneapolis: Westminster Presbyterian Church, 1982); and Guy A. Aldrich, *Seven Miles Out: The Story of Pasadena Community Church* (St. Petersburg, Fla.: Pasadena Community Church, undated).

2. For this writer's system of categories for looking at Protestant congregations see Lyle E. Schaller, *Looking in the Mirror* (Nashville: Abingdon Press, 1984), pp. 14-36.

3. David A. DeVaus, "Workplace Participation and Sex Differences in Church Attendance," *Review of Religious Research*, 25, no. 3 (March, 1984): 247-56.

4. Jon P. Alstrom, "An Assessment of the Determinants of Religious Participation," *Sociological Quarterly*, 20 (1979): 49-62.

5. For a more extensive statement of this basic concept see Daniel Pipes, "How Important Is the PLO?" *Commentary* (April 1983), pp. 17-25.

6. Charles W. Ferguson, *Organizing to Beat the Devil* (New York: Doubleday & Co., 1971).

7. Eleanor Smeal, *Why and How Women Will Elect the Next President* (New York: Harper & Row, 1984). While this impressed some as a political tract for the 1984 presidential campaign, the chapter "Getting Organized" provides an exceptionally useful discussion of some of the more sophisticated tools available today to those who seek to create a voluntary association based on a common goal.

8. For two of the classic treatments of the use of rewards and punishments as a means of creating and maintaining a political organization see Lloyd Wendt and Herman Kogan, *Bosses in Lusty Chicago* (Bloomington: Indiana University Press, 1971) and William L. Diordan, *Plunkitt of Tammany Hall* (New York: E. P. Dutton, 1969).

9. For a more extensive statement on the rule of forty and on large group dynamics see Lyle E. Schaller, *Effective Church Planning* (Nashville: Abingdon Press, 1979), pp. 17-63.

10. A remarkably provocative essay on the distinction between things and people in organizational efforts is Edward R. Dayton and Ted W. Engstrom, "Thinking About Organizing," *Christian Leadership Letter*, May 1984, published by World Vision.

11. For two biographical case studies that illustrate the futility of attempting to reform the organization from within while trying to accommodate everyone, both inside and outside that organization, see Louis T. Harlan, *Booker T. Washington: The Wizard of Tuskegee* (New York: Oxford University Press, 1984) and John G. Adams, *Without Precedent* (New York: W. W. Norton & Co., 1983).

12. For an optimistic view of the future of neighborhood organizing see Robert Fisher, "Neighborhood Organizing: Lessons from the Past," *Social Policy*, Summer 1984, pp. 9-16. That particular issue also contains other essays relating to this subject. A fascinating study on the impact of ideology on organizational efforts in the inner city, and of how these ideological considerations may turn out to be counterproductive is recounted in Harry Brill, *Why Organizers Fail: The Story of a Rent Strike* (Berkeley: University of California Press, 1971). Interesting examples of how intensive organizing efforts often create adversarial relationships among what once were perceived as allies are in the civil rights movement of the 1960s, the debate in the 1980s over abortion, and the voter registration efforts of 1984. For two excellent studies, both based on empirical evidence, that suggest the gentrification of older urban neighborhoods has been greatly exaggerated and that the forced displacement of the lower income residents of these neighborhoods is really only a modest-scale phenomenon, see Michael H. Schill and Richard P. Nathan, *Revitalizing America's Cities* (Albany: State University of New York Press, 1983) and Dennis E. Gale, *Neighborhood Revitalization and the Post Industrial City* (Lexington, Ma.: Lexington Books, 1984). A useful book on neighborhood revitalization is Howard W. Hallman, *Neighborhoods: Their Place in Urban Life* (Beverly Hills: Sage Publications, 1984).

13. Thomas H. Peters and Robert H. Waterman, Jr., *In Search of Excellence* (New York: Harper & Row, 1982). The sequel to this book offers an excellent statement on leadership roles and styles. See Tom Peters and Nancy Austin, *A Passion for Excellence* (New York: Random House, 1985).

14. Wayne A. Meeks, *The First Urban Christians* (New Haven: Yale University Press, 1983).

15. For a more extended discussion of the organizing principles used in organizing youth groups see Schaller, *Looking in the Mirror*, pp. 155-77. An excellent book on organizing adult classes is Dick Murray, *Strengthening the Adult Sunday School Class* (Nashville: Abingdon Press, 1981). The use of organizing principles in new church development is discussed in Lyle E. Schaller, *Growing Plans* (Nashville: Abingdon Press, 1983), pp. 128-33.

4. Leaders Do Lead!

1. This issue of fairness has produced an increasingly heavy workload for the United States Supreme Court as it must choose between seniority and affirmative action, between the civil liberties of students and the obligations of teachers and the limits on religious freedom.

2. For a useful survey of the research on leadership see Ralph T. Stogdill, *Handbook of Leadership: A Survey of Theory and Research* (New York: The Free Press, 1974).

3. A brief and lucid discussion on the distinctive aspects of the Christian community can be found in Edward R. Dayton and Ted W. Engstrom, "Thinking About Organizing," *Christian Leadership Newsletter* (May 1984).

4. A brief introduction to the debate on leadership and power can be found in James MacGregor Burns, *Leadership* (New York: Harper & Row, 1978), pp. 9-28.

5. A substantial body of evidence exists, however, that suggests follower satisfaction is not related to permissiveness. Stogdill, *Handbook of Leadership*, p. 375.

6. For comments on why it may be difficult to use the traditional business-like approaches for evaluation in reviewing the performance of a pastor see Schaller, *Looking in the Mirror*, pp. 38-58.

7. Donald Szantho Harrington, *Orville Dewey, Robert Collyer, John Haynes Holmes and The Community Church Today and Tomorrow* (New York: The Community Church of New York, 1975).

8. Murray Chass, "The System, Not the Stars, Keep Orioles on Top," *New York Times*, April 1984.

9. For a remarkably informative discussion on how leaders can shape the culture see Terrence E. Deal and Allen A. Kennedy, *Corporate Cultures* (Reading, Mass.: Addison-Wesley Publishing Co., 1982), pp. 141-76.

10. Robert K. Greenleaf, *The Servant as Leader* (Peterborough, N. H.: Windy Row Press, 1970), pp. 16-19.

5. Type, Role, and Style

1. Carl Dudley, *Making the Small Church Effective* (Nashville: Abingdon Press, 1978).

2. This point is discussed at greater length in Schaller, *Looking in the Mirror*, pp. 29-36.

3. Kurt Lewin and Ronald Lippitt, "An Experimental Approach to the Study of Autocracy and Democracy," *Sociometry*, 1:292-300.

4. Ronald Lippit and R. K. White, "The Social Climate of Children's Groups" in R. G. Baker et al., *Child Behavior and Development* (New York: McGraw-Hill, 1943).

5. Leland P. Bradford, Jack R. Gibb, and Kenneth D. Benne, eds., *T Group Theory and Laboratory Method: Innovation in Re-education* (New York: John Wiley & Sons, 1964).

6. Stodgill, *Handbook of Leadership*, p. 370.

7. Douglas MacGregor, *The Human Side of Enterprise* (New York: McGraw-Hill, 1960).

8. Two very useful reviews of the evolution of thinking about management and leadership in the business world are Harry Levinson, *The Great Jackass Fallacy* (Boston: Graduate School of Business Administration of Harvard University, 1973), pp. 3-33 and Peters and Waterman, *In Search of Excellence*, pp. 3-86.

9. Richard Sennett, *Authority* (New York: Vintage Books, 1981), pp. 18-19.

10. Stodgill, *Handbook of Leadership*, pp. 367-75; Peters and Waterman, *In Search of Excellence*, pp. 94-96; Levinson, *The Great Jackass Fallacy*, pp. 3-33; Ralph M. Stodgill, "Personal Factors Associated with Leadership," *Journal of Psychology*, 25:35-71; Richard Sennett, "The Boss's New Clothes," *New York Review of Books*, February 22, 1979.

11. William Ballinger, *By Vote of the People* (New York: Charles Scribner's Sons, 1946). For a more recent critique of the vulnerability of democracies, see Jean-Francois Revel, *How Democracies Perish*, trans. William Byron (New York: Doubleday & Co., 1984). Revel argues that the democratic morality of peace, civility, and reason is vulnerable to attacks from those who disdain truth, believe the end justifies the means, and ignore the rules of acceptable behavior. For a vigorous argument in favor of participatory democracy and against any system of representative government, see Benjamin R. Barber, *Strong Democracy* (Berkeley: University of California Press, 1983). One of the contemporary arguments for participatory democracy is that participation enhances the sense of community. For a classic refutation of this see Clifford Orwin, "Democracy and Distrust: A Lesson from Thucydides," *The American Scholar*, Summer 1984, pp. 313-25. Orwin argues that the natural and inevitable distrust of leaders is enhanced in direct democracy to the point it becomes disruptive. By contrast, representative democracy with relatively long terms for leaders tends to reduce this degree of distrust. That, contends Orwin, is both the key to successful representative democracies and the reason there has never been a successful direct democracy. An overview of how five countries followed different paths in determining the system of legitimate authority is Reinhard Bendix, *Kings or Power: The Mandate to Rule* (Berkeley: University of California Press, 1978). A collective approach to conceptualizing and arguing one facet of this issue is *The Case for Participatory Democracy*, ed. C. George Genello and Dimitrios Roussopoulos (New York: Viking Press, 1971). A skeptical, but scholarly appraisal of the relevance of democracy to the Third World that also underscores the fragility of democracy can be found in Ralph Buultjens, *The Decline of Democracy* (Maryknoll, N.Y.: Orbis Books, 1978). A strong defense of pluralism in the distribution of power is Nelson W. Polsby, *Community Power and Political Theory* (New Haven: Yale University Press, 1980).

12. Lyle E. Schaller, "High Demand or Voluntary Church," *The Christian Ministry*, September 1984, pp. 5-8.

13. Bradford et al., *T Group Theory and Laboratory Method*.

14. For an explanation of why that is a bad central organizing principle for creating a youth group see Glenn E. Ludwig, *Building an Effective Youth Ministry* (Nashville: Abingdon Press, 1979).

15. Selznick, *Leadership in Administration*.

16. For a more detailed discussion of the weekday nursery school as one component of a larger ministry see Schaller, *Looking in the Mirror*, pp. 178-79.

17. For a remarkably prescient statement on this tendency see B. R. Clark, *Adult Education in Transition* (Berkeley: University of California Press, 1956).

18. Lyle E. Schaller, *Activating the Passive Church* (Nashville: Abingdon Press, 1982).

19. Selznick, *Leadership in Administration*, pp. 37-38.

20. Elitism is once again a respectable concept. The historian, Barbara Tushman, declared, "Elitism is the equivalent of quality." For a brief review of the return to elitism in American educational circles see Fred M. Herhinger, "A New Elitism Appears in Higher Education," *New York Times*, November 20, 1984. For a plea that elitism is necessary for the survival of democracy see John Bunzel, "The Badge of Elitism," *Newsweek*, October 1, 1979, p. 11.

21. David A. Whetten, "Effective Administrators," *Change*, November/December 1984, pp. 38-43.

22. John P. Kolter, "What Effective General Managers Really Do," *Harvard Business Review*, November/December 1982, pp. 156-67. Another famous study reported that the typical senior manager spends an average (median) of nine minutes on each event or decision. Harvey Mintzberg, *The Nature of Managerial Work* (New York: Harper & Row, 1973). A more recent statement on this distinction between leaders and managers is Warren Bennis and Burt Nanus, *The Strategies for Taking Charge* (New York: Harper & Row, 1985).

23. Peters and Waterman, *In Search of Excellence*, pp. 279-91.

24. A sample of such research can be found in Diane Ravitch, "A Good School," *The American Scholar*, Autumn 1984, pp. 481-93; Arthur Blumberg and William Greenfield, *The Effective Principal: Perspectives on School Leadership* (Boston: Allyn and Bacon, 1980); James Traub, "Principles in Action," *Harpers*, May 1983, pp. 12-17; Daniel U. Levine et al., "Characteristics of Effective Inner-City Schools," *Phi Delta Kappan*, June 1984, pp. 707-11, and H. Dickson Corbett, "Principals' Contributions to Maintaining Change," *Phi Delta Kappan*, November 1982, pp. 190-92.

25. Examples of this call to pastors to accept their responsibility as leaders include Ernest T. Campbell, "They Also Serve Who Lead," *Pulpit Digest*, November/December 1979, pp. 367-70; Floyd Massey, Jr., and Samuel B. McKinney, *Church Administration in the Black Perspective* (Valley Forge, Pa.: Judson Press, 1976); David B. Jones and Philip B. Jones, *A Study of Fastest Growing Churches in the Southern Baptist Convention 1975-1980* (Atlanta: Home Mission Board of the Southern Baptist Convention, 1984); C. Peter Wagner, *Leading Your Church to Growth* (Venture, Ca.: Regal Books, 1984); Robert D. Dale, *Ministers as Leaders* (Nashville: Broadman Press, 1984); and Alan K. Waltz, "Stargazing into the Next Century," *Circuit Rider*, January 1985, pp. 14-15.

26. David A. Whetten, "Effective Administrators," *Change*, November/December 1984, pp. 38-43.

27. Ray Johns, *Confronting Organizational Change* (New York: Association Press, 1963).

28. James MacGregor Burns, *Leadership* (New York: Harper & Row, 1978).

29. Aaron Wildavsky, *The Nursing Father: Moses as a Political Leader* (University:University of Alabama Press, 1984). Another fascinating book by a contemporary political philosopher who builds on an Old Testament model to defend radical politics against the

charge they represent a dangerous fanaticism is Michael Walzer, *Exodus and Revolution* (New York: Basic Books, 1985). The use of Moses as a conceptual framework for looking at leadership roles also can be used to help people move from one era to another. For an interesting case study see William Boyd Grove, "Partners in Ministry: The Routinization of Charisma" (D. Min. paper, Pittsburgh Theological Seminary, 1978).

6. The Future of a New Idea

1. Rosabeth Moss Kanter, "The Middle Manager as Innovator," *Harvard Business Review*, July/August 1981, pp. 95-105. For other approaches to planned change and innovation see Victor A. Thompson, *Bureaucracy and Innovation* (University: University of Alabama Press, 1969); Lyle E. Schaller, *The Change Agent: The Strategy of Innovative Leadership* (Nashville: Abingdon Press, 1972); Harold Geutzkow, "The Creative Person in Organizations," *The Creative Organization*, Gary A. Steiner, ed. (Chicago: University of Chicago Press, 1965); Lee Grossman, *The Change Agent* (New York: Amacom, 1974); and Rosabeth Moss Kanter, *The Change Masters* (New York: Simon & Schuster, 1983). An exceptionally relevant example to the churches of mandated change in a tradition-filled organization was the introduction of women as cadets in the nation's military academies. See Judith Hicks Stiehm, *Bring Me Men and Women: Mandated Change at the U.S. Air Force Academy* (Berkeley: University of California Press, 1981). This book also speaks to those interested in the growing number of women in theological seminaries and in the pastorate.

7. Allies, Coalitions, and Meetings

1. A simple, lucid, and step-by-step statement on how to build coalitions is Edward Levin and R. V. Deuenberg, *Alliances and Coalitions* (New York: McGraw-Hill, 1984).
2. Lyle E. Schaller, *Survival Tactics in the Parish* (Nashville: Abingdon Press, 1977), pp. 42-48.
3. Robert F. Bales, "In Conference," *Harvard Business Review*, March/April 1954, pp. 44-50.
4. For several useful photographs on meeting room arrangements see B. Y. Auger, *How to Run Better Business Meetings* (Minneapolis: Minnesota Mining and Manufacturing Company, 1979), pp. 44-45. Another useful book is Winston Fletcher, *Meetings, Meetings* (New York: William Morrow & Co., 1983).

8. What Do We Seek in Our Next Minister?

1. Stodgill, *Handbook of Leadership*, pp. 35-71.
2. Jackson Carroll, "Structural Effects of Professional Schools on Professional Socialization: The Case of Protestant Clergymen," *Social Forces*, 50:61-74.
3. In the 1950s the concept that a theological seminary should be "urban, ecumenical, and university-related" began to emerge as a popular theme. Little, if any, attention was given to the probable impact this would have as a socialization factor that would influence the parish-orientation of the future graduates. This three-point emphasis could be predicted to produce a disproportionately large number of graduates who would display a strong interest in societal issues, ecumenicity, community issues, denominational concerns, teaching, scholarship; and less interest in the well-being of the parish or the parishioners.
4. Dallas A. Blanchard, "Seminary Effects on Professional Role Orientations," *Review of Religious Research*, 22, (June 1981):346-61.
5. David S. Schuller et al., eds., *Ministry in America* (New York: Harper & Row, 1980).
6. Both ministers and search committees who are involved in the traditional selection-through-interviews approach can find questions to ask at that interview in Lyle E. Schaller, *The Pastor and the People* (Nashville: Abingdon Press, 1973), pp. 16-55.
7. A useful introduction to the Myers-Briggs Type Indicator is David Kiersey and Marilyn Bates, *Please Understand Me: Character and Temperament* (Del Mar, Calif.: Prometheus Nemesis, 1978). For a provocative combination of the insights to be gleaned from the analytical psychology types of Carl Jung, the themes of the Christian gospel, and the categories used in the Myers-Briggs Type Indicator see W. Harold Grant, Magdala Thompson, and Thomas E. Clark, *From Image to Likeness* (New York: Paulist Press, 1983). The appendix offers a summary of sixteen basic personality types each divided into four developmental stages.
8. William A. Delaney, *So You Want to Start a Business?* (Englewood Cliffs, N.J.: Prentice-Hall, 1984). For some earlier comments by this writer on the usefulness of entrepreneurial skills in the process of planned change see Lyle E. Schaller, "The Municipal Executive-Entrepreneur," *Mayor and Manager*, September 1967, pp. 19-21.
9. The Bell System has been conducting a thirty-year study of its first level managers. The Edwards Personal Preference Schedule is one of the instruments used in testing these new managers. The researchers found that the new managers of the late 1970s were far more individualistic, less homogeneous, and a better educated group than their counterparts of the early 1950s, but the late 1970s group, most of whom were born in the early 1950s, displayed far less ambition to move up the corporate ladder. Ann Howard and Douglas W. Bray, "Today's Young Managers: They Can Do It, But Will They?" *The Wharton Magazine*, 5, (Summer 1981):23-30. A popular introduction to the value of tests, that inclues nine self-scoring tests designed to identify hidden talents, aptitudes, and mental abilities is James Greene and David Lewis, *Know Your Own Mind* (New York: Rawson Associates, 1983). Another book that can be useful to those seeking an associate minister or planning a collegial approach to leadership or planning to implement the dual leadership concept is Allen F. Harrison and Robert M. Bramson, *Style of Thinking* (Garden City, N.Y.: Anchor Press, 1982).
10. For an introduction to faith development see Mary M. Wilcox, *Developmental Journey* (Nashville: Abingdon Press, 1979) or James W. Fowler, *Stages of Faith* (New York: Harper & Row, 1981) or Jim Fowler and Sam Keen, *Life Maps* (Waco, Tex.: Word, 1978) or Jack R. Pressau, *I'm Saved, You're Saved . . . Maybe* (Atlanta: John Knox Press, 1977). For an introduction to ego development see Jane Loevinger, *Ego Development: Conceptions and Theories* (San Francisco: Jossey-Bass, 1976).
11. A brief account of how one senior minister and a newly arrived associate minister made productive use of the Career Counseling Center at Eckerd College is Louis S. Lunardini, "A Model for Good Staff Relationships," *Monday Morning*, June 21, 1985, pp. 6-7.
12. David C. McClelland, *The Achievement Motive* (New York: W. W. Norton & Co., 1983).
13. An excellent introduction to special competencies is Richard C. Boyatzis, *The Competent Manager* (Wiley-Interscience), 1982.

14. A beginning point for those interested in examining competency for ministry is Steve Clapp, *Ministerial Competency Report* (Sidel, Ill.: C-4 Resources, 1982). Clapp used interviews rather than tests to begin to explore the concept of special competencies.

15. A useful response to this problem can be found in Douglas W. Johnson, *The Care and Feeding of Volunteers* (Nashville: Abingdon Press, 1978).

16. An exceptionally cogent analysis of the barriers to effective leadership is David C. Jones, "What's Wrong with Our Defense Establishment?" *New York Times* Magazine, November 7, 1982, p. 38.

17. Those who believe denominations should be concerned with the nurture of future ministerial leaders may want to examine two books on this theme. Benjamin S. Bloom, *Developing Talent in Young People* (New York: Ballantine Books, 1985) documents the thesis that talent requires a long period of encouragement, nurture, education, and challenges to be fully developed. A beginning point is that the home and parents must generate pride in achievement, reinforce a belief in the value of the work ethic, and emphasize self-discipline while the most important lessons teachers can transmit are the joy of learning, the importance of accuracy and precision and to serve as models of achievement. A completely different approach was concerned with identifying and training future grassroots leaders. This $11,000,000 leadership development was financed by the Ford Foundation and provided individually tailored training experiences for seven hundred participants. A report of some of the learnings can be found in David Nevin, *Left-Handed Fastballers* (New York: Ford Foundation, 1981).